VALUE EDUCATION
AND
EDUCATION FOR HUMAN RIGHTS

VALUE EDUCATION
AND
EDUCATION FOR HUMAN RIGHTS

Editor

V. C. Pandey

ISHA

ISBN : 978-81-8205-584-1

Published, 2018
Published by

Isha Books
D-69, New Gupta Colony,
Near DDA Market
Delhi – 110009
Ph.: +91-9212142040

PREFACE

In our times, education is ubiquitous. We are offered education for today, education for yesterday, education for tomorrow, education for adjusting, education for earning, education for marriage, even education for feeling and, finally, education for death. Education is offered for all the days, in all the ways, at all the times, everywhere, and every place, for everyone of every age, in every season. One of the fundamental goals of education is to impart culture and values across the generations.

Value education, is generally understood to cut across the curriculum and is appropriately integrated into all courses as well as into the extracurricular activities and ethos of schools. It is an umbrella term for two quite different tasks and approaches. The first, which might better be called moral "socialisation" or "training," is the task of nurturing in children those virtues and values that make them good people. The second task of value education is to provide students with the intellectual resources that enable them to make informed and responsible judgments about difficult matters of moral importance. Today, the true challenge of value education remains the development of a universal conscience that puts human rights, pluralist democracy and the equality of all human beings as the most important values that we may share.

This book describes the need and importance of value education and education for human rights in the existing social scenario. It will be of interest to teachers, teacher educators and parents and will be appreciated by all who are concerned with the cause of value education.

Editor

Contents

Preface *v*

1. Socio-Moral and Cultural Context of Value Education 1
2. Nature and Concept of Morality and Moral Education 31
3. Moral Learning to Moral Education 66
4. Educating Character Development 121
5. Moral Education and Human Rights 151
6. Transactional Strategies for Moral Education and Assessment of Moral Maturity 181
7. Making Education Morally Constructivist 236

Index 265

1

Socio-Moral and Cultural Context of Value Education

Moral education, is generally understood to cut across the curriculum and is appropriately integrated into all courses as well as into the extra curricular activities and ethos of schools. There is not a lot of agreement about what moral education should be, and there is no "discipline" of moral education corresponding to the disciplines that define the courses we have discussed so far. "Moral education" is an umbrella term for two quite different tasks and approaches. The first, which might better be called moral "socialization" or "training," is the task of nurturing in children those virtues and values that make them good people. Of course, good people can make bad judgments; it's often not easy to know what is morally right. The second task of moral education is to provide students with the intellectual resources that enable them to make informed and responsible judgments about difficult matters of moral importance. Both are proper and important tasks of schools—and both cut across the curriculum.

EDUCATION AS A MORAL ENTERPRISE

Schooling is unavoidably a moral enterprise. Indeed, schools teach morality in a number of ways, both implicit and explicit. Schools have a moral ethos embodied in rules, rewards and punishments, dress codes, honor codes, student government, relationships, styles of teaching, extracurricular emphases, art, and in the kinds of respect accorded students and teachers. Schools convey to children what is expected of them, what is normal, what is right and wrong. It is often claimed that values are *caught* rather than *taught*; through their ethos, schools socialize children into patterns of moral behavior.

Textbooks and courses often address moral questions and take moral positions. Literature inevitably explores moral issues, and writers take positions on those issues—as do publishers who decide which literature goes in the anthologies. In teaching history we initiate students into particular cultural traditions and identities. Although economics courses and texts typically avoid overt moral language and claim to be "value free," their accounts of human nature, decision making, and the economic world have moral implications, as we have seen.

The overall shape of the curriculum is morally loaded by virtue of what it requires, what it makes available as electives, and what it ignores. For example, for more than a century, there has been a powerful movement to make schooling and the curriculum serve economic purposes. Religion and art, by contrast, have been largely ignored. As a result, schooling encourages a rather more materialistic and less spiritual culture—a matter of some moral significance.

Educators have devised a variety of approaches to values and morality embodied in self-esteem, community service, civic education, sex education, drug education, Holocaust education, multicultural education, values clarification, and character education programs—to name but a few. We might consider two of the most influential of these approaches briefly. For the past several decades values clarification programs have been widely used in public schools. In this approach, teachers help students "clarify" their values by having them reflect on moral dilemmas and think through the consequences of the options open to them, choosing that action that maximizes their deepest values. It is unjustifiable for a teacher to "impose" his or her values on students; this would be an act of oppression that denies the individuality and autonomy of students. Values are ultimately personal; indeed, the implicit message is that there are no right or wrong values. Needless to say, this is a deeply controversial approach—and is now widely rejected.

The character education movement of the last decade has been a response, in part, to the perceived relativism of values clarification. According to the "Character Education Manifesto," "all schools have the obligation to foster in their students personal and civic virtues such as integrity, courage, responsibility, diligence, service, and respect for the dignity of all persons".

The goal is the development of character or virtue, not correct views on "ideologically charged issues." Schools must become "communities of virtue" in which "responsibility, hard work, honesty, and kindness are modeled, taught, expected, celebrated, and continually practiced." An important resource is the "reservoir of moral wisdom" that can be found in "great stories, works of art, literature, history, and biography."

Education is a moral enterprise in which "we need to re-engage the hearts, minds, and hands of our children in forming their own characters, helping them `to know the good, love the good, and do the good'".

Finally, we note what is conspicuous by its absence: although all universities offer courses in ethics, usually in departments of philosophy or religious studies, very few public schools have such courses. Unlike either values clarification or character education programs, the major purpose of ethics courses is usually to provide students with intellectual resources drawn from a variety of traditions and schools of thought that might orient them in the world and help them think through difficult moral problems. As important as we all agree morality to be, it is striking that schools do not consider ethics courses an option worth offering.

Training and education

We distinguished between socialization, training, and indoctrination on the one hand,and education on the other. Socialzation, we suggested, is the uncritical initiation of students into a tradition, a way of thinking and acting. Education, by contrast, requires critical distance from tradition, exposure to alternatives, informed and reflective deliberation about how to think and live. Not all, but much character education might better be called *character training or socialization*, for the point is not so much to teach virtue and values by way of critical reflection on contending points of view, but to structure the moral ethos of schooling to nurturing the development of those moral habits and virtues that we agree to be good and important, that are part of our moral consensus. This is not a criticism of character education.

Children *must* be morally trained. But there are limitations to character education as a general theory of moral education; it was not designed to address critical thinking about those "ideologically charged" debates that divide us. Character education does appeal, as the Manifesto makes clear, to a heritage of stories, literature, art, and biography to inform and deepen students' understanding of, and appreciation for, moral virtue. Often such literature will reveal the moral ambiguities of life, and discussion of it will encourage critical reflection on what is right and wrong. But if the literature is chosen to nurture the development of the *right* virtues and values, it may not be well suited to nurture an appreciation of moral ambiguity or informed and critical thinking about contending values and ways of thinking and living.

One of the supposed virtues of the values clarification movement, by contrast, was its use of moral dilemmas and divisive issues; moreover, in asking students to consider the consequences of their actions, it required them to think critically about them. But the values clarification movement never required students to develop an *educated* understanding of moral frameworks of thought that could inform their thinking and provide them with critical distance on their personal desires and moral intuitions; it left them to their own inner resources.

Character education is an essential aspect of moral education, but a fully adequate theory of moral education must also address those morally divisive issues that are sufficiently important so that students must be educated about them. Of course, one of these issues is the nature of morality itself; after all, we disagree about how to justify and ground those values and virtues that the character education movement nurtures. If students are to be morally educated—and educated about morality—they must have some understanding of the moral frameworks civilization provides for making sense of the moral dimension of life. After all, morality is not intellectually free-floating, a matter of arbitrary choices and merely personal values. Morality is bound up with our place in a community or tradition, our understanding of nature and human nature, our convictions about the afterlife, our experiences of the sacred, our assumptions about what the mind can know, and our understanding of what makes life meaningful. We make sense of what we ought to do, of what kind of a person we should be, in light of all of these aspects of life—at least if we are reflective.

We have space here to offer only the briefest sketch of a theory of moral education.

— For any society to exist, its members must share a number of *moral virtues*: they must be honest, responsible, and respectful of one another's well-being. We agree about this. Public schools have a vital role to play in nurturing these consensus virtues and values, as the character education movement rightly emphasizes; indeed, a major purpose of schooling is to help develop good persons.

— If we are to live together peacefully in a pluralistic society, we must also nurture those *civic virtues and values* that are part of our constitutional tradition: we must acknowledge responsibility for protecting one another's rights; we must debate our differences in a civil manner; we must keep informed. A major purpose of schooling is to nurture good citizenship.

— But when we *disagree* about important moral and civic issues, including the nature of morality itself, then, students must learn about the alternatives, and teachers and schools should not take official positions on where the truth lies. The purpose of a *liberal education* should be to nurture an informed and reflective understanding of the conflicts.

— What shape moral education should take depends on the maturity of students. We might think of a K-12 continuum in which character education begins immediately with the socialization of children into those consensus values and virtues that sustain our communities. As children grow older and more mature they should gradually be initiated into a liberal education in which they are taught to think in informed and reflective ways about important, but controversial, moral issues.

— Character education and liberal education cannot be isolated in single courses but should be integrated into the curriculum as a whole.

We also believe, however, that the curriculum should include room for a moral capstone course that high school seniors might take, in which they learn about the most important moral frameworks of thought—secular and religious, historical and contemporary—and how such frameworks might shape their thinking about the most urgent moral controversies they face. If we are going to teach values, whose values are we going to teach?

The answer is simple, at least in principle: We teach everyone's values. When we agree with each other we teach the importance and rightness of those consensus values. When we disagree, we teach *about* the alternatives and withhold judgment. For example, we agree about democracy; it is proper, indeed important, to convey to students the value of democracy and the democratic virtues. We disagree deeply about the values of the Republican and Democratic parties, however. We can't leave politics out of the curriculum simply because it is controversial. If students are to be *educated*, if they are to make informed political decisions, they must learn something about the values and policies of the two parties. In *public* schools, teachers and texts should not take sides when the public is deeply divided; there should be no *established* political party. Schools should teach students about the alternatives fairly. And so it should be with every other major moral or civic issue that divides us—including religion.

LIBERAL EDUCATION AS MORAL EDUCATION

A good liberal education will provide students with a basic cultural literacy about those aspects of the human condition sufficiently important to warrant a place in the curriculum. History is a record of social, political, moral, and religious experiments; it provides interpretations of the suffering and flourishing of humankind.

The study of literature gives students imaginative insights into how people have thought and felt about the world in different times and places. History and literature provide students with a multitude of vicarious experiences so that they are not at the mercy of their limited and inevitably inadequate personal insights and experiences. So, for example, it is impossible to understand matters of racial justice without understanding a good deal of history, and the insights gained from imaginative literature (art, drama, and film) will be immensely valuable in making that history come alive. Indeed, one major criterion for choosing the history and literature we teach should be its relevance to deepening students' understanding of what is central to the suffering and flourishing of humankind.

A liberal education has both conservative and liberating aspects. A good liberal education will initiate students into cultural traditions, shaping their moral identities in the process. We are not social atoms, but inheritors of languages, cultures, institutions, and moral traditions. From the beginning it has been a purpose of public education to make students into good citizens, good Americans. In teaching history we provide students with a past, a sense of identity, a role in developing stories, a set of obligations.

But a good liberal education will also teach students that disagreements among us run deep: we often disagree deeply about the meaning and lessons of history—as the debate over identity and multiculturalism makes clear. We often disagree about the justice and goodness of different cultures and subcultures. We disagree about how to make sense of the world, about how to interpret it. Indeed, we often disagree about what the relevant facts are—or, even more basically, what counts as a fact, as evidence, as a good argument. We have quite different worldviews. *A good liberal education will initiate students into a discussion of the major ways civilization has devised for talking about morality and the human condition.*

Religion and moral education

Most proposals for moral education are alike in employing vocabularies sterilized of religious language. The net effect, yet again, is the marginalization of religion. The implicit message is that religion is irrelevant to the development of virtue, moral judgment, and the search for moral truth. But if students are to be liberally educated and not just trained or socialized, if schools are not to disenfranchise religious subcultures, and if they are to be neutral in matters of religion, then we must include religious voices in the discussion.

The character education movement is grounded in the conviction that there are *consensus* virtues and values. The consensus must be local, but it may also be broader; indeed, its advocates sometimes claim (rightly) that virtues such as honesty and integrity are universal and are found in all the world's religions. Nonetheless, because religion can't be practiced in public schools and because it is often controversial, the character education movement avoids it. Religion is mentioned only once in the "Character Education Manifesto"—in the claim that character education is a joint responsibility of schools, families, communities, *and churches.*

Clearly the moral ethos of *public* schools must be secular rather than religious; character education cannot use religious exercises to nurture the development of character. But character education cannot implicitly convey the idea that religion is irrelevant to morality. We have noted that character education employs literature and history to convey moral messages. Some of those stories and some of that history should make clear that people's moral convictions are often grounded in religious traditions.

When teachers and students in the higher grades discuss controversial moral issues—abortion, sexuality, and social justice, for example—they must include religious perspectives on them in the discussion. For constitutional reasons those religious interpretations cannot be disparaged or advocated.

As we've noted many times, one reason we disagree in our moral judgments is that we are committed to strikingly different worldviews. Some of us ground our moral judgments in Scripture, others in cost-benefit analyses, yet others in conscience (and there are many other alternatives). Even when we agree—about honesty, for example—we may disagree about why we should be honest. Long-term self-interest and love of humanity may both prescribe honesty as the best policy—though one's attitude and motivation, the kind of person one is, may be quite different; and, of course, there will be occasions when the requirements of love and (even long-term) self-interest will diverge. Just as in math, it is not enough that we agree about the right answer (but we must get it in the right way), so in any domain of the curriculum a good education requires more than a shallow agreement about conclusions. To be educated requires an understanding of the deep reasons for belief and values.

Historically, religions have provided the categories, the narratives, the worldviews, that provided the deep justifications for morality. From within almost any religious worldview, conservative or liberal, people must set themselves right with God, reconciling themselves to the basic moral structure of reality. They are to act in love and justice and community, being mindful of those less fortunate than themselves.

The conventional wisdom now, however, is that we can teach morality without reference to religion. Indeed, the deep justifications have changed. Health and home economics texts often ground their account of values in Abraham Maslow's humanistic psychology, whereas the economics standards and texts appeal to neoclassical economic theory and modern social science.

Modern science teaches students there is no moral structure to nature. Our whole moral vocabulary has changed: like modern culture generally, modern education often emphasizes rights over duties, individualism over community, autonomy over authority, happiness over salvation, self-esteem over self-sacrifice, and cost-benefit analysis over conscience. Indeed, students may learn that there are no right or wrong answers when moral judgments are the issue.

The problem is not just that educators ignore religious accounts of morality; it is that the secular worldview that pervades modern education renders religion suspect. How do we make sense of religious accounts of morality? A little "natural inclusion" here and there will help. A yearlong course in religious studies will help more. We also find merit in the idea of a senior capstone course in ethics in which students would study various secular and religious ways of understanding morality and several of the most pressing moral problems of our time.

Moral education and the Bible

Conservative religious parents sometimes ask that Bible courses be offered in public schools as a way of addressing the moral development of children. As we have seen, the courts have made it clear that public schools cannot teach students that the Bible is true, or that children should act in accord with Biblical morality. Nonetheless, there is a constitutional way in which study of the Bible is relevant to moral education. By studying the Bible, students will encounter a vocabulary and framework for thinking about morality and the human condition that will quite properly provide them with critical distance on the secular ideas and ideals they acquire from elsewhere in the curriculum—and from popular culture.

Morality is at the heart of all religion, and, as we've argued, one important reason for studying religion is to acquire some sense of the answers that have been given to the fundamental existential questions of life. Teachers and texts can't endorse religious answers to those questions, but they can and should expose students to them fairly as part of a good liberal—and moral—education. Students may find those answers compelling even if their teachers and texts don't require them to.

Religion and sex education

It may be helpful to sketch the relevance of religion to one particularly troublesome part of the curriculum: sex education. It is important for students to understand the biology of sexuality; but, of course, the purpose of sex education has always been something more than simple science education. Its primary purpose has been to guide students' behavior, addressing major social problems such as unwanted pregnancies and the spread of sexually transmitted diseases (STDs).

One way to address these problems is to teach students sexual abstinence. Another is to provide them with a little technological know-how regarding birth control and condoms. Not surprisingly, many parents (including many religious conservatives) view the condom approach as a legitimation of sexual promiscuity and favor "abstinence only." Many educators respond that it is naive to teach abstinence only because many adolescents will inevitably engage in sexual behavior and they must learn how to protect themselves and others. The pragmatic middle ground has become "abstinence but": teach students abstinence but include something about condoms as well.

Whichever position we take requires that we give students reasons for using condoms or foregoing the pleasures of sexuality. Three kinds of answers are common. First, it can be argued that either approach is in one's long-term self-interest, and much sex education focuses on the unhappy consequences of unplanned pregnancies and STDs. Some students will recognize the risks and alter their behavior accordingly—though adolescents are not typically strong on long-term self-interest and deferred gratification. Perhaps more important, if it is to be truly *educational*, sex education must make students aware of the fact that sexual behavior is universally held to be subject to moral as well as prudential judgments. To be ignorant of this is to be uneducated.

So, how do we introduce morality into sex education? A second approach—that taken in each of the four high school health texts we reviewed—is a variation on values clarification. Students should act responsibly: they should survey their options, consider the consequences (on themselves and on others), and then act in a way that maximizes whatever it is that they value most. Each of the health texts concludes that responsible individuals will practice abstinence. The problem, of course, is that this conclusion requires a considerable act of faith, for what students value most is up to them. The books offer no grounds for assessing the values of students as morally right or wrong; values are ultimately personal.

Health, home economics, and sex education texts and materials often use the language of *values* rather than that of *morality*. One reason is that for many educators "morality" has become synonymous either with what is "moralistic" (and hence narrow and intolerant) or what is religious. But, of course, this is an extraordinarily narrow view of morality. Indeed, no philosophers (in whose domain the field of ethics is usually taken to reside) use "morality" in such narrow ways. We suspect that the deeper problem is that much ocial science can't make sense of morality and so must translate it into talk of choices and personal values. Virtually all the health and home economics texts we reviewed start from the position of humanistic psychology. But if the authors can't cast their conceptual nets wider than this, it is not surprising that they don't catch morality in them.

One irony in all of this is that virtually everyone still believes that some actions *are* morally right and other actions *are* morally wrong. Pedophilia is morally wrong. Not telling the person with whom one proposes to have sex that he or she has an STD is morally wrong. Honesty isn't just a matter of cost-benefit analysis and personal values; it is *morally binding*. If people don't understand this, they are ignorant, and if we don't teach students this, we are irresponsible. As we have argued, the character education movement has been a widely accepted (and much needed) antidote to the relativistic tendencies of values clarification, and it offers another approach to sex education.

Sexual relationships, like all relationships, should be characterized by honesty, loyalty, and respect for the feelings, privacy, and well-being of others—and broad consensus supports this. Prudence, self-control, and a willingness to defer gratification are virtues of unquestionable importance in all aspects of life, but particularly in matters of sexuality. We agree that it is wrong for children to have sexual relationships. We might even agree that sexual modesty in dress and demeanor is an important virtue, at least for children. The moral consensus on sexuality is, no doubt, limited and fragile. Still, because there is a consensus, schools should constantly emphasize these moral virtues and principles by means of their ethos, dress codes, stories told and read, and, of course, in health, home economics, and sex education courses. Sex education must also be moral education.

We have argued that character education cannot (implicitly) give the impression that religion is irrelevant to morality. Children's stories about love and romance and marriage and the family should include religious literature. Character education builds on moral consensus, but obviously there is also a good deal of (often strong) disagreement on matters relating to sexuality—abstinence and birth control, abortion and homosexuality, for example.

Not surprisingly, we also disagree about what to teach students about these things; indeed, we often disagree about *whether* to teach about such things. Our claim is this: *if* we are to include controversial issues in the sex education curriculum, then, as always, students must hear the different voices—secular and religious, conservative and liberal—that are part of our cultural conversation. Given the importance of religion in our culture, to remain ignorant of religious ways of thinking about sexuality is to remain uneducated. Indeed, the term "sex education" is something of a misnomer; as it is usually taught, sex education is far from being truly educational, for it limits the range of voices allowed into the discussion.

Older students should learn about religious as well as secular arguments for abstinence, and they should learn how different religious traditions regard birth control. Indeed, they should learn something about the relevant Scriptural sources (in different traditions) for sexual morality, marriage, and the family. They should know, for example, that within religions, marriage is a "holy" or sacramental (and not just a legal) institution. They should understand the policy positions on controversial sexual issues taken by contemporary religious organizations and theologians. Students are *illiberally* "educated" if they learn to think about sexuality in only secular categories.

Or consider abortion. For many religious people, abortion is *the* most important moral issue of our time; for them, it is *the* most important consequence of unwanted pregnancies and sexual promiscuity. Yet most sex education ignores abortion. Of the health texts we reviewed only one mentioned it—devoting a single paragraph to explaining that it is a medically safe alternative to adoption. That paragraph concludes: "This procedure has sparked a great deal of controversy". We suggest that to be an educated human being in the United States at the end of the 20th century one must understand the abortion controversy; indeed, its relevance to sex education is immediate and tremendously important.

So what does it mean to be educated about abortion? Certainly students should understand the point of view of the Roman Catholic Church and those religious conservatives who believe that abortion is murder. They should also understand the point of view of those religious liberals (from various traditions) who are pro-choice. They should understand feminist positions on abortion. They should learn about the key Supreme Court rulings and different ways of interpreting the implications of political liberty for the abortion debate. Students should read primary source documents written from within each of these traditions. And, of course, teachers and texts should not take positions on where truth lies when we are so deeply divided.

Or consider homosexuality. The health texts we reviewed each mentioned that some people are heterosexual and others are homosexual and that we don't quite know what accounts for the difference. That's it. Like abortion, however, the issue of homosexuality is one that is tremendously important for students to understand if they are to be informed citizens and *educated* about sexuality.

One approach is for educators to decide what is right and then teach *their* views to children. New York City's *Children of the Rainbow* multicultural curriculum is a rather notorious example; it would have taught elementary school children the acceptability of homosexuality and nontraditional families had not a coalition of religious conservatives rebelled, ultimately forcing the departure of the system's chancellor. Our objection to this curriculum is not its position on homosexuality; it is that it takes a position at all. It is proper and important to teach children to respect the rights of others; name calling and gay bashing are not permissible—and there is broad consensus about this. But we disagree deeply about homosexuality on moral and religious grounds.

Given our *civic* framework, it is not permissible for a public school to institutionalize a moral or religious position on a divisive issue and teach it to children uncritically. Given our *educational* framework, students must learn about the alternative positions when we disagree; all the major voices must be included in the discussion. Of course, the New York City case was particularly troubling because the children were so young.

What then would an adequate sex education curriculum look like? It must, of course, be age appropriate. Lessons and courses for young children should adopt the character education model, and we must take great care to ensure that we don't encourage premature sexual behavior; character education continues to be appropriate for high school students—so long as it deals with matters about which we agree. Indeed, we are inclined to think that adolescents need moral guidance in matters of sexual morality rather more than they need freedom. They must learn to think about sexuality in moral terms.

We have also argued, however, that we need to educate mature students regarding some matters of great importance about which we disagree deeply. When we do this, however, we must educate them liberally, including all of the major voices—religious as well as secular—in the discussion. We have already noted that one disagreement is over whether to teach abstinence only. Unhappily, our differences here appear to be irreconcilable. We do believe that some of the controversy would dissipate if sex education were truly liberal. If it would take seriously moral and religious ways of thinking about sexuality, then discussion of condoms would be less likely to be understood as legitimizing promiscuity. Still, if schools require such courses, they should include opt-out (or opt-in) provisions. We suspect that if parents were convinced that educators took their moral and religious views seriously, fewer would have their children opt out.

We recognize that adequate materials are lacking and most teachers are not prepared to include religious perspectives on sexuality in their classes. It is no easy task to make sense of the soul when discussing abortion in a health class, sacramental understandings of marriage in a home economics class, or the sinfulness of promiscuity in a sex education class. Sex education teachers usually have backgrounds in health education, psychology, and the social sciences rather than the humanities or religious studies, and they may have no background in religious studies to help them make sense of religious perspectives on sex education. This is, once again, reason for a required course in religious studies (or a moral capstone course) that provides a sufficiently deep understanding of religion to enable students to make sense of religious interpretations of morality and sexuality. Still, for both civic and educational reasons, some attention to religion in sex education courses is absolutely essential.

Finally, we note that other teachers will sometimes find themselves drawn into both sex education and moral education. Much fiction, for example, deals with sexuality—dating, love, marriage, integrity, adultery, homosexuality, and the family. The study of literature is important for the insight and perspective it provides on the inescapable existential questions of life—a good number of which bear on sexuality. Moreover, it is tremendously important that teachers in a variety of courses provide students the moral resources for thinking critically about the portrayal of sexuality in popular culture.

One purpose of moral education is to help make children virtuous—honest, responsible, and compassionate. Another is to make mature students informed and reflective about important and controversial moral issues. Both purposes are embedded in a yet larger project—making sense of life. On most accounts, morality isn't intellectually free-floating, a matter of personal choices and subjective values.

Moralities are embedded in traditions, in conceptions of what it means to be human, in worldviews. How we ground and justify moral claims is tremendously important. It makes a huge difference if we think, for example, in terms of neoclassical economic theory and cost-benefit analyses, humanistic psychology and self-actualization, or moral theology. Inspite of religious diversity and the great differences between liberals and conservatives within religious traditions, the vast majority of religious folk agree that reality has a God-given moral structure, and this distinguishes them from most secular folk.

In their influential study of American culture *Habits of the Heart*, some argued that most Americans speak two quite different moral languages: an older, now "secondary" language derived from our civic and religious traditions; and a newer, "first" language of "utilitarian" and "expressive" individualism that is reinforced over and over again by modern culture. Unfortunately, they argue, this language of individualism is not nearly rich enough to allow us to make sense of those moral virtues and vices that are part of our civic and religious traditions.

If we haven't already become completely preoccupied with liberty and rights, self-interest and self-esteem, autonomy and individualism, we are in danger of this happening; we are losing our ability to speak meaningfully about virtue and duty, love and self-sacrifice, community and justice. The tendency is to forget the older languages, particularly when the everyday language of culture and the marketplace, schooling and scholarship are secular.

Too much education is relentlessly fixated on economic and technological development—both of which are important, of course. But, *in the end*, one of the things most people learn is that the greatest sources of meaning in life come not from wealth and technological wizardry but from altogether different realms of experience.

IMPLEMENTING GUIDELINES FOR CONSTRUCTIVIST ALTERNATIVES

To reduce the possibility that children will experience consequences as arbitrary and punitive, we suggest implementing the following constructivist teaching principles.

It is not unusual for an adult to feel that a child should be made to suffer for a misdeed. This may be vengeance based on anger, or it may derive from the common idea that if the child suffers, he or she will not do the misdeed again. Suffering may lead the child not to do the act again, or it may lead the child to resent or even hate the perpetrator of the suffering. It may lead the child to feel inwardly that he or she is bad and thereby negate self-esteem. Or it may lead the child to be more calculating next time so the adult does not find out. From the point of view of the child's psychological development, punishments are risky and most likely counterproductive if the adult wants to promote the child's moral development.

It is clear that any consequence, even the reciprocity consequences, can become expiatory if implemented with a punitive tone and attitude. To avoid turning reciprocity consequences into punishments, be matter-of-fact and supportive of the child.

Selectively allow natural consequences to occur

Teachers sometimes rescue children from natural consequences and lose an opportunity for children to construct the relation between action and consequence. For example, the teacher may separate children in a conflict without letting them experience the other's reactions. Or, the teacher may constantly put the caps back on markers. We understand the concern for waste but believe that the lesson on consequences is well worth a wasted marker.

Two kindergarten boys during a cookie-making activity were careless and did not pay close attention to the recipe.

They put in one cup of baking powder instead of one teaspoon. The teacher observed their error and could have prevented it. However, she felt that the only way the boys would become more serious and careful about cooking was to experience the result of their carelessness. At snacktime when everyone tried the cookies, children were disappointed and said they tasted "yucky." The teacher was able to review the recipe with them and help them realize their error. The next time they made cookies, they were more serious and careful.

Constructivist teachers do not "discipline" children in the sense of controlling and punishing them. Rather, the constructivist alternatives to such discipline focus on strategies to foster children's construction of convictions about relating to others in cooperative ways. Piaget's distinction between expiatory and reciprocity sanctions provides the basis for planning general responses to misdeeds.

More specifically, the criterion of reciprocity leads constructivist teachers to six types of sanctions that emphasize the social bonds broken by children's misdeeds. To reduce the possibility that children will experience consequences as arbitrary and punitive, constructivist teachers follow nine guidelines that protect children's autonomy and lead to development.

DEVELOPMENTAL DISCIPLINE

Developmental discipline describe an approach to classroom discipline for the elementary school setting. The approach is one which was developed within a more general approach to education called, "The Child Development Project" (CDP).

The CDP program

Our goal was to create a comprehensive set of home and school activities and practices that would incorporate all of the [following] experiences: warm and supportive adult-child relations; highlighting and explaining the importance of prosócia valuesl; discussion of and reflection on the reasons for moral actions; and understanding, discussing, and reflecting on the feelings, motives, and needs of others. It was also necessary that our program be learned by average teachers and parents within the constraints under which schools operate, and that it easily within the normal routines of the classroom and the home.

For a variety of reasons both our school and home programs underwent substantial change during the process of development and implementation. Sometimes these changes resulted from our aeveloping understanding of the practical limitations imposed by the fact that parents, teachers, and school administrators are very busy people and simply did not have the time to engage in all the activities that we and they deemed worthwhile.

Sometimes these changes resulted from our becoming clearer about our own theoretical perspective and better able to translate that perspective into classroom and home activities. As we worked with teachers and parents, designed specific school and home activities, observed aspects of the program in action, and reflected on our experiences, we more carefully articulated our theoretical perspective and understood its relationship to school and home activities.

What follows is a description of the school program as we currently conceive it. This is an idealized description; it is the conception that we present to teachers and that shapes the activities and materials we develop. The program in practice was sometimes far from ideal. After describing our ideal conception, we shall describe ways in which the actual implementation of the program met and failed to meet our ideal conception.

The school programme

Although we see the CDP program as an integrated whole, we have designed and taught it as five mutually consistent and somewhat overlapping components:

- *Developmental discipline*—an approach to classroom management that involves a concerted effort to create a caring community in the classroom in which each child's needs for autonomy, competence, and affection are balanced with the needs of community in order to maximize the learning and well-being of all.
- *Cooperative learning*—an approach to academic instruction in which children work together to help one another learn and have opportunities to experience and practice such prosocial values as fairness, helpfulness, responsibility, and considerateness.
- *Helping*—activities that provide children with opportunities for prosocial action both in the classroom and beyond.
- *Understanding others*—a focus on helping children understand and empathize with the situation and experience of others through literature, discussion, and direct experience.
- *Highlighting prosocial values*—a focus on explaining the importance of prosocial values and helping children see the relation of values to actions through exposure to characters and events in literature and history and through personal example.

We view the classroom as having four main functions: helping children learn a specified set of academic skills, concepts, and facts; fostering their love of learning; helping them learn a set of social skills, values, and expectations; and fostering their commitment to those values. The classroom management practices that a teacher uses must be consistent with all four goals. The teacher is inescapably engaged in socialization as well as education. Most current classroom management systems have been designed to serve the academic function only. In fact, a recent review of classroom management research does not even mention the possible socialization function of classroom management.

The socialization practices we advocate assume that most school-age children are disposed to learn and adopt the values of their community, to construct a personal moral system, and to act to benefit others as well as to satisfy personal needs. In contrast, many discipline systems are predicated on a view that children, particularly children who seem incline to misbehave, need to have good character imposed on them. Such approaches are designed to show children that the "right" thing is their self-interest. The only incentive invoked by such approaches is student self-interest - the knowledge that their behaviors will increase or decrease their receipt of positive or negative consequences. In such controlled classrooms, compliance can indeed be achieved by increasing the promise of external rewards or the threat of negative consequences. Such control may allow the teacher to achieve an environment conducive to academic learning (although probably not an intrinsic orientation to learning), but it does not teach commitment to prosocial values.

Our program holds that socialization must focus on developing an internal disposition toward prosocial action. Development discipline attempts this in four somewhat overlapping ways:

- Building a warm and supportive relationship between the teacher and each student.
- Building a community in the classroom in which the stated learning goals are being achieved and in which each child's personal needs for competence, autonomy, and respect or affiliation are being met.
- Assisting children to refine their own cognitive moral systems and their understanding of how those systems apply to everyday classroom life.

Using both proactive and reactive control techniques that enhance (or at least do not undermine) the above goals; that is, techniques that effectively control behavior but at the same time help or allow children to:

— See themselves as well-intentioned (i.e., as morally competent)
— Understand how expectations or rules are consistent with their own sense of fairness or kindness,
— Understand how behaviors affect the well-being of others,
— Feel some autonomy in compliance (by experiencing the least coercive control method possible),
— Retain their belief in the affection and good will of the authority (by experiencing means of control that are nonpunitive, the focus on solving the problem at hand, and that appear to be fair), and
— More easily satisfy the norm or expectations.

Building warm teacher-child relationship: As stated earlier, we see warm and supportive adult-child relationships as central to the development of a child's motivation to be concerned about the welfare of others. It is not a simple task for a teacher to establish a personal relationship with each of the thirty-plus students, especially when also charged with maximizing students' academic learning. In addition to increasing teachers' awareness of the importance both of the teacher-child relationship and of using information opportunities to talk with students about mutual interest, we recommend that teacher use standard academic learning situations to build these relationships. For example, teachers can introduce stories by telling a related personal experience and inviting students to tell about their own related experiences, writing assignments can be about personal experiences or viewpoints, and children can learn interview skills by interviewing the teacher. In direct contrast to the "don't smile until Thanksgiving" approach, we advise teachers, especially at the beginning of the year, to take opportunities to perform kind or helpful acts for their students in order to let them know that the teacher is personally concerned about their individual needs.

Developing children's cognitive moral understanding: Children have much to learn about what constitutes fairness and kindness and about the reasons for the many rules and procedures necessary for regulating life in a social group.

Teachers' needs to assert their power in order to maintain classroom control will be lessened if the children understand the moral principles that are being enforced. In addition to offering explanations when stating expectations and correcting misbehavior, teachers can enhance children's moral understanding by involving them in developing class rules and norms and in the responsibility for seeing that the rules and norms function well. At all grade levels teachers begin the year by asking the children to think about and talk with one another about "the way we want our class to be."

The children are specially asked to think about things they do and don't want to happen in class. The teacher then helps the children see that these things can be fit under a few general norms or values such as "be fair," "don't hurt," "be kind," and "be responsible." The norms are chosen to be general enough to cover a wide range of behaviors, and thus obviate the need for dozens of prescriptive and proscriptive rules. Regular class meetings are held throughout the year to assess how well the teacher and children are following the norms and, perhaps, to devise some procedures to help in areas where improvement is needed. We see this as a way of increasing children's understanding of such general values as kindness, fairness, and responsibility and of their application in the school and classroom setting.

Creating a caring community: Children will be more inclined to adopt the values of their community and respond to community members in a caring way if their own needs are being met. We focus on three psychological needs - autonomy, competence, and belonging.

Many different activities go into creating a classroom community that meets or addresses these needs. Each child's sense of competence, for example, can be enhanced by using individual mastery rather than normative standards to evaluate learning, by avoiding competitive learning techniques such as spelling bees and the public display of differential levels of achievement of individual class members, and by using cooperative learning structures and multiple-ability tasks to help all children find avenues to success.

Personal autonomy is always restricted in a group setting, and the classroom is no exception. However, teachers can satisfy most children's needs for autonomy by providing opportunities for choice in the timing and content of academic work, by encouraging children to develop and work toward their own personal learning goals, by relying more on explanations than external control to induce children to meet academic and behavioral expectations, and by awakening children's intrinsic interest in the learning tasks.

In addition to needing a sense of competence and autonomy, children need to interact with the feel understood and liked by their fellow class members. Our program encourages teachers to conduct a number of classroom activities that promote children's interaction while learning, and to build a sense of belonging and friendly feelings among children. These include cooperative games in which children work together to help one another, activities involving products to which all class members contribute, and partner and small-group activities in which children have opportunities to exchange personal information.

Classroom control techniques

While many think of classroom discipline as synonymous with gaining children's compliance through adult control, control techniques are only part of developmental discipline. In fact, if not exercised with restraint, the use of external control can undermine the development of prosocial motivation. However, the teacher's careful and respectful exercise of control is a necessary aspect of a classroom in which children acquire a prosocial orientation.

Setting expectations: We ask teachers to consider both the conditions that cause them to feel a need to exert control and the kinds of control to use when they feel it is needed. Teachers vary in the range of behaviors they feel they must control, and different teachers may react differently to the same student actions. Often the amount of effort a teacher has to spend exerting control can be lessened by a careful analysis of what behaviors are important to a well-functioning classroom and developmentally appropriate for the particular group of children. We ask teachers to analyze their classroom procedures and expectations with the goals of eliminating unnecessary regulation and adjusting expectations to the developmental levels of the children in the class. Is it necessary that the children complete a learning activity exactly as prescribed? Is it reasonable to expect first-graders to sit quietly for over an hour? For third-graders to keep a class meeting interesting and well-paced? For fifth-graders to handle problems on peer rejection on their own? When control is needed, we recommend that teachers use approaches that will not undermine children's sense that they are competent, cared for, and autonomous.

Indirect control: Control can be exercised in several ways. Indirectly, the teacher may organize the environment to encourage positive behaviors and discourage negative ones. Common examples of this type of teacher control are separating the children engaged in noisy tasks form those doing tasks requiring quiet contemplation, eliminating unnecessary distractions, and using a calming activity to help children make the transition from an exciting, energetic activity to a contemplative one. Indirect control is commonly used by effective teachers and is indispensable to maintaining a productive and enjoyable learning environment.

Reminders: A second type of control involves the teacher more directly, but the "force" behind the control is the child's recognition and acceptance of the teacher as a legitimate authority. This form of control often serves more as a reminder than as a threat. For example, a teacher's glance or frown can be seen by both teacher and child as a quiet way of reminding the child that he or she is not attending to the task at hand. The exercise of such control implies that the teacher believes that the child shares the underlying understanding and will willingly comply. This type of control implies mutual trust, and when such trust exists in a classroom it can take the place of more coercive forms of control.

Teaching social behaviors: A third type of control involves teaching or guiding children to more acceptable ways of behaving. This is similar to the ways teachers respond when children make mistakes in academic areas. For example, a teacher might intervene in an argument by demonstrating more tactful ways of stating opinions, or by suggesting a fairer way to reach an agreement. Such forms of control are often seen by children as helpful rather than coercive. For example, three first-grade children were pushing one another and arguing about who had the right to be first in the lunchroom line.

A CDP staff member who was standing by suggested that the children guess a number and whoever was closest would be first. The children agreed, made their guesses, and the argument was settled. The next day, upon seeing the staff member again, one of the children exclaimed, "Hey, I remember you. You're the lady who helped us solve our problem." This type of control can be an important means of helping children understand and live up to prosocial values, but it can be time consuming and difficult to exercise. It requires that the teacher understand the problem from the children's perspectives and understand children well enough to know what solutions to suggest or how to help them discover a fair or kind solution.

We believe that three forms of control are key to managing a classroom without an undue reliance or manipulative and power-assertive techniques. We encourage teachers to think of most children misbehavior as they would think of academic errors: as opportunities to teach. What is taught will depend on what skill or knowledge the child appears to be lacking: verbal self-instruction for children lacking in self-control; specific social skills such as being able to explain feelings or resolve conflicts for children lacking in skills; and provision of the moral or practical reason for a rule or expectation for children who do not see its importance.

Power assertion: Of course, not all misbehavior is the result of children's lack of knowledge, self-control, or skills. Sometimes children misbehave even when they know better. If such misbehavior is more frequent than can be explained as momentary lapses in effort, we advise the teacher to see if there is some important need that is not being met in the classroom. Is there a warm and trusting relationship with the teacher? Are there sufficient opportunities for autonomy? Are there sufficient opportunities to demonstrate competence? If any of these is lacking for a child, a group of children, or the whole class, the teacher is advised to alter the situation, if possible, to better satisfy the children's needs.

While most children can be helped to behave better by the use of these non-power-assertive techniques, some children, for one reason or another, will not respond to them, and it will be necessary to resort to the use of power assertion. Indeed, because time is frequently short in classrooms, and the need for immediate control is sometimes pressing, most teachers occasionally will find it necessary to use power-assertive techniques even with generally well-behaved children. When power assertion is used, we suggest ways to lessen the sense of coercion without lessening the effectiveness of the control. Coercion is frequently less painful if the child has room for some choice or if the authority figure express sympathy for the child's situation. For example, a teacher can send a disruptive child from the room but allow the child to determine when to return. A teacher may tell a disruptive group that he or she knows it is hard to work quietly, while still insisting on quiet.

A child's sense of self can be preserved even in the face of serious misbehavior if the teacher attributes the best possible motive to the child consistent with the facts, while simultaneously stopping or even punishing the action. The following incident is an example.

Some sixth-grade boys while trying to play a practical joke, accidentally broke a girl's wrist. When the principal had finished explaining to them the pain they had caused the girl, the boys were in tears. The principal told them that he know that they were sorry and that they had not realized the harm they could cause. He then explained that he would have to suspend them from school for a day as a message to them and the community that what they had done was serious.

The boys, on their own initiative, brought flowers to the girl. This example illustrates what we regard as constructive approach to the use of power. We do not have a specific formula for its use, but simply advise teachers that when they find it necessary to assert power, they should try to be fair and nonpunitive, and to focus on solving the problem at hand.

In the course of training teachers in developmental discipline and providing them with techniques and activities for accomplishing all four of its aspects, we have found that many hold a view of children as self-centered, manipulative, and lazy. If one see children this way, the logical way to prevent or respond to misbehavior is to use threat or punishment, and the logical way to get children to behavior well is to use rewards. We try to help teachers see children not just as self-interested but also as prosocially oriented. If one believes children are interested in learning and want to please and to be fair and kind, then the appropriate response to misbehavior is to find out why the child was not able to do the right thing, and to provide the necessary help. The way to get children to behave well is to be sure they know what is expected, have the skills required, and can see that it is a reasonable, fair, responsible, or kind thing to do.

2

Nature and Concept of Morality and Moral Education

Moral education is becoming an increasingly popular topic in the fields of psychology and education. Media reports of increased violent juvenile crime, teen pregnancy, and suicide have caused many to declare a moral crisis in our nation. While not all of these social concerns are moral in nature, and most have complex origins, there is a growing trend towards linking the solutions to these and related social problems to the teaching of moral and social values in our public schools.

However, considerations of the role schools can and should play in the moral development of youth are themselves the subject of controversy. Fortunately, systematic research and scholarship on moral development has been going on for most of this century, and educators wishing to attend to issues of moral development and education may make use of what has been learned through that work.

PIAGET'S THEORY OF MORAL DEVELOPMENT

Jean Piaget is among the first psychologists whose work remains directly relevant to contemporary theories of moral development. In his early writing, he focused specifically on the moral lives of children, studying the way children play games in order to learn more about children's beliefs about right and wrong.

According to Piaget, all development emerges from action; that is to say, individuals construct and reconstruct their knowledge of the world as a result of interactions with the environment. Based on his observations of children's application of rules when playing, Piaget determined that morality, too, can be considered a developmental process. For example, Ben, a ten year old studied by Piaget, provided the following critique of a rule made-up by a child playing marbles: "it isn't a rule! It's a wrong rule because it's outside of the rules.

A fair rule is one that is in the game". Ben believed in the absolute and intrinsic truth of the rules, characteristic of early moral reasoning. In contrast, Vua, aged thirteen, illustrates an understanding of the reasoning behind the application of rules, characteristic of later moral thinking. When asked to consider the fairness of a made-up rule compared to a traditional rule, Vua replied "It is just as fair because the marbles are far apart".

In addition to examining children's understanding of rules about games, Piaget interviewed children regarding acts such as stealing and lying. When asked what a lie is, younger children consistently answered that they are "naughty words". When asked why they should not lie, younger children could rarely explain beyond the forbidden nature of the act: "because it is a naughty word". However, older children were able to explain "because it isn't right", and "it wasn't true". Even older children indicated an awareness of intention as relevant to the meaning of an act: "A lie is when you deceive someone else. To make a mistake is when you make a mistake". From his observations, Piaget concluded that children begin in a "heteronomous" stage of moral reasoning, characterized by a strict adherence to rules and duties, and obedience to authority.

This heteronomy results from two factors. The first factor is the young child's cognitive structure. According to Piaget, the thinking of young children is characterized by egocentrism. That is to say that young children are unable to simultaneously take into account their own view of things with the perspective of someone else. This egocentrism leads children to project their own thoughts and wishes onto others. It is also associated with the uni-directional view of rules and power associated with heteronomous moral thought, and various forms of "moral realism." Moral realism is associated with "objective responsibility", which is valuing the letter of the law above the purpose of the law.

This is why young children are more concerned about the outcomes of actions rather than the intentions of the person doing the act. Moral realism is also associated with the young child's belief in "immanent justice." This is the expectation that punishments automatically follow acts of wrong-doing. One of the most famous cases of such childhood thinking was that of the young boy who believed that his hitting a power pole with his baseball bat caused a major power blackout in the New York city area.

The second major contributor to heteronomous moral thinking in young children, is their relative social relationship with adults. In the natural authority relationship between adults and children, power is handed down from above. The relative powerlessness of young children, coupled with childhood egocentrism feeds into a heteronomous moral orientation. However, through interactions with other children in which the group seeks a to play together in a way all find fair, children find this strict heteronomous adherence to rules sometimes problematic.

As children consider these situations, they develop towards an "autonomous" stage of moral reasoning, characterized by the ability to consider rules critically, and selectively apply these rules based on a goal of mutual respect and cooperation. The ability to act from a sense of reciprocity and mutual respect is associated with a shift in the child's cognitive structure from egocentrism to perspective taking.

Coordinating one's own perspective with that of others means that what is right needs to be based on solutions that meet the requirements of fair reciprocity. Thus, Piaget viewed moral development as the result of interpersonal interactions through which individuals work out resolutions which all deem fair. Paradoxically, this autonomous view of morality as fairness is more compelling and leads to more consistent behavior than the heteronomous orientation held by younger children.

Piaget concluded from this work that schools should emphasize cooperative decision-making and problem solving, nurturing moral development by requiring students to work out common rules based on fairness. This is a direct rejection of sociologists Emile Durkheim's view of proper moral education. Durkheim, similar to Piaget, believed that morality resulted from social interaction or immersion in a group. However, Durkheim believed moral development was a natural result of attachment to the group, an attachment which manifests itself in a respect for the symbols, rules, and authority of that group. Piaget rejected this belief that children simply learn and internalize the norms for a group; he believed individuals define morality individually through their struggles to arrive at fair solutions. Given this view, Piaget suggested that a classroom teacher perform a difficult task: the educator must provide students with opportunities for personal discovery through problem solving, rather than indoctrinating students with norms.

KOHLBERG'S APPROACH TO MORAL DEVELOPMENT

Lawrence Kohlberg modified and elaborated Piaget's work, and laid the groundwork for the current debate within psychology on moral development. Consistent with Piaget, he proposed that children form ways of thinking through their experiences which include understandings of moral concepts such as justice, rights, equality and human welfare. Kohlberg followed the development of moral judgment beyond the ages studied by Piaget, and determined that the process of attaining moral maturity took longer and was more gradual than Piaget had proposed. On the basis of his research, Kohlberg identified six stages of moral reasoning grouped into three major levels. Each level represented a fundamental shift in the social-moral perspective of the individual. At the first level, the preconventional level, a person's moral judgments are characterized by a concrete, individual perspective. Within this level, a Stage 1 heteronomous orientation focuses on avoiding breaking rules that are backed by punishment, obedience for its own sake and avoiding the physical consequences of an action to persons and property. As in Piaget's framework, the reasoning of Stage 1 is characterized by ego-centrism and the inability to consider the perspectives of others. At Stage 2 there is the early emergence of moral reciprocity. The Stage 2 orientation focuses on the instrumental, pragmatic value of an action. Reciprocity is of the form, "you scratch my back and I'll scratch yours." The Golden Rule becomes, "If someone hits you, you hit them back." At Stage 2 one follows the rules only when it is to someone's immediate interests. What is right is what's fair in the sense of an equal exchange, a deal, an agreement. At Stage 2 there is an understanding that everybody has his(her) own interest to pursue and these conflict, so that right is relative.

Individuals at the conventional level of reasoning, however, have a basic understanding of conventional morality, and reason with an understanding that norms and conventions are necessary to uphold society. They tend to be self-identified with these rules, and uphold them consistently, viewing morality as acting in accordance with what society defines as right. Within this level, individuals at Stage 3 are aware of shared feelings, agreements, and expectations which take primacy over individual interests. Persons at Stage 3 define what is right in terms of what is expected by people close to one's self, and in terms of the stereotypic roles that define being good - e.g., a good brother, mother, teacher. Being good means keeping mutual relationships, such as trust, loyalty, respect, and gratitude. The perspective is that of the local community or family. There is not as yet a consideration of the generalized social system. Stage 4 marks the shift from defining what is right in terms of local norms and role expectations to defining right in terms of the laws and norms established by the larger social system. This is the "member of society" perspective in which one is moral by fulfilling the actual duties defining one's social responsibilities. One must obey the law except in extreme cases in which the law comes into conflict with other prescribed social duties. Obeying the law is seen as necessary in order to maintain the system of laws which protect everyone.

Finally, the post conventional level is characterized by reasoning based on principles, using a "prior to society" perspective. These individuals reason based on the principles which underlie rules and norms, but reject a uniform application of a rule or norm. While two stages have been presented within the theory, only one, Stage 5, has received substantial empirical support. Stage 6 remains as a theoretical endpoint which rationally follows from the preceding 5 stages. In essence this last level of moral judgment entails reasoning rooted in the ethical fairness principles from which moral laws would be devised. Laws are evaluated in terms of their coherence with basic principles of fairness rather than upheld simply on the basis of their place within an existing social order. Thus, there is an understanding that elements of morality such as regard for life and human welfare transcend particular cultures and societies and are to be upheld irrespective of other conventions or normative obligations. These stages (1-5) have been empirically supported by findings from longitudinal and cross-cultural research.

Kohlberg used these findings to reject traditional character education practices. These approaches are premised in the idea that virtues and vices are the basis to moral behavior, or that moral character is comprised of a "bag of virtues", such as honesty, kindness, patience, stiength, etc. According to the traditional approach, teachers are to teach these virtues through example and direct communication of convictions, by giving students an opportunity to practice these virtues, and by rewarding their expression. However, critiques of the traditional approach find flaws inherent in this model. This approach provides no guiding principle for defining what virtues are worthy of espousal, and wrongly assumes a community consensus on what are considered "positive values".

In fact, teachers often end up arbitrarily imposing certain values depending upon their societal, cultural, and personal beliefs. In order to address this issue of ethical relativity, some have adopted the values-clarification approach to moral education. This teaching practice is based on the assumption that there are no single, correct answers to ethical dilemmas, but that there is value in holding clear views and acting accordingly. In addition, there is a value of toleration of divergent views. It follows, then, that the teacher's role is one of discussion moderator, with the goal of teaching merely that people hold different values; the teacher does attempt to present her views as the "right" views.

Kohlberg rejected the focus on values and virtues, not only due to the lack of consensus on what virtues are to be taught, but also because of the complex nature of practicing such virtues. For example, people often make different decisions yet hold the same basic moral values. Kohlberg believed a better approach to affecting moral behavior should focus on stages of moral development. These stages are critical, as they consider the way a person organizes their understanding of virtues, rules, and norms, and integrates these into a moral choice. In addition, he rejected the relativist view point in favor of the view that certain principles of justice and fairness represent the pinnacle of moral maturity, as he found that these basic moral principles are found in different cultures and subcultures around the world.

The goal of moral education, it then follows, is to encourage individuals to develop to the next stage of moral reasoning. Initial educational efforts employing Kohlberg's theory were grounded in basic Piagetian assumptions of cognitive development. Development, in this model, is not merely the result of gaining more knowledge, but rather consists of a sequence of qualitative changes in the way an individual thinks. Within any stage of development, thought is organized according to the constraints of that stage. An individual then interacts with the environment according to their basic understandings of the environment. However, the child will at some point encounter information which does not fit into their world view, forcing the child to adjust their view to accommodate this new information. This process is called equilibration, and it is through equilibration that development occurs. Early moral development approaches to education, therefore, sought to force students to ponder contradiction inherent to their present level of moral reasoning.

The most common tool for doing this was to present a "moral dilemma" and require students to determine and justify what course the actor in the dilemma should take. Through discussion, students should then be forced to face the contradictions present in any course of action not based on principles of justice or fairness. While Kohlberg appreciated the importance and value of such moral dilemma discussions, he held from very early on that moral education required more than individual reflection, but also needed to include experiences for students to operate as moral agents within a community. In this regard, Kohlberg reconciled some of the differences in orientation that existed between the theories of moral growth held by Piaget and Durkheim. In order to provide students with an optimal context within which to grow morally, Kohlberg and his colleagues developed the "just community" schools approach towards promoting moral development.

The basic premise of these schools is to enhance students' moral development by offering them the chance to participate in a democratic community. Here, democracy refers to more than simply casting a vote. It entails full participation of community members in arriving at consensual rather than "majority rules" decision-making. One primary feature of these schools is their relatively small size (often they are actually schools within schools), aimed at providing the students with a sense of belonging to a group which is responsive to individual needs. The central institution of these schools is a community meeting in which issues related to life and discipline in the schools are discussed and democratically decided, with an equal value placed on the voices of students and teachers. An underlying goal of these meetings is to establish collective norms which express fairness for all members of the community. It is believed that by placing the responsibility of determining and enforcing rules on students, they will take prosocial behavior more seriously. At the same time, this approach stems from the cognitive-developmentalist view that discussion of moral dilemmas can stimulate moral development.

However, this is not to say that just community school simply leaves students to their own devices; teachers play a crucial leadership role in these discussions, promoting rules and norms which have a concern for justice and community, and ultimately enforcing the rules. This role is not an easy one, as teachers must listen closely and understand a student's reasoning, in order to help the student to the next level of reasoning. This requires a delicate balance between letting the students make decisions, and advocating in a way which shows them the limits in their reasoning. A primary advantage to the Just Community approach is its effectiveness in affecting students actions, not just their reasoning. Students are, in effect, expected to "practice what they preach", by following the rules determined in community meetings.

DISTINGUISHING MORALITY AND CONVENTION

In the early 1970s, longitudinal studies conducted by the Kohlberg research group began to reveal anomalies in the stage sequence. Researchers committed to the basic Kohlberg framework attempted to resolve those anomalies through adjustments in the stage descriptions. Other theorists, however, found that a comprehensive resolution to the anomalous data required substantial adjustments in the theory itself. One of the most productive lines of research to come out of that period has been the domain theory advanced by Elliot Turiel and his colleagues. Within domain theory a distinction is drawn between the child's developing concepts of morality, and other domains of social knowledge, such as social convention. According to domain theory, the child's concepts of morality and social convention emerge out of the child's attempts to account for qualitatively differing forms of social experience associated with these two classes of social events. Actions within the moral domain, such as unprovoked hitting of someone, have intrinsic effects (i.e., the harm that is caused) on the welfare of another person. Such intrinsic effects occur irregardless of the nature of social rules that may or may not be in place regarding the action. Because of this, the core features of moral cognition are centered around considerations of the effects which actions have upon the well-being of persons. Morality is structured by concepts of harm, welfare, and fairness.

In contrast, actions that are matters of social convention have no intrinsic interpersonal consequences. For example, there is nothing intrinsic to the forms of address we employ that makes calling a college teacher "professor" better or worse than calling the person Mr. or Ms., or simply using their given names. What makes one form of address better than another is the existence of socially agreed upon rules. These conventions, while arbitrary in the sense that they have no intrinsic status, are nonetheless important to the smooth functioning of any social group. Conventions provide a way for members of the group to coordinate their social exchanges through a set of agreed upon and predictable modes of conduct. Concepts of convention then, are structured by the child's understandings of social organization.

These hypothesized distinctions have been sustained through studies over the past 20 years. These studies have included interviews with children, adolescents and adults; observations of child-child and adult-child social interactions; cross-cultural studies; and longitudinal studies examining the changes in children's thinking as they grow older. An example of the distinction between morality and convention is given in the following excerpt from an interview with a four-year-old girl regarding her perceptions of spontaneously occurring transgressions at her preschool.

Moral issue: Did you see what happened? Yes. They were playing and John hit him too hard. Is that something you are supposed to do or not supposed to do? Not so hard to hurt. Is there a rule about that? Yes. What is the rule? You're not to hit hard. What if there were no rule about hitting hard, would it be all right to do then? No. Why not? Because he could get hurt and start to cry.

Conventional Issue: Did you see what just happened? Yes. They were noisy. Is that something you are supposed to or not supposed to do? Not do. Is there a rule about that? Yes. We have to be quiet. What if there were no rule, would it be all right to do then? Yes. Why? Because there is no rule.

Morality and convention, then, are distinct, parallel developmental frameworks, rather than a single system as thought of by Kohlberg. However, because all social events, including moral ones, take place within the context of the larger society, a person's reasoning about the right course of action in any given social situation may require the person to access and coordinate their understandings from more than one of these two social cognitive frameworks. For, example, whether people line up to buy movie theater tickets is largely a matter of social convention. Anyone who has traveled outside of Northern Europe or North America can attest to the fact that lining up is not a shared social norm across cultures. Within the United States or England, for example, lining up is the conventional way in which turn-taking is established.

The act of turn-taking has a moral consequence. It establishes a mechanism for sharing - an aspect of distributive justice. The act of breaking in line within the American or British context is more than merely a violation of convention. It is a violation of a basic set of rules that people hold to maintain fairness. How people coordinate the possible interactions that may arise between issues of morality and convention is a function of several factors including: the salience of the features of the act; and the developmental level of the person.

It was Turiel's insight to recognize that what Kohlberg's theory attempts to account for within a single developmental framework is in fact the set of age-related efforts people make at different points in development to coordinate their social normative understandings from several different domains. Thus, domain theory posits a great deal more inconsistency in the judgments of individuals across contexts, and allows for a great deal more likelihood of morally based decisions from younger and less developed people than would be expected from within the traditional Kohlberg paradigm. Current work from within domain theory has sought to explore how the child's concepts of moral and conventional regulation relate to their developing understandings of personal prerogative and privacy.

Moral and social values education

The implications of domain theory for values education are several. First, the identification of a domain of moral cognition that is tied to the inherent features of human social interaction means that moral education may be grounded in universal concerns for fairness and human welfare, and is not limited to the particular conventions or norms of a given community or school district. By focusing on those universal features of human moral understanding, public schools may engage in fostering children's morality without being accused of promoting a particular religion, and without undercutting the basic moral core of all major religious systems. Second, educational research from within domain theory has resulted in a set of recommendations for what is termed "domain appropriate" values education. This approach entails the teacher's analysis and identification of the moral or conventional nature of social values issues to be employed in values lessons. Such an analysis contributes to the likelihood that the issues discussed are concordant with the domain of the values dimension they are intended to affect.

A discussion of dress codes would constitute a poor basis for moral discussion, since mode of dress is primarily a matter of convention. Likewise, consideration of whether it is right to steal to help a person in need, would be a poor issue with which to generate a lesson intended to foster students' understandings of social conventions. A related function of the teacher would be to focus student activity on the underlying features concordant with the domain of the issue. Thus, students dealing with a moral issue would be directed to focus on the underlying justice or human welfare considerations of the episode. With respect to conventions, the focus of student activity would be on the role of social expectations and the social organizational functions of such social norms. On the basis of this kind of analysis teachers are also better enabled to lead students through consideration of more complex issues which contain elements from more than one domain. By being aware of the developmental changes that occur in students' comprehension of the role of social convention, and related changes in students understanding of what it means to be fair or considerate of the welfare of others, teachers are able to frame consideration of complex social issues in ways that will maximize the ability of students to comprehend and act upon the moral and social meaning of particular courses of action.

UNDERSTANDING CHARACTER EDUCATION

Part of the difficulty in studying moral behavior from a cognitive developmental perspective is that moral stages are formal structures of thought that have only a probablistic relationship to moral content. As The Standard Issue Scoring Manualshows, opposed resolutions of moral dilemmas can be justified at any stage. Moreover, appeals to specific virtues and values can be made at almost any stage. Although moral stages are too abstract to yield straightforward predictions to moral action, they do provide a context of meaning lacking in accounts focusing on the mere content of values and virtues.

Cognitive developmental researchers are now beginning to examine the development of virtues within a cognitive developmental framework. This marks a dramatic shift from Hartshorne and May's studies of character. Hartshorne and May started with the common sense assumption that being virtuous presupposed possessing certain attitudes and information or knowledge. Yet their tests of attitudes and knowledge did not consistently predict to behavior. In fact, their most significant finding was that children could not be divided as virtuous or unvirtuous, but that moral behavior appeared to be situation specific. Although reanalyses of the Hartshorne and May data indicate that virtuous behavior maybe somewhat more consistent than Hartshorne and May originally found (Burton, 1963), the correlations remain weak. A more fruitful approach to the study of virtue and character may be one that examines virtue from a cognitive developmental perspective.

COMMUNITY APPROACH AS CHARACTER EDUCATION

A cognitive developmental approach to virtue and character may seem strange to those familiar with Kohlberg's critique of character education as the "the bag of virtues" approach. Yet Kohlberg based that critique on the understanding of character and virtue found in the Hartshorne and May Studies. Kohlberg later entertained a far more sympathetic view of the Aristotlean approach to the teaching of virtue as a result of his just community experiments.

The just community approach to moral education involves establishing a democratic community of students and teachers. The key institution this approach is the community meeting where the members make and enforce the rules and policies that express the shared aspirations of the group. In practice, rules and policies were established and redefined in response to particular disciplinary problems. For example, rules about attendance and respecting property were made in response to incidents of skipping class and stealing.

The purpose of the rule making exercise is to engage students in a moral discussion of why a community needed to have particular rules and give students responsibility for upholding the rules. Community meetings succeeded to the extent that the students agreed to hold each other accountable for maintaining certain standards understood to express the values of community.

Thus, for example, the meetings that established a rule about stealing had as their goal the establishment of a commitment to the value of trust. From the standpoint of the group, the just community has as its aim the development of collective norms and values. From the perspective of the individual, however, the just community approach has as its aim the development of specific virtues.

In this sense, virtues are patterns or habits of action accompanied by requisite reasons and feelings. For example, the establishment of a collective norm of trust, entailed fostering a personal commitment to act regularly in a trustworthy manner out of an understanding and valuing of trusting relationships. Students thus learned the virtue of trust not through an academic lesson but by experiencing need for and the fruit of trust in a small school.

The just community research indicated that the specific norms and virtues of community developed discretely, that is the development of a norm of trust with reference to property did not entail the corresponding development of a norm of participation in the classroom. The norms were, nevertheless, related to each other, such that the development of each norm made its easier for the next one to develop. All of the different norms, after all, express in different ways a common conception of community. Although the just community approach arguably fostered virtue and character, the research on the approach focussed on assessing the moral atmosphere of the school and not the development of individual virtue and character.

The development of responsibility

The just community research did, however, find that members of the just community schools were more likely than their peers in the comparison high schools to develop a sense of responsibility for upholding the norms and rules of their school. This sense of responsibility was defined as a particular kind of moral orientation and judgment, much along the lines suggested by Gilligan.

The communal emphasis of the just community schools called students' attention to value of helping others for the sake of group solidarity and the democratic institutions encouraged personal accountability for their behavior. The strong influence of the environment n the students in the just community programs, raised questions, however, about the lasting effects of the intervention. Would the students still feel responsible to act in prosocial ways without the support of their community? Had the just community approach influenced the students' character?

Responsibility judgments

Kohlberg introduced a conception of responsibility in his later reflections on the judgment action question and on the significance of the just community approach. Following Blasi, he hypothesized that the deliberative process leading to moral action involves two kinds of judgments: a deontic judgment about the rightness or wrongness of a particular course of action and a responsibility or an aretaic judgment about whether one should follow through. The responsibility judgment entails a response to the question. How important or necessary is it for me to do what we believe to be right in this particular situation? Individuals may recognize that particular action is the right thing to do without feeling a strong personal obligation to act. Real life decision-making is complicated by the fact that competing values are at stake. To do what is morally right may mean sacrificing a career opportunity or hurting a friend. Therefore, individuals may not be consistent in acting upon what they know to be right.

Analyzing McNamee's experimental study of helping in a situation of drug abuser, Kohlberg noted that consistency between a decision that one should help and actual help offered increased in a monotonically from 25% to 88% from stage 2 to stage 5. Kohlberg attempted to explain this increasing consistency as due to a corresponding "decrease in ... excuses or 'quasi-obligations' at each higher stage". For example, in the McNamee study, stage 4 participants typically excused their inaction by referring to the fact that the drug abuser had been denied help from a psychologist, who was the authority in this situation.

Although he claims that responsibility judgments are related to individuals' self-definition, Kohlberg's explanation of the judgment-action relationship simply extends his cognitive stage model a step further by showing how the stages prior to stage 5 can generate excuses for doing what one thinks to be right. Yet this explanation fails to explain why many individuals at the lower stages act consistently. As Blasi (1983) argues, the impetus to act one way or another depends to some degree on the kind of person one thinks one is and wishes to become. Individuals are more likely to feel responsible to act morally if moral concerns are crucial for their self-definition.

Self-consistency and moral justification

In our current research, we are examining the extent to which judgments of self-worth depend on moral criteria. In attempting to build a bridge to moral judgment research, we ask a number of questions probing why an individual should keep a promise or generally act in a moral way if no one were likely know how he or she acted. These questions are designed to elicit some reference to the self as moral.

Self-Esteem and Character

Jennifer tells us that by acting morally in one develops a positive sense of self, which in turn increases the likelihood that one will act morally in the future. Her sense of the role of self-esteem in the moral life deepens the common view that simply building self-esteem fosters good character. This common view presupposes that a high sense of self-esteem can inoculate children and adolescents from having to find alternative, anti-social means of gaining approbation. Children appear to resort to anti-social behavior if they fail to meet conventional norms of success or if they are denied approval from parents, teachers, coaches, and popular peers. Delinquency research, however, fails to support the common view.

Although most theorists assume that self-esteem has a moral basis, the empirical data indicate that there is no necessary relationship between the two. Moral behavior is but one of several components of self-esteem and apparently not an essential one. As Harter has shown, self-esteem is based on such non-moral sources as success in school and sports, popularity, and physical appearance. Furthermore, individuals vary in the importance that they attribute to sources of self-esteem. Some children value athletic achievements, others good grades. There is no reason that individuals will derive a sense of self-esteem from acting morally unless becoming a moral person is an important feature of their self-definition.

Character development and self-esteem

Character refers to the moral dimension of one's self-understanding or self-definition. People of good character place moral concerns at the center of their identity. Although they derive self-esteem from many sources, their self-esteem is deeply influenced by their moral behavior. Character is thus that dimension of the self that leads to responsible action. This notion of character is consistent with Aristotle's depiction of character in a general sense as the kind of person one is and in a more specific sense as the kind of person possessing the virtues.

Aristotle's depiction of character and virtue has a key cognitive component insofar as it includes phronesis as well as a behavioral component, habit, a term that often leads to confusion. Habits seem to imply automatic behaviors that are learned through simple repetition. Yet Aristotle speaks of habits as regular patterns of behavior that are done for the right reason, on the proper occasion, experiencing the appropriate pleasures. The character educators' emphasis on habit as distinct from reason does not do justice to Aristotle's complex view. On the other hand, the moral educator's almost exclusive emphasis on reasoning about the morality of actions appears shortsighted as I have noted in discussing the moral judgment/ moral action relationship.

If moral educators wish to have an impact on moral responsibility, as well they should, then must begin to explore how character is formed. Here we can learn from children and adolescents, who, like Jennifer in the example above, tell us that character involves building a positive self-image or positive self-esteem through moral deeds. Yet there is a circularity about all of this that Aristotle saw very clearly. If moral deeds presuppose moral character, how can moral character be formed through moral deeds? Aristotle believed that virtue could be taught in some ways like a craft through an apprenticeship of guided practice.

Aristotle recognized, however, that virtue differed from craft because virtuous action presupposed a capacity for decision-making based on right reason and a stable disposition. Aristotle's view of character education thus includes within an apprenticeship model a concern for the development of moral judgment and moral responsibility. The character educator must not focus action alone but on the intentions and internal state of the apprentice.

The just community approach provides a concrete illustration of an apprenticeship model of character education. This approach has a strong behavioral component; all the students are expected to participate in the democratic process of decision-making and to abide by the norms of the community. The teachers in the just community schools are like the masters of a craft who model the kinds of actions that they expect the students to perform. With each new class of students, the teachers need to work particularly hard to demonstrate how to participate democratically and how to build community.

The teachers generally face a two-fold challenge: 1) students are generally unfamiliar with the institutions of direct participatory democracy and community and 2) the impersonal bureaucratic organization of schools is hardly conducive to fostering democratic and communitarian values.

Character education as apprenticeship

The easiest way to illustrate how the just community approach functions as an apprenticeship is to analyze the often cited example of the way in which the first just community school, Cluster, dealt with the problem of cheating. As in most urban public schools, incidents of cheating surfaced in the early days of Cluster. Typically teachers and students respond by not bringing valuables to school or by exercising greater caution (e.g., making sure that students lock their lockers with sturdy locks).

In Cluster, the teachers made cheating an issue for community meeting discussion and deliberation. When they did so, the students expressed surprise that the teachers were making a "big deal" out of something that "goes on all the time." One student put it this way: "Just because a few things are stolen you don't have to cry about it." The teachers criticized the students' indifference and attempted provoke some expression of moral indignation: "Don't people think that it [stealing] is wrong? When the students tried to foreclose the discussion by moving that harsher punishments for stealing be instituted, the teachers asked the students to reflect on stealing as a matter of conscience rather than as an external nuisance: "Maybe someone can explain why stealing has been going on."

Although the students initially reject the ideal of community, the teachers act as if the school already was a community. From a character education perspective, the teachers may be seen as habituating the students to participate in a democratic community and more specifically to stop stealing themselves and not to tolerate stealing by others. The teachers encourage the performance of certain behaviors, such as expressing their views, following a speaking order, analyzing the problem, and acting honestly. The habituation process includes a focus on students' reasoning, judgment, and emotions.

The teachers engage the students in a moral discussion that will terminate in a vote. In the course of discussion, the teachers attend to the students' affectivity by evoking feelings of disappointment and indignation at the revelations of stealing and by fostering a desire for the security and freedom that comes with trusting relationships. Finally the teachers direct the students to look at stealing as an expression of an attitude toward others and the group as a whole.

The research on the just community demonstrated that students' attitudes as well as behavior changed as a result of participating the in just communities. For example, as students resolved the stealing problem, they began to exhibit the kinds of reactions that the teachers modeled in the initial meeting on stealing. After what would be the last occurrence of stealing in Cluster, a student leader admonished, "It's everyone's fault that she [the victim] don't have no money. It was stolen because people don't care about the community."

The use of community as a motivation for moral responsibility thus contributes to the character development process. In the initial discussion of stealing, students did not take responsibility for the problem beyond establishing a strong deterrent. In the later meetings students began to say "As members of this community, we should care about others in the community." This statement indicates a dramatic shift in both moral judgment and moral responsibility.

Moral self-evaluation

In what follows, we present an approach to character development that focuses on the development of the categories used in moral self-evaluation. we accept the belief, shared by many psychologists and teachers, that self-esteem plays a significant role in the moral life. We submit, however, that conventional measures of global self-esteem focus too narrowly on self-esteem as either high or low. Judgments of self-esteem vary radically, in our view, depending on their sources (moral and non-moral) and their developmental level. Building self-esteem is an important part of character development insofar as building self-esteem involves the construction of moral standards of self-evaluation.

Most self-esteem research focuses on self-esteem as the fruit of individuals' achievement. This is especially true with respect to James's formula that self esteem equals successes over pretensions. It is true to a lesser extent with respect to Cooley's observation that self-esteem is influenced by the responses of significant others. Clearly the most reliable way of influencing others' judgments of the self is to act in ways that impress others.

An earned sense of self-esteem appears to depend upon living up to one's ideals, as Harter, and Strauman & Higgins have shown, as well as avoiding the negative or fared possibilities for one's life. These ideals may be thought of as congealing in an ideal self and these negative possibilities may be represented in a dreaded self. Moral self-esteem appears to depend upon judging one's actual self to be at least directed toward one's ideal self and away from one's dreaded self. In our research, we describe how these conceptions of the self develop and what extent individuals incorporate moral criteria into these definitions.

Our preliminary analysis indicates that ideal, dreaded, and real selves develop in a sequential pattern of cognitive levels with similarities to the moral judgment stages, ego development stages, faith stages, and self understanding levels. We use term levels rather than stages because without longitudinal data, we do not wish to make strong claims about invariant sequence or structured wholeness. The specifically moral characteristics of the first four levels are described below.

Level one: Individuals describe their ideal and real moral attributes with general labels, such as "nice." Often their descriptions of their ideal selves reflect either explicitly or implicitly parental expectations. Individuals descriptions of their ideal selves are consistent with their real selves. They rarely engage at this level or at the next in spontaneous self-criticism. When they do criticize themselves, they generally refer to specific acts of disobedience, but not to bad habits or negative traits. Conscience and guilt are expressed as anxiety caused by the anticipation of external punishment (imminent justice) for a moral transgression.

Level two: Individuals describe their ideal and real selves in terms of dispositions for action. In describing moral attributes, they often mention helpfulness or kindness, understood as meeting the concrete needs or interests of others. Ideal are justified in term of their instrumental value, for example as leading to success. The dreaded self is of ten described as being unsuccessful or as a person with bad habits.

Level three: Individuals describe their ideal selves in terms of traits and attitudes, which typically reflect a concern for being caring and unselfish. They also describe their dreaded selves with such traits, focusing especially on a fear of becoming self-centered. At this level, many individuals describe their dreaded self as a genuine threat if they are not vigilant. Spontaneous self-criticism is common in their descriptions of their actual selves as is self-acceptance in spite of their faults..

Level four: Individuals describe their ideal selves as having an identity character. Some individuals express a desire to make a difference to their society or to the world. Descriptions of the dreaded self focus on a failure to live up to one's ideals or role expectations often because of real word pressures. In describing their real selves, individuals sometimes distinguish their "true" inner self from an outer superficial self. This leads them to criticize hypocrisy. As they focus on their inner identity, individuals become conscious of the complexity of their motives and the possibility of self-deception.

These levels indicate that individuals do not develop an awareness of themselves as having a character in the sense of a unified self until high school at the earliest. The sequence of levels suggests, nevertheless, that the bedrock for character development is laid throughout the early levels. Moral actions play a significant role in children's depictions of themselves as good and nice at level one. At level two, they begin realize that good and bad habits are formed through their actions and they describe themselves as having dispositions to act in one way or another.

This level is also one in which children begin to describe their ideal selves in terms of images of success. Some notions of success emphasize the acquisition of wealth and status; other notions emphasize acting in ways that reflect both personal achievement and a responsiveness to others' needs. This latter, active sense of self appears more conducive to later character development, but future longitudinal study will be necessary to explore this crucial question.

Although social psychologists focus on self-esteem principally as an achievement, self-esteem may also be thought of as intrinsic to the self. Theories of justice, emphasizing equality and respect for persons, abstract the fundamental value of personhood from both natural and achieved characteristics. Thus in his Theory of Justice, Rawls states that individuals have value apart from their age, gender, race, educational level, occupation, etc.

This notion of personal worth leads to judgments that, for example, individuals have a right to life, even if they are strangers, have low status, or break the law. Related to this concern for the dignity of others based on their personhood is a concern for the dignity of the self. If individuals have worth simply because they are persons, then they have a basis for defending themselves against injury and insult, even when they may not earned respect through their actions.

A sense of intrinsic self-worth not only serves to protect the self, but also to empower and to challenge it. If one has a sense of inherent dignity, then one may be challenged act in ways that bring this dignity to realization. While an appreciation of one's intrinsic self-worth may thus be a source of comfort, it is also a goad to achievement. We assess individuals' sense of intrinsic self-esteem by presenting them with stories in which individuals confront failure. We ask how these individuals should cope with failure and whether an individual has a duty to respect herself or himself. We find that individuals at the first two levels of development simply assert that no one should feel that they are worthless, but that it is only at the third level that individuals begin justify an intrinsic sense of self-esteem as based such notions as the value of all human life or the dignity of being a child of God.

EDUCATIONAL IMPLICATIONS

Our research suggests that character education must begin with an understanding of how character itself develops. Static views of character education that emphasize rewards and punishments, moral exemplars, and strong authority fail to take into account the extent to which children begin to construct or themselves ideals about their future and images of their negative possibilities.

These ideals and images bear the influence of their culture, particularly as that culture is reflected in their school. Our children learn at an early age the importance given to outward success and the corresponding lack of recognition given to the practice of virtue. They find, for example, that teachers reward good grades, not honesty and that peers reward clique loyalty, not kindness to outcasts.

As can be learned from Aristotle's Nicomachean Ethics and the research on just community programs, the best approach to character education is one that provides a communal environment supportive of the virtues of trust, care, participation, and responsibility. I believe that it is also essential that students have opportunities to participate in decisions about the discipline of the classrooms and school, such participation affirms their sense of intrinsic self-worth while at the same time underscoring their responsibilities as members of an academic community. This democratic participation provides an apprenticeship in the virtues, encouraging students to form good habits and make sound decisions with the guidance of their teachers.

DOMAIN APPROACH TO VALUE EDUCATION

One of the most significant advances made during the past 15 years of research and theory on social development has been the discovery that children's conceptions of morality and social convention are not aspects of single developmental system of morality, but constitute distinct conceptual and developmental domains.

More recently we have begun to make progress in applying these findings from developmental psychology to what we call "domain appropriate" values education. What follows are examples of ways in which American History curricula and English writing classes can be used to foster development of students' moral and conventional concepts. These practices also increase students' ability to coordinate moral concerns of fairness and human welfare with the needs of social systems for conventions which structure social organization.

The specific practices that are outlined are ones that have been successfully used with adolescent students in grades eight, and nine.

The domain approach to values education emerges from the discovery that children's social concepts do not form a single conceptual system, but are structured within discrete areas of social knowledge that account for qualitatively differing aspects of societal and interpersonal regulation. Within this framework, morality pertains to the set of interpersonal actions such as hitting and hurting that have nonarbitrary consequences for the rights or welfare of persons.

Moral issues, then, are treated as categorical, and universalizable; specific moral concepts are structured by underlying conceptions of justice, rights, and welfare (beneficence). Whereas morality deals with issues inherent in interpersonal relations, social conventions such as modes of dress, forms of address, sex roles, manners, and aspects of mores regarding sexuality are the arbitrary and agreed-upon uniformities in social behavior determined by the social system in which they are formed.

Thus, conventions are seen as alterable, and context dependent. Through accepted usage, however, these standards serve to coordinate the interactions of individuals within systems by providing them with a set of expectations regarding appropriate behavior. In turn, the matrix of social conventions and customs serves as one element in the structuring and maintenance of the general social order. Judgments about social convention are structured by underlying conceptions of social organization.

Over 30 published studies have reported results consistent with the claim that morality and convention constitute distinct domains. In brief three forms of evidence are offered in support of the moral - conventional distinction. First, interview studies with children as young as 2 ½ years-of-age have reported that subjects distinguish between matters of morality and social convention. In these studies it has been found that subjects view moral transgressions as wrong irrespective of the presence of governing rules, while conventional acts are viewed as wrong only if they are in violation of an existing standard.

Interview studies have also found that individuals view conventional standards as alterable, while moral prescriptions are viewed as universal and unchangeable. The second form of evidence comes from observational studies of children's and adolescents' social interactions in family, school, and playground contexts.

These studies have reported that the forms of social interactions in the context of moral events differ qualitatively from interactions in the context of conventions. It was found that children's and adults' responses to events in the moral domain focus on features intrinsic to the acts, while responses in the context of conventions focus on aspects of social order.

The general pattern of results reported in the interview and observational studies have been replicated with subjects in other cultures (Brazil, Hong Kong, India, Indonesia, Israel, Nigeria, US. Virgin Islands, Zambia) indicating that the distinction between morality and convention is not confined to subjects reared in Western societies. The third piece of evidence comes from developmental studies examining age-related changes in children's moral and conventional judgments.

These studies have reported that concepts in the moral and conventional domains follow distinct developmental patterns. The sequence of changes observed in the moral domain indicates that as children develop, they form increased understandings of benevolence, equality, and reciprocity. In the conventional domain development entails transformation in the child's underlying conceptions of social organization and moves toward an understanding of convention as constitutive of social systems and as important for the coordination of social interactions.

Morality and Convention in Interaction Often social situations will contain elements from both domains. For example, conventions sometimes result in injustices, as in the case of sex conventions that discriminate against women. In other cases, conventions, such as waiting in line to purchase theater tickets, act in the service of fairness. When people reason about such issues they tend to do one of three things:

— emphasize on one domain and subordinate the other

For example, people worried about, or committed to maintaining the existing social order may not even recognize the potential injustice in existing sex role conventions that give greater privileges to men than women. Others, on the other hand, focusing on such injustices may not take into account the impact on social organization in such contexts as family structure, that might result from a single-minded focus on rights and equality.

— experience conflict between the two, and engage in inconsistencies and vacillation with an absence of resolution or reconciliation of the components

— coordination of the two components, so that the two are taken into account in consideration of the issue.

For example, concerns for fairness and equality are coupled with changes in the conventions regarding household tasks, child care, etc., that allow for family life to go forward in an organized and functional way.

This view of social reasoning is consistent with a reinterpretation of earlier, global theories of social development, such as Kohlberg's stages of moral development, as an approximation of the age-related changes in domain coordinations.

From the distinct domains perspective, however, one would not interpret such interdomain coordinations as representing a stable context-independent cognitive structure.

From this perspective one would predict a great deal more intraindividual, and cross-cultural variation in social reasoning than is permitted by Kohlbergian stages of moral judgment, since morality is but one element to be interrelated in the process of generating actions in multifaceted social contexts.

Basic Principles of Domain Education

One educational implication of these psychological findings is that values instruction be coordinated with domain of the issues addressed in a given lesson. The first step in such an approach, would entail the teacher's analysis and identification of the moral or conventional nature of social issues employed in values lessons. Such an analysis would be necessary to ensure that the issues discussed are concordant with the domain of the values dimension they are intended to affect.

A related function of the teacher would be to focus student activity (verbal or written) on the underlying features concordant with the domain of the issue. Thus, students dealing with a moral issue would be directed to focus on the underlying justice or human welfare considerations of the episode. With respect to conventions, the focus of the student activity would be on the role of social expectations and the social organizational function of such social norms. As we noted earlier, not all issues of social right and wrong fall simply into one domain or the other.

Cases of domain overlap would involve both the domain concordant practices just outlined as well as activities that would involve students in reasoning that necessitates the coordination of knowledge from more than one social dimension. The second general principle is that the activities and questions posed to students be appropriate for their developmental level.

Students in the 8th grade and 9th grades are approximately 13 to 15 years-old. In terms of their conceptions of convention, the majority of such young adolescents are either at Level 4 negation, in which conventions are viewed as the arbitrary and unimportant dictates of authority, or are in the process of shifting toward Level 5 affirmation, in which conventions are understood to be constitutive of social systems.

Sometimes, as in the case of teacher names, Level 4 adolescents will go along with conventions in order not to cause moral harm in the form of perceived hurt feelings or disrespect that may come from violating someone else's strongly held convention. These Level 4 adolescents, however, do not understand why anyone's feelings should be hurt, and simply conform in order not to be gratuitously hurtful.

It is at Level 5 that the person's conceptions of convention can first be described as reflecting an understanding of society as a system. For the first time, students clearly perceive that while individual conventions are arbitrary, they form the set of norms that structures society in particular ways. People who are members of a society are obligated (as a general rule) to adhere to conventions in order for society to function. History teachers, particularly those given the responsibility to teach the US Constitution, or World History are probably familiar with the kinds of difficulties that arise when students are not at a point where they have achieved this Level 5 understanding of social systems and their relations to conventions and customs.

Many school districts respond to this developmental transition by delaying the teaching of World history until the sophomore year of high school when most students are 15 to 16 years of age and generally at Level 5 in their conventional understandings.

In doing so, schools wait for development, rather than contributing to it. The materials and practices described below are based on a different premise, namely that the transition point from Level 4 and 5 presents a great opportunity to link the teaching of particular school subject matter with the dynamics of development. Done well, such a link carries with it payoffs in the form of student motivation, and interest in the subject matter as well as increased sophistication in their understanding of the academic content.

In the moral domain adolescents are generally beyond childhood conceptions of fairness as "raw justice", and are beginning to apply their moral understandings to issues that require an integration of concerns for equal treatment with concerns for equity. Fairness is understood as requiring more than a simple tit-for-tat approach to social interactions. At this age, adolescents are also beginning to couple their moral understandings with a broadening sense of their moral community. By engaging students at this age in coordinating their concerns for morality with their emerging conceptions of society, teachers can begin to contribute to the ability of students to take a moral perspective in relation to society as a whole.

The following examples are taken from lessons that were used with students in American History and English writing classes. The questions that are provided here were used to structure in-class discussions and students' homework assignments. Some teachers have used these materials to do both. In the latter case students were first placed in small groups of 5 and asked to discuss the questions among themselves in class. Students were then given the same questions to take home and answer in written form as homework to be graded the next day by the teacher.

Examples of conventional issues

We will begin first with issues that primarily involved matters of social convention. Conventional issues addressed in the English course essays included such things as contemporary dating patterns, modes of dress, and table manners. Among the conventional issues drawn from American history were such things as adjustments in modes of dress, work conventions (such as time schedules), and dating patterns that resulted in part from the influx of immigrants and the shift from an agrarian to an industrial society.

Students' conceptions of convention in relation to societal organization were also stimulated through discussion of such events as the Marbury versus Madison Supreme Court decision which dealt with governmental separation of power, and which helped to establish the American legal norm of judicial precedent.

The following example illustrates how conventional issues may be presented to students. It is taken from a history discussion involving conventions of forms of address. The targeted incident occurred in the period just after the American Revolution and revolved around the early negotiations regarding the establishment of diplomatic relations between the newly formed United States, and their former colonial master, England. The following summary paragraph, based on the course text was presented to the students to begin the discussion.

Examples of moral issues

Moral issues which can be drawn from American history are those which bring to focus facets of fairness such as distributive and retributive justice, and issues of individual and social welfare. These elements of moral understanding may be evoked through discussion of such things as the moral courses of action available to a nation attempting to respond to the impressment of its own citizens by another country, as in the Chesapeake incident of the early 1800s in which United States sailors were captured and forced to man British ships.

This incident may be compared to contemporary hostage taking situations in the Middle-East. The forced removal of Indians from their lands as illustrated during the period of the Jackson presidency, and a number of incidents related to the Civil war, such as the raids of John Brown, and Sherman's march through Georgia, may also be included as stimuli for moral discussion.

Finally, history can provide the context for discussion of moral issues of deception and interpersonal exploitation through such things as the Whiskey Ring scandal during Grant's presidency, and the behavior of the "robber barons" during the period of industrial expansion. These "distant" moral issues may be reiterated through essays in either American history or English writing courses which put them into everyday contexts.

Examples of domain overlap

These issues pit conventional concerns for social organization and coordination against moral concerns of justice and human welfare. Issues of overlap which may be employed in American history are such things as changes in suffrage laws which over the course of American history have extended the vote to women, African-Americans, and persons who do not own property. Other issues of overlap may be drawn from the existence of slavery in the ante-bellum south, and contemporary debate over sex role conventions as they relate to family structure and opportunities for women. In English composition classes students may be asked to write essays on such issues as an event reported in the local newspapers in which a high school principal had censored an article in the student newspaper concerning the impact of divorce on children. That particularly rich incident brings the conventions regulating the roles and relative status of adults and children into play with issues of freedom of expression and responsible journalism. The following example taken from American history course materials illustrates the way in which mixed domain issues may be presented to students.

"By the 1870s public schools were established in the Southern states. At first the schools were open to all children black and white. However, few white parents permitted their children to attend schools with the children of former slaves. As a result, public schools in the South were segregated by race, with children attending different schools from blacks."

A domain-appropriate treatment of this issue would direct students to consider the moral issues involved, as well as the implications for the overall conventional structure of society. A good way to start is to have students first dealt separately with the conventional and moral aspects of the episode, and then ask them to take both into account in their resolution of issues.

The issue of segregation in the United States has many parallels to contemporary events in South Africa. There the laws and norms established separate ways of life for blacks and whites. In both cases, considerations for maintaining the social system (segregation in the US.; apartheid in South Africa) were, or are in conflict with consideration of human rights and justice.

3

Moral Learning and Moral Education

As in many areas of educational research, the field of moral education is rife with controversy. These disputes are not limited to psychological accounts of the nature of moral development or character formation, but extend to the very definition of educational aims in this area. Arguments surrounding the aims of values education capture the essential quandary for any pluralist democracy attempting to construct a shared civil society without privileging the particular values of any one group.

The contribution which educational psychology can make with regard to these issues is to clarify how moral and social values are formed, and to address the social and psychological factors which contribute to the tendency of individuals to act in ways that are concordant with their own well-being and the welfare of others.

Controversies notwithstanding, the past several decades have witnessed a great deal of progress with regard to our understanding of these issues. This chapter will address those aspects of what has been learned in the areas of developmental and educational psychology that can help educators engage in meaningful moral and character education.

Historically, these issues have been approached from two perspectives with divergent, though overlapping, interests and differing sets of assumptions about the nature of social development and socialization. On the one hand have been traditional character educators whose emphasis has been on processes of internalization and self control that would ostensibly result in virtuous conduct.

On the other hand have been cognitive developmentalists whose emphasis has been on the development of structures of moral reasoning which ostensibly underlie action choices. These two points of view, one emphasizing non-rational mechanisms of self-control and behavioral follow-through, and the other emphasizing rationality in the form of moral decision-making, are irreconcilable in terms of underlying philosophy.

Moreover, at the level of educational policy, these two perspectives have tended to take turns over the past thirty years in dominating the attention of educators interested in fostering children's social as well as academic growth. Yet, neither point of view, in their traditional form provides a sufficient basis for guiding educational policy. There can be no meaningful moral action in the absence of moral judgment since morality by definition requires choice and intent.

Thus, proponents of educational policies that ignore the development of moral decision making have generally absented themselves from offering suggestions in the area of moral education. Conversely, the development of moral judgment, though necessary, is not a sufficient aim of moral education.

For moral judgment, in and of itself, does not lead to a particular course of action. It would appear then, that the divergent aims of these two points of view for the development of moral reasoning, and the development of characterological propensities for moral follow through are both desirable and necessary components of any educational contribution to children's moral growth. Therefore, will pull information from diverse areas of research to construct a coherent picture integrating both sets of concerns.

In order to reconcile these points of view, we will need to appeal to contemporary cognitive theories of personality formation, and recent work on the development of the moral "self", rather than restrict discussion to the behavioral and social learning perspectives that have been traditionally used in support of character education.

DEVELOPMENT OF MORAL AND SOCIAL UNDERSTANDINGS

What Do We Mean by Morality? A large part of the controversy surrounding moral or character education has to do with how morality is to be defined. In everyday discourse morality refers simply to the norms of right and wrong conduct. At issue, however, is what is meant by moral right and wrong, and whose criteria shall be used to judge the wrongness of actions. As it turns out, this diversity at the level of public opinion, has a corollary in the underlying heterogeneity of the structures of the individual's social concepts.

Within the individual, concepts of social right and wrong are not all of one type, but are organized within distinct conceptual and developmental frameworks. In research conducted over the past twenty years, it has been discovered that individuals treat some forms of social behavior as moral universals, other forms of social conduct as subject to determination by local cultural or social norms, and still others as matters of personal choice.

More specifically, these conceptual differences emerge when formal criteria for morality are employed which define morality as those interpersonal behaviors that are held to be right or wrong independent of governing social rules, and maintained as universally binding. Prescriptions which meet these criteria are those which refer to actions, such as hitting and hurting, stealing, slander, which have an impact on the welfare of others.

Accordingly, concepts of morality have been found to be structured by underlying conceptions of justice and welfare. Morality, then, may be defined as one's concepts, reasoning, and actions which pertain to the welfare, rights and fair treatment of persons.

Morality can be distinguished from concepts of social conventions, which are the consensually determined standards of conduct particular to a given social group. Conventions established by social systems such as norms or standards of dress, how people should address one another, table manners and so forth derive their status as correct or incorrect forms of conduct from their embeddedness within a particular shared system of meaning and social interaction.

The particular acts in and of themselves have no prescriptive force in that different or even opposite norms could be established to achieve the same symbolic or regulatory function. The importance of conventions lies in the function they serve to coordinate social interaction and discourse within social systems. In keeping with this definition, concepts of social convention have been found to be structured by underlying conceptions of social organization.

The distinctions which have been drawn between morality and social convention have been sustained by findings from over 50 studies conducted since 1975. This research has indicated that children, adolescents, and adults treat violations of morality, such as harming another, as wrong whether or not there is a governing rule in effect, and generalize these judgments of wrongness to members of other cultures or groups which may not have norms regarding such actions.

Conventions, on the other hand, are viewed as binding only within the context of an existing social norm, and only for participating members within a given social group. While there is some controversy over whether the distinction between morality and convention is made by members of all cultural groups, a number of studies have demonstrated that subjects from a wide variety of the world's cultures do differentiate between matters of morality and convention.

Evidence in support of the morality/convention distinction has been obtained from subjects in Brazil, India, Israel, Korea, Nigeria, Virgin Islands, and Zambia. Moreover, recent research has demonstrated that something parallel to the distinction between morality and social convention operates within the moral and normative conceptions of religious children and adolescents with respect to their conceptions of religious rules. It has been found that children and adolescents from observant religious groups judged certain religious norms in conventional terms in that they regarded these as contingent on religious authority or the word of God, and as particular to their religion. In contrast, moral issues were regarded as prescriptive independent of the existence of a rule established by religious authority or by God's word, and as obligatory for members of all other religious groups.

The discovery of these psychological distinctions between moral and conventional forms of social right and wrong provides an empirical basis for beginning to address some of the definitional issues vexing moral education. In differentiating what is moral from what is socially "proper", these findings can allow educators to focus the discussion of moral education on questions of how best to develop children's moral understandings, and their tendencies to act in accord with such moral principles, rather than being captured by heated arguments over which set of local conventions or religious norms ought to be included within the collection of values to be addressed by the curriculum. In keeping with the broad cross cultural generalizability of this research, the identification of morality as centered around issues of justice and human welfare is consistent with common sense construals of the basic task of values education as fostering the development of people who don't lie, cheat, steal, or hurt others.

At the same time, the grounding of these definitions of the content of morality in basic developmental research, avoids falling into the trap of what Lawrence Kohlberg so aptly and perjoratively labeled the "bag of virtues" approach to establishing the aims of moral education. These core moral concerns for fairness and welfare are not virtues in the usual sense, but constitute the central issues for moral judgments and consequent actions.

The distinction between morality and convention also allows the educator to give convention its due. Earlier analyses of children's moral development, such as Kohlberg's stage theory, interpreted attention to convention as characteristic of the reasoning of persons at lower stages of moral development, and therefore as something to be overcome through moral education. As stated above, concepts of conventions are now understood as distinct from moral understandings, and structured by children's and adolescents' emerging conceptualizations of social systems and social organization.

Conventions are constituent elements of social systems. Just as morality is fundamental to interpersonal interaction, conventions are essential to the operation of society. The development of children's and adolescents' understandings of the functions and purposes of social convention, therefore, have educational worth in their own right. In sum, current research on the structure of children's social concepts, provides an empirical basis for differentially addressing development within each of these conceptual systems rather than reducing either morality or conventional norms to a single framework.

Context, and the inevitability of controversy: While the discovery of distinct domains of social knowledge can help to focus the aims of moral education by identifying the core content of morality, the heterogeneity in people's social understandings, and the contextual overlap of moral and non-moral normative components in everyday life means that an honest approach to moral education will always need to contend with contradiction and controversy. Such overlap is inevitable given that all social interactions take place within societal systems framed by conventions.

Thus, although many everyday issues are straightforward instances of either morality or convention, many others contain aspects from more than one domain. In such cases, people may differ from one another in terms of the information they may bring to a situation, or the weight they may give to one or another feature of a given issue.

Two basic forms of overlap occur between morality and convention. In one form, called domain mixture, conventional norms sustaining a particular organizational structure are in harmony or conflict with what would objectively be seen as concerns for fairness or rights. Examples of such overlap would be conventions for lining up to purchase tickets, or gender role conventions which proscribe areas in which men or women may participate.

In the former case, the convention, while a morally neutral and arbitrary way to arrange people, could be used to serve a distributive justice function, and cutting in line would, therefore, become unfair. In the latter case, the convention may be in conflict with fairness if the convention prevents members of one gender from obtaining opportunities afforded the other.

The second type of moral/convention overlap, labeled second order moral events, occurs when the violation of a strongly held convention is seen as causing psychological harm to persons maintaining the convention. In our culture, for example, attending a funeral in a bathing suit would generally be seen as insensitive toward the deceased and the grieving family, and not merely an instance of unconventional conduct.

In responding to issues that involve elements from more than one domain, individuals may either subordinate the issue to a single dimension and reduce an issue of overlap to one that is primarily either moral or conventional, or engage in an effort to coordinate the multifaceted nature of the issue taking the moral as well non-moral aspects of a given situation or event into account.

These responses to overlap at an individual level help to account for the inconsistencies we observe within people as they respond to events in different contexts. They also help to explain how cultural groups, or subgroups arrive at different readings of social issues they consider to be morally neutral or charged with moral meaning. Within western society, those instances of overlap in which convention and morality are in harmony account for the moral component of what is generally viewed as mannerly and respectful conduct, and for the moral aspect of norms and procedures that sustain participatory forms of government.

For the most part, within democratic societies, these areas of overlap are non-controversial inasmuch as they represent values concordant with morality and the conventional status quo. Consequently, values education programs purporting to foster such conventional values enjoy wide public support.

Controversies are likely to emerge, however, whenever the relations between moral and non-moral components of issues are not in accord, and, therefore likely to be viewed differently by the affected parties. In the case of second-order issues such as disputes over what constitutes modesty in forms of dress, the essentially conventional nature of such issues generally allows for local consensus to settle the matter. While some civil libertarians might protest any constraint on student choice with respect to personal conduct, and some conservative religious people might protest as immoral, any alteration in the norms of public conduct, such second-order issues are generally resolved by elected school boards, or school policy.

More problematic for curriculum designers and educational policy makers are potential conflicts between morality and convention embedded within the norms that sustain existing social order, and by implication benefit members of the privileged social classes.

While this incident from America's past is easy to look at in the cool light of history, such issues are not easily dealt with when they concern contemporary practices. Two of the elements that lend to the difficulty in dealing with these issues are captured in the above example.

First, the conventionalized practices in and of themselves are morally neutral and play themselves out in the course of everyday life. Thus, people steeped in a particular way of life may not be cognizant of the moral implications of their particular social system. The problem here, of course, is that inequitable systems may simply perpetuate themselves, and educational curricula based on transmitting the values of the community may become the hand-maidens of immorality.

Second, because such issues are multifaceted, they lend themselves to more than one interpretation, raising the specter of controversy for the educational system. This is particularly problematic for public schools since such controversies tend to have political ramifications. Generally, people in positions of relative power and privilege are more likely to view such issues in conventional terms and favor maintenance of the status quo, since the conventional system serves their personal interests.

People on the receiving end of such conventionalized inequities, on the other hand, are less likely to subordinate such overlapping issues to convention, and more likely to be cognizant of their moral status.

The moral dilemma these overlapping issues pose for educators is how to allow students to address the moral contradictions posed by some of society's conventions in areas such as gender and race relations without themselves becoming subject to the positions held by political groups that inevitably align themselves with one or another side of such issues.

Moral diversity and informational assumptions: Variations in the moral meanings people attribute to particular actions stem not only from the areas of overlap between morality and the conventions of social systems, but also arise as a result of the differences in factual assumptions people make about given acts. Within our own culture, for example, people hold different views about whether it is morally wrong or all right to engage in the physical punishment of children. In her research on this issue, Wainryb found that pro corporal punishment parents held the view that this behavior was all right because it was a highly effective, educative act rather than one of unprovoked harm or abuse of the child. When such parents were presented with information that spanking is no more effective than other methods of disciplining children, significant numbers of parents shifted in their view of corporal punishment and maintained that it was not all right for parents to engage in the behavior. Conversely, when parents who maintained that it was wrong to engage in corporal punishment were presented with information that experts had found spanking to be the most efficient method to teach young children, there was a tendency for such parents to shift toward a view that corporal punishment would be all right.

In the above example, the morality of an action shifted as a function of the informational assumptions people had regarding the effect of the act. In other cases, informational assumptions can alter people's views of the moral culpability of the actor. Many people in our culture, for example, have been found to hold to the view that homosexuality is an immoral lifestyle choice.

From that perspective, being a homosexual entails a conscious decision to engage in behavior which they consider to be offensive and indecent. Leaving aside such questions as to whether homosexuality should be viewed in such normative terms or as a matter of private, personal conduct, the issue of choice is central to whether the individual may be held accountable for his or her sexual orientation. Information that would bear on that issue would undoubtedly impact the moral evaluation many people would make of homosexuals, even if it had no impact on their view of homosexual acts.

In sum, the moral worlds within which people act out their lives are affected by informational as well as contextual variables which enter into the evaluations people generate about particular courses of action. As with issues of domain overlap, the impact of new information regarding the causes or effects of social behaviors both complicates and enriches the role of education in preparing students to deal with social and moral issues. From a policy standpoint, we are once again confronted with the need to recognize that values education within a pluralistic, information rich, democratic society means preparing students to coordinate fundamental moral understandings of fairness and human welfare with potentially changing conventions and informational assumptions.

Understanding inconsistencies in individual conduct: The existence of domain overlap and differences in informational assumptions helps to account not only for disagreements between people about the moral meaning of social issues, but also helps to explain some of the inconsistencies we observe within individuals. Just as different groups of people may disagree over the moral meaning of contextualized social issues, individuals may differ in their attribution of moral meaning of actions within different contexts.

In relatively unambiguous cases, deciding upon the moral or conventionally correct course of action is fairly straightforward. However, in cases where moral and conventional expectations are in conflict, where the information regarding the meaning of the action is ambiguous, or when moral concerns run counter to highly salient pragmatic or personal desires of the actor, individuals display inconsistency in their social judgments and subsequent actions.

From the point of view of domain theory, such inconsistencies are the inevitable consequence of applications of a multifaceted conceptual framework in the context of varying heterogeneous social contexts. This is not a case of situational ethics. People do not make up their morality on the spot. The place of morality within a given context, however, will vary as a function of the person's application of the totality of their social understandings and concerns to a given situation.

Reconceptualizing the developmental aims of moral education: Given what we currently know about moral cognition, it is sensible to propose that the core focus of moral education be upon students conceptions of fairness, human welfare and rights, and the application of those moral understandings to issues of everyday life. Research on the development of children's moral understandings has shown that morality begins in early childhood with a focus upon issues of harm to the self and others.

Preschool aged children are very concerned with their own safety, and understand that it is objectively wrong to hurt others. Even three - year - olds, for example, understand that it is wrong to hit and hurt someone even in the absence of a rule against hitting because, "When you get hit, it hurts, and you start to cry." Young children's morality, however, is not yet structured by understandings of fairness as reciprocity.

Fairness for the young child is often expressed in terms of personal needs and the sense that one isn't getting one's just desserts. "It's not fair.", often means, "I didn't get what I want.", or that someone's actions caused the child to experience harm. By age 10 nearly all children have constructed an understanding of fairness as reciprocity, but have difficulty in coordinating their sense of fairness as equality with notions of equity.

Expanding the sense of fairness to include compassion, and not raw justice, and to tie that sense of compassionate justice to a conceptually compelling obligation to all people and not just the members of one's community is the developmental task of adolescence and adulthood. Similar research on the development of children's understandings of social convention indicate that constructing an understanding of why conventions matter is a long process. Unlike morality, there is nothing intuitively obvious about the functions of convention. Even though most children have learned the content of their society's conventions by early elementary school, the purpose of such rules is not easily understood.

In fact it is not until middle to late adolescence that children develop a coordinated understanding of conventions as constituent elements of social systems. It is little wonder then that children so often seem disconnected from society's rules even when their normative content has been repeatedly presented to them.

This developmental research can be of enormous value to educators interested in developing "good" children. It provides curriculum designers and classroom teachers a framework from which to direct educational efforts at moral education which are appropriate for students at different points in development, and provides a basis from which to differentially address both the moral and conventional dimensions of social values. In doing so, educators will contribute to the development of a fair and compassionate moral citizenry that also understands and respects the need for convention.

As we have just seen, however, contextualized moral judgments may often call upon the person's ability to weigh or coordinate moral and non-moral considerations. Defining the aims of moral education in such circumstances becomes more complex. Put simply, the moral educator is not simply interested in developing the students moral and conventional understandings in such contexts, but is also interested in whether or not the student will be aware of, and prioritize the moral elements of such issues when deciding upon a course of action.

In the past this issue was dealt with rather neatly by Kohlberg's six stage sequence of moral development. According to Kohlberg's standard account, moral development moves from early stages in which moral understandings of fairness are intertwined with prudential self interest and concrete concerns for social authority, to conventional moral understandings in which morality is intertwined with concerns for maintaining social organization defined by normative regulation. Finally, at the highest, principled stages of morality attained by a minority of the general population, morality as fairness is fully differentiated from non-moral prudential or conventional considerations, and morality serves as the basis from which the individual not only guides personal actions, but is able to evaluate the morality of the conventional normative system of society. This progression has been appealing to moral educators for several reasons.

First, because the sequence was empirically based and purportedly described a universal developmental progression, this description of development offered educators an "objective" non-political basis from which to engage in moral education.

Second, because the stages were presumably "content free" in that they do not pertain to particular issues, but instead refer to structures of reasoning, educators did not need to be concerned about the specific positions students take with respect to given issues.

Finally, the sequence moved ultimately to a principled moral resolution of the kinds of complex issues of overlap discussed above. In other words, from the teacher's point of view, philosophical and political conundrums were resolved by the natural logic of the developmental process.

What we have now come to understand is that the progression identified through Kohlberg's paradigmatic research program does not adequately capture the ways in which people make socio-moral judgments, and cannot therefore, serve as the sole guide to moral education.

Kohlberg described the sequence of age-related changes in the ways in which moral and non-moral concerns are typically integrated in overlapping contexts. For example, Stage 4 moral reasoning as described in the Kohlberg system reflects the emergence in middle to late adolescence of understandings in the conventional domain that social norms are constituent elements of social systems.

Although these age-typical integrations are captured by Kohlberg's stage descriptions, they do not represent the full range of socio-moral decision-making patterns that individuals present. For example, in the process of conducting their careful and extensive research aimed at standardizing moral stage scoring, the Kohlberg group discovered that individuals at all points in development may respond to Kohlberg's moral dilemma's by reasoning from a perspective of either rules and authority or justice and human welfare.

From the vantage point of our current understanding of the domain related heterogeneity in people's social cognition, such within-stage variation can be accounted for by recognizing that the Kohlberg tasks generate reasoning employing knowledge from more than one conceptual system.

In moving beyond Kohlberg's landmark research on children's moral development, educators are both liberated in terms of how they might conceptualize the opportunities they have to engage students in moral reflection and behavior, and are also vested with greater responsibility for stimulating students to think and act in such moral terms. If in fact, children at all points in development are capable of considering moral issues from a moral perspective of justice and welfare, then it becomes important to increase the likelihood that children will "read" and prioritize the moral component of contextualized social issues, rather than simply attempting to move students toward a distal "principled" stage of moral judgment where such moral prioritization becomes a matter of course.

This is not say that development doesn't matter. Achieving principled moral understandings in the full sense of Kohlberg's theory, presupposes a fully developed understanding of societies as social systems, an understanding that is only arrived at in middle to late adolescence. In addition, the ability of children to "see" the morality of certain actions requires a similar, late adolescent, level of sophistication in the area of convention. For example, when we presented the issue of a person wearing a bathing suit to a funeral, many young adolescents failed to see any problem. In their minds, since conventions were nothing other than the arbitrary dictates of authority, and since the important issue in this case was attendance at the funeral, there was nothing wrong in going to a funeral in a bathing suit.

Older adolescents, however, who had constructed an understanding of conventions as constituent elements of social systems, were able to see the second-order moral implications that might arise from violating this social convention, and tended to view it as wrong to wear a bathing suit to a funeral, since within the societal framework of the funeral party, dress conveyed a sense of respect for the deceased, and sensitivity to the feelings of the grieving family.

The point being made here is that attention to develop within moral education needs to be accompanied by attention to students' reading of overlapping social issues. In focusing upon development within each of these conceptual frameworks, educators contribute to students' capacity to understand and function within their social and moral worlds. However, because these systems interact in context, strictly developmental aims as set forth in the traditional Kohlbergian position need to be reconsidered.

Since it has been found that students' reasoning about such complex issues is not the result of reasoning structures within a single system, the weight that students give to moral and non-moral considerations, and not just their reasoning within the moral domain becomes of interest. Unfortunately, even those individuals judged within the Kohlberg framework to be at post-conventional stages of reasoning have been found to be subject to social pressures and situational cues in their reading of the moral meaning of actions.

There is research which demonstrates that teachers can impact the ways in which students read social issues, and the tendencies of students to attempt to address both the moral and conventional aspects of complex social issues. In their study, Nucci & Weber divided students into three discussion groups which met for 4 weeks.

During these groups, students discussed issues that were primarily moral, conventional, or overlapping both morality and convention. Throughout the course of these weekly discussions, one group was directed to treat all issues in terms of moral concerns for fairness and human welfare; a second group was directed to treat all issues as matters of social convention and social order, and the third group was directed to treat moral issues from a moral perspective, conventional issues from a conventional perspective, and to coordinate moral and conventional components of multifaceted issues.

Following this intervention, students levels of moral and conventional reasoning were assessed through interviews. Students in all three groups were able to clearly respond to unambiguous moral or conventional issues. However, when asked to write their views about the values contained in an incident which had both moral and conventional features, subjects in the moral only group subordinated complex issues to moral concerns, and subjects in the convention only group subordinated complex issues to matters of norms and social organization.

Only the third group spontaneously looked at both features of issues and attempted to coordinate them. As this relatively benign and short-term treatment illustrates, education can be influential in framing the meaning individuals will give to complex social situations.

Given that many of the moral issues of everyday life are enmeshed within conventionalized norms and contexts, it seems imperative that children be given the intellectual and attitudinal tools necessary to deal with these realities. What this means in practice is that students not only be given opportunities to develop their understandings and ways of reasoning about morality and convention, but that they be engaged in the more complex task of evaluating and coordinating the moral and social organizational elements of multifaceted social issues. These processes will necessarily be different at differing points in development. Adolescents with complex understandings of societies as systems will address such issues in ways that are more integrative and complex than will children.

Nonetheless, meaningful discourse about the moral component of multifaceted social standards, can be addressed across a broad age range. Furthermore, the contexts in which morality and convention may overlap are not confined to the distal world of adult society, but also arise in contexts structured by the norms of children and adolescents. For example, engaging children in "seeing" the moral implications of group norms of exclusion which might arise within cliques which don't want "geeks" as members, or in helping them to deal with masculine norms of toughness in the context of playground disputes can help them to formulate ways of constructing "societies" that are non-discriminatory, just, and safe.

Thus, helping students come to terms with the difficult task of integrating what is moral with the need for social order and organization need not be seen as far afield from the straight forward business of raising "good" children who don't lie, cheat, steal, or hurt others. If we have learned anything over the past 30 years, it is that moral education cannot be isolated to one part of the school day, or to one context, but must be integrated within the total school experience.

Bringing the approach described here to the curriculum as a whole, however, may prove unsettling for some. Engaging children in critical moral reflection about issues raised in literature, or about existing or historical social standards contained within social studies or history texts may seem threatening to those who maintain the recapitulation view of the mission of public schools to foster citizenship. From that point of view, values education serves the purpose of bringing the young into the existing social order so that society may be preserved and perpetuated.

Unfortunately for that perspective, pluralist democracies are dynamic, and efforts to stifle critique run counter to the very nature of the democratic society such people hope to preserve.

Whether we wish to engage the resources of our schools to develop the ability of our citizenry to engage in thoughtful moral critique of our culture is a political and moral decision. As I have laid out, the knowledge base from which to construct such an approach to moral and social education is available.

CHARACTER FORMATION

The preceding discussion has highlighted the basic reasons why moral education must attend to issues of social cognition and moral reasoning. Knowing right from wrong is more than a simple process of being aware of specific social rules, and doing the right thing is not a simple matter of putting those rules into practice. Social contexts are not fixed and, therefore, do not always lend themselves to habitual or formulaic ways of responding.

Moreover, extant social rules may themselves require changes to bring them in line with morality. Reading and evaluating what is morally right, therefore, entails judgment. Being a good person, however, is more than a matter of understanding what is morally right. In philosophy a distinction is made between deontic judgments of what is morally right and aretaic judgments of responsibility which involve a commitment to act on one's deontic judgment. In everyday language we use the term "character" to refer to the tendency to act in ways that are consistent with what one understands to be morally right. A person of good character is someone who attends to the moral implications of actions and acts in accordance with what is moral in all but the most extreme of circumstances.

This everyday usage of the term character captures an important feature of what is ordinarily meant by a good person. The question for us as educators becomes one of understanding how these common sense notions of character map onto actual human psychology, and what aspects of the educative process can contribute to character formation.

Unfortunately, most of the current rhetoric about character education has little to do with what people are actually like, and more to do with a political agenda that would return us to mistaken practices of the past. It is important to remember as we move forward in our efforts to engage schools in meaningful moral and character education just why character education fell out of favor in the first place.

Limitations of character education

Traditional character education, which had its heyday in the early part of this century, had as its central aim fostering formation of elements of the individual's personality and value structure which would constitute socially desirable qualities or virtues. In the late 1920s a major research effort was undertaken by Hugh Hartshorne and Mark May to identify the factors that contributed to the formation of character. The design of their research was based on the reasonable premise that the first step should be to identify those individuals who possessed moral virtues. What they had expected to find was that the population of 8000 students they studied would divide up into those who displayed virtuous conduct nearly all of the time, and those who would not. To the surprise and disappointment of the researchers they discovered that few students were virtuous, and that instead, most children cheated, behaved selfishly, and lacked "self control" a large amount of the time.

Virtue, according to their data, seemed to be context dependent as students cheated, or lied et cetera in some situations and not in others. As Clark Power noted: Hartshorne and May concluded that there were no character traits per se but "specific habits learned in relationship to specific situations which have made one or another response successful."

The reference to habit by Hartshorne and May is concordant with traditional views of character formation. Since Aristotle, the development of virtue has been thought to emerge out of the progressive building up of habits. Contemporary character educators likewise rely heavily on psychological theories that emphasize punishment and reward systems to reinforce desired behavior, and systems of inculcation which are presumed to instill values and virtues in the young. It is worth remembering that in response to their findings, Hartshorne and May concluded that such traditional approaches to character education through the use of didactic teaching, exhortation, and example probably do more harm than good since such practices do not take into account the practical demands of social contexts. In other words, such rigid instruction runs counter to the evaluative and contextualized nature of moral life. By focusing solely on efforts to instill proper values and habits, such approaches fail to develop students' capacities to make the social and moral judgments that contextualized actions require. Moreover, these rigid approaches run counter to the multifaceted and complex nature of human personality.

Research on personality conducted over the past 30 years has served to confirm the view of character offered by Hartshorne and May by demonstrating that people cannot be accurately described in terms of stable and general personality traits since people tend to exhibit different and seemingly contradictory aspects of themselves in different contexts.

The moral self

Findings that individual personality and character are multifaceted, complex and responsive to contextual cues, seems to comport with such common experiences as knowing people who are shy in some contexts and gregarious in others, and fits our general common sense understanding that people are not always consistent in their moral positions or actions. On the other hand, our awareness of such inconsistencies also runs counter to shared experiences that people are more or less shy than others, kinder and more trustworthy than others, and so forth.

In other words, there seems to be a sense in which human personality or character is consistent Resolving this apparent contradiction in the nature of persons has been the task of contemporary personality and social psychology. Resolution with respect to issues of morality and character seems to rest on a recognition that judgments and not just habits are operating when people respond to social contexts. In this light, observed consistencies within individuals across contexts may be accounted for with reference to the ways in which individuals address moral consistencies or inconsistencies within themselves.

In other words, if individual moral actions are guided by choices and not simply the result of unreflective habit, then the issue for character education rests not with inculcation and habit formation, but in understanding how it is that people judge the worth of their own actions in relation to their world view and sense of themselves as moral beings. We need to move away from the notion of character as a set of externally provided traits and habits to a view of the moral self as constructed rather than absorbed and as being updated and reconstructed continuously.

Self in this view is not so much an entity as it is a story or a narrative we tell ourselves in which we are the featured character. Who we are emerges as we engage the social world and attempt to provide ourselves an account of how we initiate actions, and of who that agent is, and who we wish that agent to be. What we call the self, is a psychological construction which we form in social contexts. Before we are born, aspects of the content of who we will become are already laid out for us. Each of us lives in a particular time period, cultural and historical context, and family situation.

We are given a name, assigned a gender, and live in a society in which race matters or doesn't matter. All of which comes without our asking, and none of which comes with prepackaged understandings. Personal development, then is in part a function of how one interprets the hand one is dealt at birth, and the meanings and ways in which one enacts the different roles (e.g., boy, girl, athlete, scholar, gang member, professor, someone named Larry or Maria) which we assume in context. In a sense such social roles imply scripts, and some social learning theorists have mistakenly reduced social conduct to knowledge of social scripts.

Social life, however, is not rigidly scripted, and to the extent that one can use this metaphor it would be more in the sense of a broad outline in which persons present an interpretation of a given role (e.g., mother) which they enact and modify in social context. In addition, social roles are not simply accepted by individuals, but are evaluated and modified to comport with individuals' constructions of what a social role should be as it relates to themselves. Finally, personhood and a sense of agency requires personal choice, and individuals engage in choices which would establish their uniqueness.

The connection between this drammaturgical or narrative view of self, and the present discussion of character has to do with how individuals construct a view of themselves as moral beings, or what some have called the moral self, and the relation between this moral self and the more general narrative we construct which constitutes our personal identity. Self as singular, that is who we refer to when we speak about ourselves, look at our own baby pictures, and experience the sense of agency when we engage in actions, is in fact multifaceted.

Those facets of who we are vary in terms of their salience or importance both as a function of the general narrative we have constructed about ourselves, and the particular situation we find ourselves in. Our "moral selves", what some have been calling character, is only a part of and functions in relation to the totality of who we are. When we act in context, our reading of the social situation may or may not engage our moral understandings. And when our moral understandings are involved, it may or may not be the case that the moral part of who we are is the most salient. Richard Nixon, for example, argued that being President was different from being an ordinary citizen in that the Presidency required one to act in extra- legal and amoral ways when the pragmatic self interests of the United States were at stake.

In essence, Nixon's understanding of the role of President meant that morality was secondary to political pragmatics. Implicit in his argument was the notion that Nixon's moral self remained intact, but on hold while he was acting from pragmatics. We see similar forms of argument in the self reports of adolescents who engage in aggressive acts to steal from others. Often these adolescents explain their actions in means - end terms in which the moral consequences of their actions are placed well below the pragmatic goal of obtaining goods. While these adolescents will describe themselves in moral terms in relation to general dealings with people , especially family members, they define their actions in very "business" like terms when describing their actions on the street.

In Blasi's work on the moral self, he makes the point that morality may or may not be a central element of the general narrative we construct about who we are. In other words, morality may or may not be a salient issue in constructing one's personal identity.

The fact that virtually all children construct basic moral understandings about fairness and human welfare does not mean that being a person who acts on that knowledge in relation to others is necessarily an important part of how one self defines. For the adolescents described above, or for some businessmen for that matter, being moral may not be as integral to their self definition as are other facets of their personal identities.

According to Blasi, the experience of "guilt" or moral responsibility emerges in those situations in which one acts counter to what one knows to be morally right only for those for whom morality is an integral part of personal identity. In other words, from Blasi's work, we can infer that a central feature of what we mean by moral character is the degree to which being a moral person attains salience as a part of one's self definition. Acting in consonance with one's deontic moral judgments is for someone of "good" character important for that person's sense of intrapersonal coherence in the vast majority of contexts.

From an educational standpoint this means that character formation is not a curricular issue in the usual sense of a course or program designed to teach a particular content. Character emerges from the more general individual environment interactions from which students construct their sense of themselves.

There is no simplistic model or formula for "building" character. And, as much as those of us who each year brave Chicago's character building Winters would like to believe, no specific set of experiences that lead to good or strong character. Schools contribute to character to the degree to which they constitute environments conducive to more general social and emotional development, and more specifically moral environments in which students are treated fairly and with respect, and which convey and enact through teacher behavior and school policy a general climate in which morality is valued. Having said that, there are some policies and practices which schools can engage in that raise the likelihood that schooling will contribute to students moral development and character.

Limitations of individual responsibility

Much of what we see in present day society by way of criminal activity, and juvenile crime in particular needs to be understood as a rational response to objective social conditions rather than simply a lack of morality or character of individuals. A study which we conducted in Brazil of adolescents' and young adults' conceptions of everyday forms of corruption is highly instructive.

Nearly all of our young subjects across social classes and economic levels engaged in what they considered to be corrupt social practices at least some of the time. When asked to evaluate these practices nearly all of our subjects argued that they were wrong. However, lower class subjects irrespective of educational level were five times as likely as upper middle class young people to state that engaging in such practices was justified in the face of an overwhelmingly corrupt social system.

In contrast upper-middle class university students were more than twice as likely as lower class subjects irrespective of educational level to argue that it was important to not engage in such practices in order to offer individual resistance to the corrupt social system and thereby change it. What is instructive for us at the policy level is to recognize that these observed class and educational differences in orientation to the immorality of corrupt public behavior did not reflect a difference in the morality of individuals, but rather social class differences in the sense of political and social empowerment to effect change in the objective social situation, and the belief on the part of the poor and uneducated that such actions constituted a rational form of self protection from victimization by the general system.

While the US. is not Brazil, the lesson to be drawn is that we should not expect school approaches to moral and character education aimed at individual responsibility to completely compensate for broader changes that need to take place with respect to social policies which impact America's poor and disenfranchised.

IMPLICATIONS FOR EDUCATIONAL PRACTICE

Educational practices and policies with respect to moral development and character formation. These practices divide more or less into those which concern academic or intellectual content and reflection, and school policies or practices which affect general school climate or student activities. We begin first with academic practices.

— *The focus of moral education should be on students' concerns for and conceptions of fairness and the welfare of others*. These moral issues are treated by children and adults as universalizable, and as independent of the specific norms and rules of their particular culture. Morality is distinct from social conventions which are the agreed upon social norms particular to social or cultural groups. This definition of morality is consistent with individual psychology and may serve as the basis for a common and shared values focus for moral education.

— *Educational practices should be coordinated with student development*: While young children have an intuitive sense of morality, they do not have fully developed understandings of fairness. Nor do they have an understanding of the function of conventions in organizing social systems. For educators to be effective in fostering students' moral and social growth they need to match educational practices with student developmental level.

— *Educational practices should take into account the fact that morality and convention develop out of qualitatively differing types of social experiences*: Morality deals with justice and human welfare. Thus, children's moral concepts are fostered by school experiences that focus on such issues, engage children in reflection upon such concerns, and ask them to resolve genuine moral problems in ways that are the most fair and compassionate for all parties. Issues of convention, on the other hand, deal with concerns for social organization. Thus, children's understandings of the meaning and importance of convention emerge out of efforts to come to agreed upon norms for coordinating the actions of members of a group. In daily school experience this emerges in the context of discourse over dress codes, rules for hand raising and the like. In the curriculum these issues emerge as children attempt to understand the meaning or function of different conventional norms throughout history, or within differing cultural groups. Specific suggestions for what is termed "domain appropriate education" are provided in Nucci and Weber.

— *Moral development is fostered by moral discussion and moral problem solving*: Moral reasoning develops when students recognize inconsistencies and inadequacies in their moral positions. One of the most effective ways to bring this about is through small group discussions which are characterized by transactive discourse. In such discussions, students are asked to arrive at a resolution of a moral problem in such a way that it would be most fair to all parties. In the process students must listen carefully to what group members are saying and come to terms with positions at variance from their own. Discussions can be stimulated by readings as well as actual events, and are not limited to particular educational subject matter.

— *Moral discussion may also make use of moral exemplars*: Traditional character education has generally included reading literature about morally exemplary figures as an important way to provide students with moral role models. While over-reliance on this approach is unjustified, there is a place for providing students with opportunities to consider the thoughts and actions of exemplary figures such as Martin Luther King, and morally charged situations from literature as way to allow students to consider how they might construct their own sense of self with respect to morality. What is critical is that students be actively engaged in constructing a connection between themselves and the role model. Otherwise, such exercises are a waste of everyone's time.

— *Opportunities for self reflection can be used to foster moral character*: Stimulating students to raise the salience of their "moral self" and integrate it within their overall identity can often be accomplished through classroom activities and assignments which ask students to reflect upon who they are and wish to become. While this can be misused in futile attempts to generate student guilt, it can be productive when students view the activity as serving their own intrinsic interest in learning about themselves. Teachers can encourage students to address inconsistencies and lacunae within their views of self which can help focus student attention on the moral content of their character. This has been successfully used not only as a vehicle for self examination, but also as a context within which students can develop literacy and communication skills.

— *Moral discussion is most effective when it concerns actual student behavior or issues:* Student motivation and attention is heightened when the moral problems they are asked to address concern real life issues, and when the consequences of their decisions have real impact on subsequent policies or actions. This approach also engages students in role enactment related to their construction of a sense of self. Thus, this approach touches not only upon deontic judgments, but aretaic judgments of moral responsibility and character. A widely studied approach which makes use of this technique is the "Just Community".

— *Moral concerns are often embedded within conventionalized practices:* Since moral actions take place within cultural contexts, many moral issues are embedded within, or overlap with morality. This has the following educational ramifications.

— *Concerns for fostering moral development should include concerns for fostering moral sensitivity:* Because issues of morality are often embedded within existing conventional practices, the moral meaning of such practices may be overlooked. If schools are committed to moral education, then one function of such education should be to heighten the likelihood that students will attend to the moral consequences of conforming to the norms of the existing social order. One way to do this is to present students with issues which involve an overlap between morality and convention, and ask them to consider both the moral and conventional aspects of such issues. Examples of this type of approach are provided in Nucci and Weber.

— *Moral educators need to be prepared to deal with controversy:* Because issues of overlap often involve established conventional practices, the potential unfairness or harm caused by such practices may be overlooked by the majority of society, or may be important to the interests of particular social groups. A moral dilemma faced by educators and policy makers is whether and to what extent to engage students in consideration of such controversial matters. Engaging such issues prepares students to contribute to the moral growth of society. However, schools which take on such issues risk alienating their constituent base. Balancing the educator's moral duty to enable students to deal with the contradictions inherent in any complex value system, with the educator's role as an agent of that very society defines the core moral dilemma faced by any teacher

Issues of school climate and student activity

— *General school climate should foster fairness and respect for others*: Moral development and character education are not limited to discrete academic subject areas, but are infused throughout school life. The school climate should be one characterized by mutual respect for all persons. School rules should be ones which protect student safety, and promote respect for others. Enforcement of school policies should be characterized by firmness, fairness, and flexibility. School authority should not be characterized by harshness or intolerance.

— *Provide students with opportunities to develop social problem solving skills*: While not a component of moral development per se, knowledge of conflict resolution, and social problem solving allows students greater ability to engage in non-confrontational peer interactions which allow for dialogue and construction of moral orientations toward others. This works best when students are encouraged to use these skills in resolving actual conflicts while at school.

— *Students should be given opportunities to assume roles that entail moral responsibility:* Much of school life requires little more of students than passive obedience. Opportunities for students to build a sense of themselves as moral beings, such as actively participating in meeting the needs of their own school and local community if coupled with opportunities for meaningful reflection can provide content for students to construct a moral sense of self.

A CRITICAL OUTLOOK OF CHARACTER EDUCATION

The phrase character education also has two meanings. In the broad sense, it refers to almost anything that schools might try to provide outside of academics, especially when the purpose is to help children grow into good people. In the narrow sense, it denotes a particular style of moral training, one that reflects particular values as well as particular assumptions about the nature of children and how they learn.

Unfortunately, the two meanings of the term have become blurred, with the narrow version of character education dominating the field to the point that it is frequently mistaken for the broader concept. Thus educators who are keen to support children's social and moral development may turn, by default, to a program with a certain set of methods and a specific agenda that, on reflection, they might very well find objectionable.

This character is to subject these programs to careful scrutiny and, in so doing, to highlight the possibility that there are other ways to achieve our broader objectives. Let me get straight to the point. What goes by the name of character education nowadays is, for the most part, a collection of exhortations and extrinsic inducements designed to make children work harder and do what they're told. Even when other values are also promoted - caring or fairness, say - the preferred method of instruction is tantamount to indoctrination. The point is to drill students in specific behaviors rather than to engage them in deep, critical reflection about certain ways of being. This is the impression one gets from reading articles and books by contemporary proponents of character education as well as the curriculum materials sold by the leading national programs. The impression is only strengthened by visiting schools that have been signaled out for their commitment to character education. To with:

> A huge, multiethnic elementary school in Southern California uses a framework created by the Jefferson Center for Character Education. Classes that the principal declares "well behaved" are awarded Bonus Bucks, which can eventually be redeemed for an ice cream party. On an enormous wall near the cafeteria, professionally painted Peanuts characters instruct children: "Never talk in line."

A visitor is led to a fifth-grade classroom to observe an exemplary lesson on the current character education topic. The teacher is telling students to write down the name of the person they regard as the "toughest worker" in school. The teacher then asks them, "How many of you are going to be tough workers?" "Can you be a tough worker at home, too?" (Yes.) A small, almost entirely African American school in Chicago uses a framework created by the Character Education Institute. Periodic motivational assemblies are used to "give children a good pep talk," as the principal puts it, and to reinforce the values that determine who will be picked as Student of the Month. Rule number one posted on the wall of the kindergarten room is "We will obey the teachers." Today, students in this class are listening to the story of "Lazy Lion," who orders each of the other animals to build him a house, only to find each effort unacceptable. At the end, the teacher drives home the lesson: "Did you ever hear Lion say thank you:" (No.) "Did you ever hear Lion say please?" (No.) "It's good to always say ... what? (Please.) The reason for using these words, she points out, is that by doing so we are more likely to get what we want.

A charter school near Boston has been established specifically to offer an intensive, homegrown character education curriculum to its overwhelmingly white, middle-class student body. At weekly public ceremonies, certain children receive a leaf that will be hung in the Forest of Virtue. The virtues themselves are "not open to debate," the headmaster insists, since moral precepts in his view enjoy the same status as mathematical truths. In a first-grade classroom, a teacher is observing that "it's very hard to be obedient when you want something.

Some of the most popular schoolwide strategies for improving students' character seem dubious on their face. When President Clinton mentioned the importance of character education in his 1996 State of the Union address, the only specific practice he recommended was requiring students to wear uniforms. The premises here are first, that children's character can be improved by forcing them to dress alike, and second, that if adults object to students' clothing, the best solution is not to invite them to reflect together about how this problem might be solved, but instead to compel them all to wear the same thing.

A second strategy, also consistent with the dominant philosophy of character education, is an exercise that might be called "If It's Tuesday, This Must Be Honesty." Here, one value after another is targeted, with each assigned its own day, week, or month. This seriatim approach is unlikely to result in a lasting commitment to any of these values, much less a feeling for how they may be related. Nevertheless, such programs are taken very seriously by some of the same people who are quick to dismiss other educational programs, such as those intended to promote self-esteem, as silly and ineffective.

Then there is the strategy of offering students rewards when they are "caught" being good, an approach favored by rightwing religious groups[1] and orthodox behaviorists but also by leaders of - and curriculum suppliers for - the character education movement. Because of its popularity and because a sizable body of psychological evidence germane to the topic is available, it is worth lingering on this particular practice for a moment.

In general terms, what the evidence suggests is this: the more we reward people for doing something, the more likely they are to lose interest in whatever they had to do to get the reward. Extrinsic motivation, in other words, is not only quite different from intrinsic motivation but actually tends to erode it. This effect has been demonstrated under many different circumstances and with respect to many different attitudes and behaviors. Most relevant to character education is a series of studies showing that individuals who have been rewarded for doing something nice become less likely to think of themselves as caring as helpful people and more likely to attribute their behavior to the reward.

"Extrinsic incentives can, by undermining self-perceived altruism, decrease intrinsic motivation to help others," one group of researchers concluded on the basis of several studies. "A person's kindness, it seems, cannot be bought." The same applies to a person's sense of responsibility, fairness, perseverance, and so on. The lesson a child learns from Skinnerian tactics is that the point of being good is to get rewards. No wonder researchers have found that children who are frequently rewarded - or, in another study, children who receive positive reinforcement for caring, sharing, and helping - are less likely than other children to keep doing those things. In short, it makes no sense to dangle goodies in front of children for being virtuous. But even worse than rewards are awards - certificates, plaques, trophies, and other tokens of recognition whose numbers have been artificially limited so only a few can get them. When some children are singled out as "winners," the central message that every child learns is this: "Other people are potential obstacles to my success."

Thus the likely result of making students beat out their peers for the distinction of being the most virtuous is not only less intrinsic commitment to virtue but also a disruption of relationships and, ironically, of the experience of community that is so vital to the development of children's character. Unhappily, the problems with character education are not restricted to such strategies as enforcing sartorial uniformity, scheduling a value of the week, or offering students a "doggie biscuit" for being good. More deeply troubling are the fundamental assumptions, both explicit and implicit, that inform character education programs. Let us consider five basic questions that might be asked of any such program: At what level are problems addressed? What is the underlying theory of human nature? What is the ultimate goal? Which values are promoted? And finally, How is learning thought to take place?

1. *At what level are problems addressed?*

One of the major purveyors of materials in this field, the Jefferson Center for Character Education in Pasadena, California, has produced a video that begins with some arresting images - quite literally. Young people are shown being led away in handcuffs, the point being that crime can be explained on the basis of an "erosion of American core values," as the narrator intones ominously. The idea that social problems can be explained by the fact that traditional virtues are no longer taken seriously is offered by many proponents of character education as though it were just plain common sense. But if people steal or rape or kill solely because they possess bad values - that is, because of their personal characteristics - the implication is that political and economic realities are irrelevant and need to be addressed. Never mind staggering levels of unemployment in the inner cities or a system in which more and more of the nation's wealth is concentrated in fewer and fewer hands; just place the blame on individuals whose characters are deficient. A key tent of the "Character Counts!" Coalition, which bills itself as a nonpartisan umbrella group devoid of any political agenda, is the highly debatable proposition that "negative social influences can [be] and usually are overcome by the exercise of free will and character." What is presented as common sense is, in fact, conservative ideology.

Let's put politics aside, tough. If a program proceeds by trying to "fix the kids" - as do almost all brands of character education - it ignores the accumulated evidence from the field of social psychology demonstrating that much of how we act and who we are reflects the situations in which we find ourselves. Virtually all the landmark studies in this discipline have been variations on this them. Set up children in an extended team competition at summer camp and you will elicit unprecedented levels of aggression. Assign adults to roles of prisoners or guards in a mock jail, and they will start to become their roles. Move people to a small town, and they will be more likely to rescue a stranger in need. In fact, so common is the tendency to attribute to an individual's personality or character what is actually a function of the social environment that social psychologists have dubbed this the "fundamental attribution error."

A similar lesson comes to us from the movement concerned with Total Quality Management associated with the ideas of the late W. Edward Deming. At the heart of Deming's teaching is the notion that the "system" of an organization largely determines the results. The problems experienced in a corporation, therefore, are almost always due to system flaws rather than a lack of effort or ability on the part of individuals in that organization. Thus, if we are troubled by the way students are acting, Deming, along with most social psychologists, would presumably have us transform the structure of the classroom rather than try to remake the students themselves - precisely the opposite of the character education approach.

2. *What is the view of human nature?*

Character education's "fix-the-kids" orientation follows logically from the belief that kids need fixing. Indeed, the movement seems to be driven by a stunningly dark view of children - and, for that matter, of people in general. A "comprehensive approach [to character education] is based on a somewhat dim view of human nature," acknowledges William Kilpatrick, whose book Why Johnny Can't Tell Right from Wrong contains such assertions as: "Most behavior problems are the result of sheer 'willfulness' on the part of children."

Despite - or more likely because of - statements like that, Kilpatrick has frequently been invited to speak at character education conferences. But that shouldn't be surprising in light of how many prominent proponents of character education share his views. Edward Wynne says his own work is grounded in a tradition of thought that takes a "somewhat pessimistic view of human nature." The idea of character development "sees children as self-centered," in the opinion of Kevin Ryan, who directs the Center for the Advancement of Ethics and Character at Boston University as well as heading up the character education network of the Association of Supervision and Curriculum Development. Yet another writer approvingly traces the whole field back to the bleak world view of Thomas Hobbes: it is "an obvious assumption of character education," writes Louis Goldman, that people lack the instinct to work together. Without laws to compel us to get along, "our natural egoism would lead us into 'a condition of warre one against another."

This sentiment is echoed by F. Washington Jarvis, headmaster of the Roxbury Latin School in Boston, one of Ryan's favorite examples of what character education should look like in practice. Jarvis sees human nature as "mean, nasty, brutish, selfish, and capable of great cruelty and meanness. We have to hold a mirror up to the students and say, 'This is who you are. Stop it.' " Even when proponents of character education don't express such sentiments explicitly, they give themselves away by framing their mission as a campaign for self-control. Amitai Etzioni, for example, does not merely include this attribute on a list of good character traits, he defines character principally in terms of the capacity "to control impulses and defer gratification." This is noteworthy because the virtue of self-restraint - or at least the decision to give special emphasis to it - has historically been preached by those, from St. Augustine to present, who see people as basically sinful.

In fact, at least three assumptions seen to be at work when the need for self-control is stressed: first, that we are all at war not only with others but with ourselves, torn between our desires and our reason (or social norms); second, that these desires are fundamentally selfish, aggressive, or otherwise unpleasant; and third, that these desires are very strong, constantly threatening to overpower us if we don't rein them in. Collectively, these statements describe religious dogma, not scientific fact. Indeed, the evidence from several disciplines converges to cast doubt on this sour view of human beings and, instead, supports the idea that it is as "natural" for children to help as to hurt. We will not rehearse that evidence here, partly because done so elsewhere at some length. Suffice it to say that even the most hard-headed empiricist might well conclude that the promotion of prosocial values consists to some extent of supporting many facets of the self. Any educator who adopts this more balanced position might think twice before joining an educational movement that is finally inseparable from the doctrine of original sin.

3. *What is the ultimate goal?*

It may seem odd even to inquire about someone's reasons for trying to improve children's character. But it is worth mentioning that the whole enterprise - not merely the particular values that are favored - is often animated by a profoundly conservative, if not reactionary, agenda. Character education based on "acculturating students to conventional norms of 'good' behavior ... resonates with neoconservative concerns for social stability," observed David Purpel. The movement has been described by another critic as a "yearning for some halcyon days of moral niceties and social transquility." But it is not merely a social order that some are anxious to preserve: character education is vital, according to one vocal proponent, because "the development of character is the backbone of the economic system" now in place.

Character education, or any kind of education, would look very different if we began with other objectives - if, for example, we were principally concerned with helping children become active participants in a democratic society (or agents for transforming a society into one that is authentically democratic). It would look different if our top priority were to help students develop into principled and caring members of a community or advocates for social justice. To be sure, these objectives are not inconsistent with the desire to preserve certain traditions, but the point would then be to help children decide which traditions are worth preserving and why, based on these other considerations. That is not at all the same as endorsing anything that is traditional or making the preservation of tradition our primary concern. In short, we want to ask character education proponents what goals they emphasize - and ponder whether their broad vision is compatible with our own.

4. *Which values?*

Should we allow values to be taught in school? The question is about as sensible as asking whether our bodies should be allowed to contain bacteria. Just as humans are teeming with microorganisms, so schools are teeming with values. We can't see the former because they're too small; we don't notice the latter because they're too similar to the values of the culture at large. Whether or not we deliberately adopt a character or moral education program, we are always teaching values. Even people who insist that they are opposed to values in school usually mean that the are opposed to values other than their own.

And that raises the inevitable question: Which values, or whose, should we teach: It has already become a clich to reply that this question should not trouble us because, while there may be disagreement on certain issues, such as abortion, all of us can agree on a list of basic values that children ought to have. Therefore, schools can vigorously and unapologetically set about teaching all of those values. But not so fast. Look at the way character education programs have been designed and you will discover, alongside such unobjectionable items as "fairness" or "honesty," an emphasis on values that are, again, distinctly conservative - and, to that extent, potentially controversial. To begin with, the famous Protestant work ethic is prominent: children should learn to "work hard and complete their tasks well and promptly, even when they do not want to," says Ryan. Here the Latin question Cui bono? comes to mind. Who benefits when people are trained not to question the value of what they have been told to do but simply to toil away at it - and to regard this as virtuous?

Similarly, when Wynne defines the moral individual as someone who is not honest but also "diligent, obedient, and patriotic," readers may find themselves wondering whether these traits really qualify as moral - as well as reflecting on the virtues that are missing from this list. Character education curricula also stress the importance of things like "respect," "responsibility," and "citizenship." But these are slippery terms, frequently used as euphemisms for uncritical deference to authority. Under the headline "The Return of the 'Fourth R' " - referring to "respect, responsibility, or rules" - a news magazine recently described the growing popularity of such practices as requiring uniforms, paddling disobedient students, rewarding those who are compliant, and "throwing disruptive kids out of the classroom."

Indeed, William Glasser observed some time ago that many educators "teach thoughtless conformity to school rules and call the conforming child 'responsible.' By this he meant specifically that they should turn in their friends who used drugs. Exhorting students to be "respectful" or rewarding them if they are caught being "good" may likewise mean nothing more than getting them to do whatever the adults demand. Following a lengthy article about character education in the New York Times Magazine, a reader mused, "Do you suppose that if Germany had had character education at the time, it would have encourage children to fight Nazism or to support it?"

In place of traditional attributes associated with character education, Deborah Meier and Paul Schwarz of the Central Park East Secondary School in New York nominated two core values that a school might try to promote: "empathy and skepticism: the ability to see a situation from the eyes of another and the tendency to wonder about the validity of what we encountered." Anyone who brushes away the question "Which values should be taught?" might speculate on the concrete differences between a school dedicated to turning out students who are loyal, patriotic, obedient, and so on. Meanwhile, in place of such personal qualities as punctuality or perseverance, we might emphasize the cultivation of autonomy so that children come to experience themselves as "origins" rather than "pawns," as one researcher put it. We might, in other words, stress self-determination at least as much as self- control. With such an agenda, it would be crucial to give students the chance to participate in making decisions about their learning and about how they want their classroom to be. This stands in sharp contrast to a philosophy of character education like Wynne's which decrees that "it is specious to talk about student choices" and offers students no real power except for when we give "some students authority over other students.

Even with values that are widely shared, a superficial consensus may dissolve when we take a closer look. Educators across the spectrum are concerned about excessive attention to self-interest and are committed to helping students transcend a preoccupation with their own needs. But how does this concern play out in practice? For some of us, it takes the form of an emphasis on compassion; for the dominant character education approach, the alternative value to be stressed is loyalty, which is, of course, altogether different.

Moreover, as John Dewey remarked at the turn of the century, anyone seriously troubled about rampant individualism among children would promptly target for extinction the "drill-

and- skill" approach to instruction: "The mere absorbing of facts and truths is so exclusively individual an affair that it tends very naturally to pass into selfishness." Yet conservative champions of character education are often among the most outspoken supporters of a model of teaching that emphasizes rote memorization and the sequential acquisition of decontextualized skills.

Or take another example: all of us may say we endorse the idea of "cooperation," but what do we make of the practice of setting groups against one another in a quest for triumph, such that cooperation becomes the means and victory in the end? On the one hand, we might find this even more objectionable than individual competition.

On the other hand, "school-to-school, class- to-class, or row-to-row academic competitions" actually have been endorsed as part of a character education program, along with contests that lead to awards for things like good citizenship. The point, once again, is that it is entirely appropriate to ask which values a character education program is attempting to foster, notwithstanding the ostensible lack of controversy about a list of core values. It is equally appropriate to put such a discussion in context - specifically, in the context of which values are currently promoted in schools.

The fact is that schools are already powerful socializers of traditional values - although, as noted above, we may fail to appreciate the extent to which this is true because we have come to take these values for granted. In most schools, for example, students are taught - indeed, compelled - to follow the rules regardless of whether the rules are reasonable and to respect authority regardless of whether that respect has been earned.

Students are led to accept competition as natural and desirable, and to see themselves more as discrete individuals than as members of a community. Children in American schools are even expected to begin each day by reciting a loyalty oath to the Fatherland, although we call it by a different name. In short, the question is not whether to adopt the conservative values offered by most character education programs, but whether we want to consolidate the conservative values that are already in place.

5. *What is the theory of learning?*

We come to now to what may be the most significant, and yet the least remarked on, feature of character education: the way values are taught and the way learning is thought to take place. The character education coordinator for the small Chicago elementary school also teaches second grade. In her classroom, where one boy has been forced to sit by himself for the last two weeks, she is asking the children to define tolerance. When the teacher gets the specific answers she is fishing for, she exclaims, "Say that again," and writes down only those responses. Later comes the moral: "If somebody doesn't think the way you think, should you turn them off?" (No.)

Down the hall, the first-grade teacher is fishing for answers on a different subject. "When we play games, we try to understand the - what?" A moment later, the children scramble to get into place so she will pick them to tell a visitor their carefully rehearsed stories about conflict resolution. Almost every child's account, narrated with considerable prompting by the teacher, concerns name-calling or some other unpleasant incident that was "correctly" resolved by finding an adult. The teacher never asks the children how they felt about what happened or invites them to reflect on what else might have been done. She wraps up the activity by telling the children. "What we need to do all the time is clarify - make it clear - to the adult what you did."

The schools with character education programs that we have visited are engaged largely in exhortation and directed recitation. At first one might assume this is due to poor implementation of the programs on the part of individual educators. But the program themselves - and the theorists who promote them - really do seem to regard teaching as a matter of telling and compelling. For example, the broad-based "Character Counts!" Coalition offers a framework of six core character traits and then asserts that "young people should be specifically and repeatedly told what is expected of them."

The leading providers of curriculum materials walk teachers through highly structured lessons in which character-related concepts are described and then students are drilled until they can produce the right answers. Teachers are encouraged to praise children who respond correctly, and some programs actually include multiple-choice tests to ensure that students have learned their values. For example, here are two sample test questions prepared for teachers by the Character Education Institute, based in San Antonio, Texas: "Having to obey rules and regulations (a) gives everyone the same right to be an individual, (b) forces everyone to do the same thing at all times, (c) prevents persons from expressing their individually [sic]"; and "One reason why parents might not allow their children freedom of choice is (a) children are always happier when they are told what to do and when to do it, (b) parents aren't given a freedom of choice; therefore, children should not be given a choice either, (c) children do not always demonstrate that they are responsible enough to be given a choice." The correct answer, according to the answer key, are (a) and (c) respectively.

The Character Education Institute recommends "engaging the students in discussions," but only discussions of particular sort: "Since the lesson have been designed to logically guide the students to the right answers, the teacher should allow the students to draw their own conclusions. However, if the students draw the wrong conclusion, the teacher is instructed to tell them why their conclusion is wrong." Students are told what to think and do, not only by their teachers but by highly didactic stories. Most character education programs also deliver homilies by way of posters and banners and murals displayed throughout the school. Children who do as they are told are presented with all manner of rewards, typically in front of their peers.

Does all of this amount to indoctrination? Absolutely, says Wynne, who declares that "school is and should and must be inherently indoctrinative." Even when character education proponents tiptoe around that word, their model of instruction is clear: good character and values are instilled in or transmitted to students. We are "planting the ideas of virtue, of good traits in the young," says William Bennett. The virtues or values in question are fully formed, and, in the minds of many character education proponents, divinely ordained.

The children are - pick your favorite metaphor - so many passive receptacles to be filled, lumps of clay to be molded, pets to be trained, or computers to be programmed. Thus, when we see Citizen-of-the-Month certificates and "Be a good sport!" posters, when we find teachers assigning preachy stories and principals telling students what to wear, it is important that we understand what is going on.

These techniques may appear merely innocuous or gimmicky; they may strike us as evidence of a scattershot, let's-try-anything approach. But the truth is that these are elements of a systematic pedagogical philosophy. They are manifestations of a model that sees children as objects to be manipulated rather than as learners to be engaged.

Ironically, some people who accept character education without a second thought are quite articulate about the bankruptcy of this model when it comes to teaching academic subjects. Plenty of teachers have abandoned the use of worksheets, textbooks, and lectures that fill children full of disconnected facts and skills.

Plenty of administrators are working to create schools where students can actively construct meaning around scientific and historical and literary concepts. Plenty of educators; in short, realize that memorizing right answers and algorithms doesn't help anyone to arrive at a deep understanding of ideas. And so we are left scratching our heads. Why would all these people, who know that the "transmission" model fails to facilitate intellectual development, uncritically accept the very same model to promote ethical development? How could they understand that mathematical truths cannot be shoved down students' throats but than participate in a program that essentially tries to shove moral truths down the same throats?

In the case of individual educators, the simple answer may be that they missed the connection. Perhaps they just failed to recognize that "a classroom cannot foster the development of autonomy in the intellectual realm while suppressing it in the social and moral realms," as Constance Kamii and her colleagues put it not long ago."

In the case of proponents of character education, we believe the answer to this riddle is quite different. The reason they are promoting techniques that seem strikingly ineffective at fostering autonomy or ethical development is that, as a rule, they are not trying to foster autonomy or ethical development. The goal is not to support or facilitate children's social and moral growth, but simply to "demand good behavior from students," in Ryan's words.

The idea is to get compliance, to make children act the way we want them to. Indeed, if these are the goals, then the methods make perfect sense - the lectures and pseudo-discussions, the slogans and the stories that conk students on the head with their morals. David Brooks, who heads the Jefferson Center for Character Education, frankly states, "We're in the advertising business."

The way you get people to do something, whether it's buying Rice Krispies or becoming trustworthy, is to "encourage conformity through repeated messages." The idea of selling virtues like cereal nearly reaches the point of self-parody in the Jefferson Center's curriculum, which includes the following activity: "There's a new product on the market! It's Considerate Cereal. Eating it can make a person more considerate. Design a label for the box. Tell why someone should buy and eat this cereal. Then list the ingredients."

If "repeated messages" don't work, then you simply force students to conform: "Sometimes compulsion is what is needed to get a habit started," says William Kilpatrick. We may recoil from the word "compulsion," but it is the premise of that sentence that really ought to give us pause. When education is construed as the process of inculcating habits - which is to say, unreflective actions - then it scarcely deserves to be called education at all. It is really, as Alan Lockwood say, and attempt to get "mindless conformity to externally imposed standards of conduct." Notice how naturally this goal follows from a dark view of human nature. If you begin with the premise that "good conduct is not our natural first choice," then the best you can hope for is "the development of good habits" - that is, a system that gets people to act unthinkly in the manner that someone else has deemed appropriate. This connection recently became clear to Ann Medlock, whose Giraffe Project was designed to evoke "students' own courage and compassion" in thinking about altruism, but which, in some schools, was being turned into a traditional, authoritarian program in which students were simply told how to act and what to believe.

The character education movement's emphasis on habit, then, is consistent with its view on children. Likewise, its process matches its product. The transmission model, along with the use of rewards and punishments to secure compliance, seems entirely appropriate if the values you are trying to transmit are things like obedience and loyalty and respect for authority. But this approach overlooks an important distinction between product and process.

When we argue about which traits to emphasize - compassion or loyalty, cooperation or competition, skepticism or obedience - we are trafficking in value judgments. When we talk about how best to teach these things, however, we are being descriptive rather than just prescriptive. Even if you like the sort of virtues that appear in character education programs, and even if you regard the need to implement those virtues as urgent, the attempt to transmit or instill them dooms the project because that is just not consistent with the best theory and research on how people learn.

The techniques of character education may succeed in temporarily buying a particular behavior. But they are unlikely to leave children with a commitment to that behavior, a reason to continue acting that way in the future.

You can turn out automatons who utter the desired words or maybe even "emit" the desired actions. But the words and actions are unlikely to continue - much less transfer to new situations - because the child has not been invited to integrate them into his or her value structure. As Dewey observed, "The required beliefs cannot be hammered in; the needed attitudes cannot be plastered on." Yet watch a character education lesson in any part of the country and you will almost surely be observing a strenuous exercise in hammering and plastering. For traditional moralists, the constructivist approach is a waste of time. If values and traditions and the stories that embody them already exists, then surely, "we don't have to reinvent the wheel," remarks Bennett.

Likewise an exasperated Wynne: "Must each generation try to completely reinvent society?" The answer is no - and yes. It is not as though everything that now exists must be discarded and entirely new values fashioned from scratch. But the process of learning does indeed require that meaning, ethical or otherwise, be actively invented and reinvented, from the inside out. It requires that children be given the opportunity to make sense of such concepts as fairness or courage, regardless of how long the concepts themselves have been around.

Children must be invited to reflect on complex issues, to recast them in light of their own experiences and questions, to figure out for themselves - and with one another - what kind of person ought to be, which traditions are worth keeping, and how to proceed when two basic values seem to be in conflict.

In this sense, reinvention is necessary if we want to help children become moral people, as opposed to people who merely do what they are told - or reflexively rebel against what they are told. In fact, as Rheta DeVries and Betty Zan add. "If we want children to resist [peer pressure] and not be victims to others' ideas, we have to educate children to think for themselves about all ideas, including those of adults."

Traditionalists are even more likely to offer another objection to the constructivist approach, one that boils down to a single epithet: relativism! If we do anything other than insert moral absolutes in students, if we let them construct their own meanings, then we are saying that anything goes, that morality collapses into personal preferences. Without character education, our schools will just offer programs such as Values Clarification, in which adults are allegedly prohibited from taking a stand.

In response, we would offer several observations. First, the Values Certification model of moral education, popular in some circles a generation ago, survives today mostly in the polemics of conservatives anxious to justify an indoctrinative approach. Naturally, no statistics are ever cited as to the number of school districts still telling students that any value is as good as any other - assuming the program actually said that in the first place.

Second, conservative critics tendentiously try to connect constructivism to relativism, lumping together the work of the late Lawrence Kohlberg with programs like Values Clarification. The truth is that Kolberg, while opposed to what he called the "bag of virtues" approach to moral education, was not much enamored of Values Clarification either, and he spent a fair amount of time arguing against relativism in general.

If Kohlberg can fairly be criticized, it is for emphasizing moral reasoning, a cognitive process, to the extent that he may have slighted the affective components of morality, such as caring. But the traditionalists are not much for the latter either;

caring is seen as an easy or soft virtue that isn't sufficiently "binding or absolute". The objection to constructivism is not that empathy is eclipsed by justice, but that children - or even adults - should not have an active role to play in making decision and reflecting on how to live.

They should be led instead to an uncritical acceptance of ready-made truths. The character educator's job, remember, is to elicit the right answer from students and tell those who see thing differently "why their conclusion is wrong." Any deviation from this approach is regarded as indistinguishable from full-blown relativism; we must "plant" traditional values in each child or else either/or thinking, long since discarded by serious moral philosophers, continues to fuel character education and to perpetuate the confusion of education with indoctrination.

To say that students must construct meaning around moral concepts is not to deny that adults have a crucial role to play. The romantic view that children can basically educate themselves so long as grown-ups don't interfere is not taken seriously by any constructivists wel know of - certainly not by Dewey, Piaget, Kohlberg, or their followers. Rather, like Values Clarification, this view seems to exist principally as a straw man in the arguments of conservatives. Let there be no question, then: educators, parents, and other adults are desperately needed to offer guidance, to act as models, to pose challenges that promote moral growth, and to help children understand the effects of their actions on other people, thereby tapping and nurturing a concern for other that is present in children from a very young age.

Character education rests on three ideological legs: behaviorism, conservatism, and religion. Of these, the third raises the most delicate issues for a critic; it is here that the change of ad hominem argument is most likely to be raised. So let us be clear: it is of no relevance that almost all of the leading proponents of character education are devout Catholics. But it is entirely relevant that, in the shadows of their writings, there lurks the assumption that only religion can serve as the foundation for good character. It is appropriate to consider the personal beliefs of these individuals if those beliefs are ensconced in the movement they have defined and directed. What they do on Sundays is their own business, but if they are trying to turn our public schools into Sunday schools, that becomes everybody's business.

Logically, its supporters should be those who firmly believe that we should focus our efforts on repairing the characters of children rather than on transforming the environments in which they learn, those who assume the worst about human nature, those who are more committed to preserving than to changing our society, those who favor such values as obedience to authority, and those who define learning as the process of swallowing whole a set of preexisting truths. It stands to reason that readers who recognize themselves in this description would enthusiastically endorse character education in its present form. The rest of us have a decision to make. Either we define our efforts to promote children's social and moral development as an alternative to "character education," thereby ceding that label to the people who have already appropriated it, or we try to reclaim the wider meaning of the term by billing what we are doing as a different kind of character education.

The first choice - opting out - seems logical: it strains the language to use a single phrase to describe practices as different as engaging students in reflecting about fairness, on the one hand, and making students dress alike, on the other. It seems foolish to pretend that these are just different versions of the same thing, and thus it may be unreasonable to expect someone with a constructivist or progressive vision to endorse what is now called character education. The problem with abandoning this label, however, is that it holds considerable appeal for politicians and members of the public at large. It will be challenging to explain that "character education" is not synonymous with helping children to grow into good people and, indeed, that the movement associated with the term is a good deal more controversial than it first appears.

Whether we relinquish or retain the nomenclature, though, it is vital that we work to decouple most of what takes place under the banner of "character education" from the enterprise of helping students become ethically sophisticated decision makers and caring human beings. Wanting younger people to turn out that way doesn't require us to adopt traditional character education programs any more than wanting them to be physically fit requires us to turn schools into Marine boot camps.

What does the alternative look like? Return once more to those five questions: in each case, an answer different from that given by traditional character education will help us to sketch the broad contours of a divergent approach. More specifically, we should probably target certain practices for elimination, add some new ones, and reconfigure still others that already exist. We have already offered a catalogue of examples of what to eliminate, from Skinnerian reinforcers to lesson plans that resemble sermons. As examples of what to add, we might suggest holding regular class meetings in which students can share, plan, decide, and reflect together.

We might also provide children with explicit opportunities to practice "perspective talking" - that is, imagining how the world looks from someone else's point of view. Activities that promote an understanding of how others think and feel, that support the impulse to imaginatively reach beyond the self, can provide the same benefits realized by holding democratic class meetings - namely, helping students become more ethical and compassionate while simultaneously fostering intellectual growth.

A good example of an existing practice that might be reconfigured is the use of literature to teach values. In principle, the idea is splendid: it makes perfect sense to select stories that not only help students develop reading skills but also raise moral issues. The trouble is that many programs use simplistic little morality tales in place of rich, complex literature. Naturally, the texts should be developmentally appropriate, but some character educators fail to given children credit for being able to grapple with ambiguity. Perhaps the concern is not that students will be unable to make sense of challenging literature, but that they will not derive the "correct" moral.

This would account for the fact that even when character education curricula include impressive pieces of writing, the works tend to be used for the purpose of drumming in simple lessons. As Kilpatrick sees it, a story "points to these [characters] and says in effect, 'Act like this; don't act like that.' This kind of lesson often takes the form of hero worship, with larger-than-life characters - or real historical figures presented with their foibles airbrushed away - held up to students to encourage imitation of their actions.

Rather than employ literature to indoctrinate or induce mere conformity, we can use it to spur reflection. Whether the students are 6-year-olds or 16-year-olds, the discussion of stories should be open-ended rather than relentlessly didactic. Teachers who refrain from tightly controlling such conversations are impressed again and again by the levels of meaning students prove capable of exploring and the moral growth they exhibit in such an environment. Instead of announcing, "This man is a hero; do what he did," such teachers may involve the students in deciding who (if anyone) is heroic in a given story - or in contemporary culture and why. They may even invite students to reflect on the larger issue of whether it is desirable to have heroes.

More than specific practices that might be added, subtracted, or changed, a program to help children grow into good people begins with a commitment to change the way classrooms and schools are structure - and this brings us back to the idea of transcending a fix-the-kid approach. Consider the format of classroom discussions. A proponent of character education, invoking such traditional virtues as patience or self-control, might remind students that they must wait to be recognized by the teacher. But what if we invited students to think about the best way to conduct a discussion?

Must we raise our hands? Is there another way to avoid having everybody talk at once? How can we be fair to those who aren't as assertive or as fast on their feet? Should the power to decide who can speak always rest with the teacher? Perhaps the problem is not with students who need to be more self-disciplined, but with the whole instructional design that has students waiting to be recognized to answer someone else's questions. And perhaps the real learning comes only when students have the chance to grapple with such issues.

A proponent of character education says we must make students understand that it is wrong to lie; we need to teach them about the importance of being honest. But why do people lie? Usually because they don't feel safe enough to tell the truth. The real challenge for us as educators is to examine that precept in terms of what is going on in our classrooms, to ask how we and the students together can make sure that even unpleasant truths can be told and heard. Does pursuing this line of inquiry man that it's acceptable to fib? No. It means the problem has to be dissected and solved from the inside out. It means behaviors occur in a context that teachers have helped to establish; therefore, teachers have to examine that context even at the risk of some discomfort to themselves. In short, if we ant to help children grow into compassionate and responsible people, we have to change the way the classroom works and feels, not just the way each separate member of the class acts. Our emphasis should not be on forming individual characters so much as on transforming educational structures.

Happily, programs do exist whose promotion of children's social and moral development is grounded in a commitment to change the culture of schools. The Child Development Project, (CDP's) premise is that, by meeting children's needs, we increase the likelihood that they will care about others. Meeting their needs entails, among other things, turning schools into caring communities. The CDP offers the additional advantages of constructivist vision of learning, a positive view of human nature, a balance of cognitive and affective concerns, and a program that is integrated into all aspects of school life.

Is the CDP an example of what character education ought to be - or of what ought to replace character education? The answer to that question will depend on tactical, and even semantic, considerations. Far more compelling is the need to reevaluate the practices and premises of contemporary character education. To realize a humane and progressive vision for children's development, we may need to look elsewhere.

4

EDUCATING CHARACTER DEVELOPMENT

There is currently great interest around the world in both character education and education for democracy. Whereas character education tends to be more widely acclaimed, education for democracy is of particular interest in countries which are newly democratic or are attempting to increase or bolster their democratic nature. Fortunately, there are currently many such countries in both hemispheres.

Unfortunately this field is rife with problems of language and terminology. Terms vary both between cultures and historically within cultures. So what a term may connote in one place and time may be quite different than what it connotes in another place or time. In the US alone during the 20th century, the favored rubric shifted from "character education" to "values education" to "moral education" and back presently to "character education." Character education and moral education often have negative connotations in other cultures, conjuring up images of authoritarian religious sermons about eternal salvation and damnation.

The specific aim of Character Education (CE) may be an increase in the ability to reason about right and wrong, an increase in the motivation to do pro-social work or engage in pro-social behaviors, an increase in knowledge about right and wrong, etc. Or it may focus on a combination of these and other related aims. Education for democracy is any form of intentional education aimed at instilling the skills and knowledge necessary to function effectively in, and thereby contribute to, the democratic process.

At the most mundane level this includes literacy to allow one to be aware of issues and processes of the democratic process. At a somewhat more direct level, it entails teaching about the democratic process. More fundamentally, however, Education for Democracy (EFD) includes the fostering of the development of the citizen or future citizen, so they may be able to understand, evaluate, and advocate for the citizenry, the state, and the democratic process.

It is this last aspect, fostering civic development, that underscores the considerable overlap between CE and EFD. Benjamin Franklin stated that "only a virtuous people are capable of freedom" and Theodore Roosevelt claimed that "educating a person in mind and not in morals is to educate a menace to society." When Alexis de Tocqueville came to explore American character to find out how this great experiment in democracy was working, he observed that "America is great because she is good; but if America ever ceases to be good, she will cease to be great." Thomas Lickona, a foremost character educator, has argued that: Educating for virtue is especially crucial in a democracy in which people govern themselves. A democratic people, the American founders believed, must grasp and be committed to democracy's moral foundation: respect for the rights of others, concern for the common good, voluntary compliance with law, and participation in the public life. Furthermore, Lawrence Kohlberg has argued that a democratically run school is the ideal context for moral education, just as John Dewey argued that a democratically run school is essential for educating for citizenship.

Kohlberg's Just Community Schools are based in part upon the structure of a direct democracy, which is justified by the argument that participation in collaborative egalitarian governance is a rich context for the development of moral maturity. Marvin Beckerman and Timothy O'Rourke argue that EFD has the potential for character-building, for promoting basic democratic values, and for developing patterns of responsible citizenship behavior. Well-designed programs...can enhance the social, psychological and intellectual development of youth and help them to become informed, engaged, and effective citizens.

Verba and colleagues, in a study of political participation, conclude that it is the "hands-on training" in US schools, rather than "teaching about" democracy that promotes political participation. So we can see that EFD promotes character development and requires elements of CE. It is also true that good citizenship requires good character. Whereas some experts focus on the practice of democracy as the central ingredient in preparation for citizenship, Patricia White, in her book Civic Virtues and Public Schooling: Educating Citizens for a Democratic Society, argues that it is the character of the citizenry that truly defines a democracy. Indeed, many experts believe that left to nature, humans would be ultimately hedonistic. If humans are to develop democratic (or any moral form of) character, then society must intervene and foster it.

When government and law urge me to support the common good, the may find an ally in my reason and my soul, but they must expect resistance from my body and my senses... Civic virtue requires that we govern some or our strongest feelings and desires. In that sense, Aristotle argued, to rule free men–and hence, to be a citizen of a democracy–one must first learn how to be ruled.

Regardless of how pessimistic one is about human nature, it is clear that moral character is part of democratic functioning. Thomas Jefferson argued that democracy depends upon the cultivation of "public-spiritedness" which will not flourish spontaneously, but must be educated.

Not only is character routinely included in models of citizenship, but citizenship is often included in models of character. The Josephson Instititue for Ethics' Youth Summit meeting of 30 experts in youth character in 1992 identified six core character traits that were assumed to be universal goals of CE. The sixth of these was "civic virtue and citizenship."

Clearly there are many intimate links between CE and EFD. But the overlap between CE and EFD is not complete. There are some important differences as well, to which we now turn. First of all, the goals are different. For CE, character is the end. For EFD, character is a means toward the end, which is effective citizenship in a democratic society. Second, character development is only one of the targets of EFD. EFD, to be comprehensive and effective, must also target practical skills such as literacy and knowledge of the structure of government and the legal processes of democratic law-making.

Third, CE may choose as a option to include participation in democratic education as a means toward the end of character development, whereas it has been argued that EFD must include democratic participation as part of its curriculum to provide practical experience in what is the end goal of EFD; i.e., democratic competency.

GOALS OF EDUCATING FOR DEMOCRACY

Ultimately, as we have already suggested, the goal of EFD is to produce future effective citizens of the democratic state. But what exactly comprises such a citizen? In addition to the "bedrock" democratic values such as justice, tolerance, and personal autonomy that undergird the democratic enterprise, Patricia White identifies seven traits or dispositions of democratic character: hope and confidence; courage; self-respect and self-esteem; friendship; trust; honesty; decency.

She goes so far as to argue that it is the values of the democratic institutions and the dispositions of its citizens, and not the democratic procedures or "machinery," that comprise a democracy. In a separate analysis, David Sehr differentiates between private democracy and public democracy. It is the latter, he argues in his book Education for Public Democracy, which is the legitimate conceptualization of democracy.

Public democracy requires active commitment to and participation in the public arena and rests upon five characteristics of the democratic citizen: an ethic of care and responsibility; respect for the equal right of everyone to the conditions necessary for their development; appreciation of the importance of the public; critical/analytical social perspective; capacities necessary for participation in public democracy (e.g., verbal analytical skills, habits of active listening, self-confidence, cooperation, etc.). In essence, democracy rests on the character of both its institutions (including its schools) and its citizens.

Dewey further felt that the way students experience their schools is central to the way they will learn to experience and relate to their broader social contexts when they are adults. Or as John Minkler of the Bonner Center for Character Education and Citizenship in Fresno (CA) has stated, "While factual knowledge is essential, it is not enough. Schools have a profound obligation to reorganize curriculum and instruction to teach the knowledge, participation skills, and civic values that students need to become responsible citizens."

Thomas Jefferson, one of the principle architects of the great American experiment in democracy, reinforced the last element indirectly in his appeal for public education when he argued that "In every government on earth is some trace of human weakness, some germ of corruption, and degeneracy, which cunning will discover, and wickedness insensibly open, cultivate and improve." He perceived education to be a partial but vital piece of the antidote to this human failing. In a similar vein, Jefferson's contemporary, James Madison, argued that "What is government itself but the greatest of all reflections on human nature? If men were angels, no government would be necessary."

So we can see that EFD requires at least four central elements. First, there is certainly need for learning about democracy and the role of citizens in a democratic state. Second, there is the need to experience or practice democracy. Third, there is the need for more general education as a foundation for the capacities of democratic participation. And, fourth, there is the need for the development of character. Hence government quells our selfish nature and education makes us both governable and governors.

IMPLEMENTING EDUCATION FOR DEMOCRACY

The four elements of EFD (foundational capacities, knowledge about democracy, practice at democracy, moral character), then this allows us to begin to explore how these outcomes can best be achieved through education. Each will be explored in turn, but it is the last, character, which will receive the greatest emphasis here.

Lawrence Kohlberg has argued that the right to an education in the US is really the right to read the founding documents of our democratic republic. Literacy becomes necessary for optimal functioning as a citizen in a democracy. This is one example of a foundational capacity for democratic functioning. As noted above, David Sehr lists other such capacities:

(a) Analysis of written, spoken and image language

(b) Clear oral and written expression of one's ideas

(c) Habits of active listening as a key to communication

(d) Facility in working collaboratively with others

(e) Knowledge of constitutional rights and political processes

(f) Knowledge of the complexities and interconnections of major public issues to each other and to issues in the past

(g) Self-confidence, self-reliance, and ability to act independently (within context of the community)

(h) Ability to learn more about any issue that arises

The items (e) and (f) in the category of democratic knowledge and others of these capacities may be better construed as aspects of character, e.g., item (g). Nonetheless it should be clear that there are certain skills of communication and social cooperation, among others, that schools need to instil in students in order to successfully accomplish the central goals of EFD. Skill-building such as this is a fundamental goal of education in general and should not be difficult to implement, nor will it be examined in detail here. It may require some less traditional forms of education to foster specifically democratic skills. Such forms may be service learning, cooperative learning, etc., which embody the communicative and cooperative competencies required for citizenship in a democracy.

Educating for democratic knowledge

This is probably the simplest of the four goals of EFD, as it is most centrally what educators know how to do; i.e., the transmission of knowledge. Of course this assumes that the educators are professionally familiar with the knowledge domain. This is a bit trickier in newly democratized nations. One of the typical constraints on implementing EFD in such cultures is that the socializing agents (parents, teachers, etc.) have little familiarity with democracy. They don't know what the practices and institutions of a democracy are, nor can they articulate their nuances or justifications.

Hence, educating for democratic knowledge may presuppose professional training of educators and altering the curriculum of students studying to be teachers. In addition to this is the problem of motivation. Do citizens who have not previously experienced a democracy value the new democracy? If they are not committed to its value and future success, then they may be fairly ineffective in teaching about democracy. Obviously this qualification is not limited to this element. As has long been known, teachers who do not value what they are teaching are unlikely to teach it effectively.

Practicing democracy

We have already demonstrated that most experts agree that one cannot produce democratic character and skills without allowing for the practice of such skills. As Beckerman and O'Rourke argue "social studies teachers have long recognized that civics is no less a laboratory science than, say, chemistry or biology". Unfortunately, schools have historically not been places where students can legitimately exercise their democratic rights of self-governance. Schools have been authoritarian and hierarchical in structure.

Hence, advocates of EFD tend to argue for alterations in the traditional structure of schools. On the more extreme end are experts like Kohlberg, who has designed the Just Community Schools to function as direct democracies. Similarly Berman and Mosher have argued for increasing the democratic nature of schools, in Berman's case to instill social responsibility and activism and for Mosher to prepare future citizens in a democracy. Others rely on somewhat less direct means, such as the role-playing curriculum for younger children Educating for Citizenship or the limited weekly open forum used for 10-11 year old children at the Heath School in Brookline Massachussetts. John Dewey strongly argued that experience lies at the core of education. Mosher, Kenny and Garrod pick up that theme in their detailed articulation of the value of participation in democratic processes as central to preparing future citizens in adolescence. For this to work, however, educators need to embrace the philosophical justifications for such a form of education and to confront their own fears and misgivings about doing so. Educators often either fear that giving up control will lead to anarchy and chaos, or that they are somehow violating their professional obligations to "run" schools by allowing students to take some control for the functioning of the classroom or school.

First, there are degrees of doing so. Some programs merely use periodic open discussions of school issues. Others run the school as a complete direct democracy, with one vote per "citizen" whether they be a teacher or a student. Some teachers clearly delineate the domains that are open to student decision-making and those that are not. Indeed, even Kohlberg's Just Community approach has been successfully implemented in prisons, where limits are clearly placed on the domains that are under inmate control.

Secondly, when students are given control of their schools they are less likely to be alienated from them and therefore more likely to take responsibility for them. When one has a say in forming legislation, then one is more likely to respect and obey that legislation. Hence schools with democratic aspects do not become anarchies, just as democratic nations do not become anarchies.

BUILDING DEMOCRATIC CHARACTER

This fourth and final piece of the puzzle is the most complex. This is partly so because it invokes all of the complexities and controversies in the field of character education. Some experts differentiate between moral character and non-moral character; others do not. Some view character as holistic and others see it as a list of disparate traits. Some believe that character is formed before school begins (in the family); others believe school can be a significant force in shaping character.

Most disagree as to what comprises character. And most disagree to some degree as to how to foster character development, however it is defined. Therefore it is important to understand that what will be argued here is decidedly biased.

Character educators are unfortunately in great disagreement as to how to foster character development in schools. Some rely on teaching and lecturing. Others rely on active experimentation. Some use specific curricula, others do not. Some alter the governance structure of traditional schools. Etc. We will argue here, from an admittedly biased perspective, that (1) character is a complex set of psychological attributes and (2) character education requires a pervasive and differentiated set of educational initiatives.

Elsewhere we have described a model of character that we refer to as the "moral anatomy." Essentially it argues that there are seven interrelated parts of the moral person (person with moral character): moral behavior; moral values; moral personality; moral reasoning; moral affect; moral identity; meta-moral characteristics. We will not elaborate on this model here but invoke it simply to reinforce the idea that being a good person is not a unitary phenomenon and certainly not a simple one.

This leads to my second point, that character education is complex and multi-faceted. Promoting moral reasoning requires educational components that challenge one's existing moral reasoning capacities. Such components may be the periodic classroom discussion of moral problems or the experience of having to collectively solve real problems in the classroom, school, or community.

Promoting moral values relies more heavily on role-modeling and reinforcement as well as guided introspection. Nurturing moral behavior relies on role-modeling and learning, but is also derivative of all the other components of the moral anatomy; i.e., a student with moral values, personality, reason, etc. is more likely to engage in moral behavior.

There are two possible approaches to designing character education for democratic functioning. The first is generic. Simply implement a successful character education program and assume that good character will support democratic functioning. The second is targeted. Identify those character attributes that are considered essential to democratic functioning and implement an intervention designed specifically to promote their development. It may seem at face value that the "targeted" option is decidedly preferable; however, there are three reasons for the preferability of the "generic" option.

First, there is disagreement on what comprises specifically democratic character as can be seen from the examples offered above. Second, the "science" of character education is too new to be able to validly identify which character education components produce which character development outcomes; thus greatly reducing the likelihood of accurate "targeting." Third, many of the character traits associated with democratic functioning tend to be outcomes of many generic character education initiatives. For example, the Child Development Project, frequently cited as a model CE program, reports increased spontaneous prosocial behavior, democratic values, and social competence in students, all of which are identified by others as aspects of democratic character.

What then is generic character education? We will describe six facets of CE. First it relies on the climate of the school. Recent studies of the Child Development Project suggest that schools where the perception of a sense of community in the school increases are also schools that promote social competency, critical thinking, democratic values, prosocial motivation, and reduced violence and substance use. Kohlberg argued for the formation of communities of justice and caring in schools. At the minimum, how people treat each other in the school is critical to the effectiveness of character education. This clearly includes how students treat each other and how teachers treat students, but also must include how teachers treat each other, how other staff and administrators treat each other and how they treat teachers and students, etc. This leads naturally to a second dimension of effective character education; i.e., role modeling.

Educators cannot effectively promote character if they do not practice what they preach. Just as a parent will not effectively reduce their child's aggressive behavior if they spank the child while chastising them for hurting another child or if they get in fights with other adults, a teacher will not instill good character if they do not themselves manifest good character. A dishonest teacher will not effectively promote honesty in students, for example. Also, identifying other role models in the local community is a popular addendum to character education programs.

Students also need to develop the capacity for ethical reflection and analysis. They need to develop mature moral reasoning capacities. Furthermore, it is difficult to enter into and contribute to civic debate in a democracy without such capacities. It has been well-demonstrated that guided peer discussions of moral issues and problems and participation in democratic governance promote the development of such capacities. Exposure to moral ideas and examples is also central.

Formal curricula are often very useful here, and are often targeted to specific character outcomes; e.g., courage, honesty, responsible sexuality, etc. Even where such curricula are not available, however, the traditional curriculum is rife with adaptable examples. Every history or social studies or civics curriculum is full of examples of desirable and undesirable character traits. Literature is also a rich source of such examples. Teachers can readily develop their own curricula from such existing sources.

Because parents are the primary influences on the development of character, it is important to include them in any comprehensive character education initiative. The Child Development Project has found it valuable to include families in the curriculum. They have developed extensive curricula to be taken home and completed with family members. As noted earlier, parents may in a newly democratized nation may not have the inclinations and/or skills to aid in EFD. Then training of parents may be necessary before including them in the EFD initiative.

Just as practice at democracy is critical for EFD, practice at being moral is critical for CE. In the US, a currently very popular form of this is service learning, which although quite variable in implementation, is basically using community service as a means of learning about educational content. For example, if students are studying environmental conservation in science class, then a service learning component would be to have them either join an existing conservation initiative in the local community or start their own initiative aimed at a real existing local environmental problem.

Cooperative learning is another form of CE practice. Whereas schools, at least in the US, tend to be very competitive, recent advances in education have tried to promote team learning and small group cooperative projects and classroom exercises. Such activities tend to require cooperation, sharing, altruism, effective communication, etc.

A generic CE initiative would include the following key elements: promotion of a moral atmosphere in the school and/or classroom; role modeling of good character by school members and community members; guided peer discussions of moral issues and/or participation in school or classroom governance; learning about character through the curriculum; inclusion of families, especially parents, in the CE initiative; practical experience in moral behavior.

Assessing Education for Democracy

Assessment is both one of the historically more neglected and currently more popular topics in CE. The Character Education Partnership has a new task force on assessment which has produced a primer and is currently producing an anthology and review of assessments and instruments. The Bonner Center for Character Education and Citizenship recently convened a Character Education Assessment Forum in Fresno, California. Despite this recent flurry of activities, the state of assessment technology in character education is very underdeveloped. Hence, we will present a general model for assessing EFD after first presenting some general tips on assessing CE. In A Primer for Evaluating a Character Education Initiative, published by the Character Education Partnership, we introduce 12 questions that one should ask and answer before beginning a character education assessment project.

In the primer each of these questions is elaborated and discussed in some detail. Clearly, these issues apply as well to other educational initiatives, including non-character aspects of EFD. It is advisable to plan evaluation in advance of an initiative, if possible, and to budget resources for the evaluation. It is also advisable to contract with an outside evaluation expert, again if feasible. In assessing a specifically EFD initiative, we can return to the four elements discussed already: foundational capacities, knowledge about democracy, practice at democracy, democratic character. Each of these will be assessed somewhat differently, so a sound evaluation will depend in part on which of these four elements are focal aspects of the initiative to be evaluated. We will therefore address each of these elements in turn.

Assessing foundational capacities will depend upon which foundational capacities are targeted. Literacy and verbal skills certainly can be assessed with standardized instruments that are quite prevalent in education. In fact, in many settings, these data are already being collected for other purposes. Social competencies and communication skills may require observation of behavior and coding schemes, but there are some more objective measures available as well. If possible, baseline measures should be taken before the EFD initiative begins and matched comparison groups who do not receive the EFD initiative should be assessed simultaneously.

These suggestions apply to each of the other three elements as well, although less centrally to the practice of democracy. Knowledge about democracy is the simplest element to assess, as it is what educators typically assess; i.e., acquired knowledge and understanding resulting from the educational experience. A recent evaluation of a Boy Scouts of America CE curriculum entitled "Learning for Life" offers an excellent model of assessing the acquisition of CE-based teaching. Similarly, John Minkler of the Bonner Center has outlined a more comprehensive assessment model for EFD that includes suggestions for assessing knowledge about democracy.

A slightly different approach is suggested for assessing practice at democratic functioning. First, this requires both process and outcome evaluation. Because participation in democratic practices is part of the intervention, it is important to establish whether students actually participated. This may include simple presence during democratic functions (e.g., town meetings, judicial hearings, etc.) which can be accomplished with simple attendance records. Or it may include analyses of the amount of participation at a given function (e.g., how often one spoke during the meeting) which will likely require more demanding analyses of transcripts or other recordings of meetings. These are examples of process evaluation.

To assess the outcome of participation, it is likely necessary to evaluate how well one participates rather than how much one participates. This would necessitate either analyses of transcripts or other recordings of democratic functions or analyses of role playing of democratic functions. The assessment of democratic character is more complex than the other three elements, largely because the aspects of character in general or specifically democratic character more specifically are so controversial and variable.

As we stated in the CEP Primer, "it is critical to identify which character components you are trying to address in your initiative so that you can choose the evaluation procedures and instruments that are most relevant to your approach." Ask yourself "If your initiative should prove successful, what effects do you expect it to have?". For instance, one Child Development Project evaluation identified two aspects of each of six outcome domains: school-related (e.g., academic motivation); intellectual (e.g., critical thinking skills); social (e.g., social competence); personal (e.g., self-esteem); ethical (e.g., democratic values); prevention (e.g., reduced drug and alcohol use). Not all of these are aspects of character and certainly not all are relevant to EFD, but they exemplify the need to elaborate reasonably anticipated outcomes of a particular initiative.

A more relevant model is offered by John Minkler who identifies six civic values (liberty, justice, social responsibility, respect, trustworthiness, unity) plus civic responsibility as anticipated character outcomes of an EFD initiative. As noted earlier, character can be any or all of the seven parts of the moral anatomy. Hence one may need to measure values, which can be assessed fairly easily with written attitude type scales. Or one may need to observe ethical (or unethical) behavior. Sometimes such behaviors are archival (school records of student infractions, for example) or may need to be assessed directly.

If one is interested in moral reasoning, then various written and interview methods are available. Personality scales may be used to measure moral personality, although accuracy of self-reporting may be a problem (for example, in measuring honesty). Obviously, it is prudent to begin with a consideration of what the initiative is likely to affect, and then to find valid ways of assessing those anticipated outcomes. It should be clear that a useful assessment needs to be well-planned and well-executed. Furthermore, its structure and content will depend upon the resources available as well as the specific nature of the EFD initiative to be assessed.

Steps 1: Getting Started: Now that we have introduced the differences and relations between CE and EFD, have described the elements of EFD, and have discussed some aspects of evaluating EFD, it is time to step back for a moment and consider how to get started in designing and implementing an EFD initiative. Admittedly, this discussion will be general, because it is always best to work with a consultant to customize your initiative to fit your context. Nonetheless, some general suggestions may be helpful for those beginning or considering such an initiative.

Step 1: Identify Resources: We want to reiterate what we just stated; i.e., optimally one would work with a consultant (1) whose expertise is in EFD and (2) whose orientation is to customize the initiative's design to fit your needs, wishes, and circumstances. This may not always be possible, due to financial or other constraints, but where it is possible, it is highly recommended. Such a consultant can assist you in identifying your goals, both in terms of structure or process and in terms of specific outcomes.

The consultant can help you avoid common mistakes and therefore increase accuracy and efficiency. Etc. You may wish to wait upon hiring a consultant until after Step 2. However, there are additional resources that should be identified before embarking on implementation. The ease of finding such resources electronically is particularly helpful in places that don't have direct access to expertise. A few such World Wide Web sites are listed in the bibliography. Financial resources, staff, etc. are other types of resources that should be in place early in the process.

Step 2: Collaborate: Identify the stake-holders in the endeavor. For an EFD initiative they certainly include the educators, students, and parents of those students, but likely they also include community leaders, clergy, politicians, business owners, and others in the local community. Then invite them to be partners in the conceptualization, justification, and design of the initiative. This serves multiple purposes. It tends to prevent opposition by sharing control. It brings in multiple perspectives. It creates a pool of potential advocates and collaborators. Perhaps most importantly, it is democratic. It would not only be counterproductive but also hypocritical to create an EFD program through authoritarian means. Proceeding democratically models democracy and reinforces the justification for the initiative in the first place. This strategy should not apply merely at the planning phase. It should continue during implementation and assessment as well. For example, when training staff, other stakeholders as well as staff and administrators should be involved, whether in planning the training or actually participating in the training.

Step 3: Dream...Realistically: Think big but be realistic. Now this may sound like an impossibility or a contradiction. Not necessarily. If one truly wants to produce good citizens, then a trivial intervention is likely to produce trivial results. Shaping people is not readily or superficially accomplished. Too many CE and EFD initiatives aim to change a few attitudes, for example, through a half dozen or a dozen 45 minute lessons. This is unlikely to make a great impact either on those students or on their republic. However, one should not design an initiative on such a grand scale that it becomes unrealistic and impractical. It must be implementable in the real world, for which it is intended.

Step 4: Enlist Support: Be sure to enlist the support of key players. Begin with the school administrator (headmaster, head teacher, principal, etc.). This is a critical piece. If the school administrator is skeptical about the initiative or simply does not understand the justification and philosophy of EFD, then the implementation is either unlikely to ever occur or likely to fail when attempted. Again, the enlistment of the school administrator should actually be part of Step 2. But the enlistment of support of others may be delayed until now. However, their representatives are likely already part of the collaborative planning team; e.g., a few teachers or parents may be on the planning team, but the rest of the teachers and parents may not be approached until this fourth step. Keep in mind that the sequencing of these steps is fairly flexible.

Step 5: Plan, Plan, and then Plan Some More : Plan well. Think out your conceptualization, your goals, your rationale, your design, your resources, your time and task plan, etc. before beginning. This should continue the collaborative democratic process you have already begun. Be sure to include your assessment plans in this process, as they will likely affect the nature of the implementation. Action research models, which are now being advocated by many CE experts, include continuous feedback loops between implementation and assessment, for example.

Step 6: Training: Be sure to include appropriate and adequate training. Preferably all stakeholders, or at least their representatives, should participate in training when and where it is feasible and appropriate. Often, CE and EFD initiatives fail because the staff do not have the skills and knowledge required for competent implementation. Training may simply be a matter of introduction and orientation to the initiative, but more likely will include some skill-building. A consultant again may be invaluable in either providing training or identifying training resources. Training may be sequential and varied for different groups. It is frequently advisable to train school administrators first as part of Step 4 or even Step 2 to enlist their enthusiastic and informed support. The actual implementing staff need not be trained until Step 6 however.

In summary, be sure to identify resources and build consensus among stakeholders early in the planning process. If a consultant or consultants can be identified and enlisted, that too should occur early in the process. Make sure the planning is collaborative and democratic. Then be sure to plan well, think big but realistically, and train participants as necessary.

EFD is necessary for creating or nurturing a democratic society. EFD has four elements (instilling foundational capacities, teaching knowledge about democracy, providing opportunities for practice at democracy, developing democratic character) and is closely related to character education, but is not identical with it. A society which makes provision for participation in its good of all its members on equal terms...is in so far democratic. Such a society must have a type of education which gives individuals a personal interest in social relationships and control, and the habits of mind which secure social changes without introducing disorder. Such a form of education is democratic in nature. Its mandate is clear, but the path toward implementation is poorly marked and riddled with obstacles... as is the path toward a democratic society.

MORAL EDUCATION IN THE INFORMATION AGE

Families and schools must assume a leadership role in preparing youth for success in the emerging information age. This preparation goes beyond skills in mathematics, understanding of scientific principles, and effective writing. Preparation for success in the information age must include:

— A respect for the laws and standards that society has agreed upon for governing behavior related to the use of information technologies, including appropriate ways to work with others to change laws which are not in the best interests of society;

— The ability engage in moral reasoning and decision-making, especially when there are conflicts in values and interests; and

— The moral motivation and self-control to engage in appropriate and ethical behavior, even in situations where there is the freedom to do otherwise.

Research in moral development, while not specifically addressing issues related to information technologies, brings insight to factors that affect behavior. This insight includes: a) an understanding of underlying moral/cognitive development process and issues related to moral reasoning; b) moral motivation and the role of empathy; and c) the factors influencing moral control and behavior. The research provides a basis for initiating an analysis of issues raised through the use information technologies and the Internet.

It is important to understand the context in which schools and families will be addressing moral development in the information age. The Internet, which can be viewed as a paradigm for the information technology environment, was created by the U.S. military to withstand a nuclear attack. To do so, the network technology was designed to function without centralized control and with the ability to route around technological barriers.

This "open systems" capability virtually guarantees that whenever a technological barrier is developed, the technology to get around this barrier follows shortly thereafter. The decision by the U.S. government to make the technology publicly available for international and commercial use has led to the rapid emergence of a global network of networks, transmitting massive amounts of data every second. The bottom line is that while there will always be a role for laws and technical security and blocking systems, ultimately, decisions about information sent or received and the activities engaged in through the use of information technologies will largely be controlled by individual choice.

The word "anarchy" comes to mind when considering the Internet. "Anarchy" comes from Greek word "anarchos" , which means without a ruler or without leadership. The definitions provided for this word are seemingly in opposition.

The generally recognized definition of anarchy includes concepts of a state of lawlessness, disorder due to the absence of governmental authority, and confusion, chaos, and despair. But "anarchy" also refers to a Utopian or ideal society, with the absence of coercive government, built and managed instead through voluntary cooperative action of individuals and groups. To achieve an ideal society in the absence of central control would necessarily require that the individuals within that society will chose to act in accord with common values and with regard to their responsibilities to others.

Internet Ethics Issues and Concerns

The terms "Internet ethics," "cyberethics," "cyberlaw," "netiquette," "appropriate use," and others such terms have been applied to discussions or analysis of the legal, ethical and moral issues raised by this emergence of information technologies. It is helpful to more clearly define and categorize the kinds of behavioral issues that parents and educators must deal with as their children or students are going online. The following is a preliminary classification system of these issues:

1. *Respect for property:* Respect for property issues include: system security issues, such as computer hacking and respect for intellectual property rights, such as copyrights.
2. *Respect for territory and privacy:* Respect for territory and privacy issues also include system security issues as well as the dissemination and/or gathering of private information.
3. *Respect for others and common courtesy:* Respect for others involves respectful communication and the avoidance of irresponsible speech. Irresponsible speech includes defamation, harassment, flaming /abusive language, and spamming. A related problem is the use of e-mail forgery to disguise the source of the irresponsible speech.
4. *Respect for institution:* Respect for the institution addresses the use of a limited purpose Internet account in accord with its limited purpose. The activities that are permitted through a particular Internet account may be restricted due to the source or institution providing that account, such as limited purpose accounts provided by educational institutions and business or government employers.
5. *Respect for self:* Respect for self issues include those activities that generally do not have an impact on others but can be injurious to the self, such as addiction, personal safety, and "garbage" activities.

Based on a preliminary analysis, there appear to be four key factors that have an influence on behavior in the use of information technologies and the Internet. These include:

1. *Lack of affective feedback and remoteness from harm:* When people communicate or do some other action in cyberspace, they do not receive strong affective feedback about the hurtful impact of their communication or actions. Electronic text alone, without visual and auditory clues,

provides little insight about the impact of communications or actions. Users of technology are also distanced from the potential harm they may cause by their actions. The intangible nature of cyberspace creates the impression that actions or words have no real impact.

2. *Reduced fear of risk of detection and punishment:* Negative consequences will only work as a deterrent to misbehavior if there is a high enough risk of detection and punishment. On the Internet, there is a reduced likelihood of detection and punishment for activities that are illegal or could lead to civil liability, much less actions that are merely unethical or rude. The Internet is simply not a "law and order" paradigm.

3. *New environment means new rules:* Many rationalizations make the basic argument that "real world" concepts and values do not have any standing in cyberspace. This is an issue that must be evaluated carefully because we are moving into a new era which will require new rules. Basic values of respect for property and territory will likely continue to exist in the new era, but some of the rules and laws that accompany these values will need to be reshaped. The need to reshape some rules and laws, creates an environment that supports disregard for the underlying values. Peer and authority support for new rules is a related factor. It is quite possible to find authority support for the proposition that it is or should be perfectly appropriate for people to break into computer systems or to engage in copyright infringement.

4. *Perceptions of social injustice and corruption:* Issues related to social injustice and corruption of business and government are frequently raised rationalizations for inappropriate behavior. For those who have the perception that they are the "have-nots" and that individuals or organizations who have power and wealth (the "haves") are corrupt or unjustly enriched, information technologies provide the means to even the score.

A FRAMEWORK FOR MORAL DEVELOPMENT RESEARCH

The following is an analysis of moral development research which has been developed to serve as a preliminary framework for inquiry into information technology ethics issues.

1. Moral Reasoning

a. Cognitive-moral development

Kohlberg's theories on cognitive moral development emerged from the cognitive development understandings introduced by Piaget together with Kantian concepts of justice which emerged from the work of Rawls. On the basis of his research, Kohlberg identified six stages in the development of moral reasoning, grouped into three major levels. The progression through the stages reflects cognitive development in the understanding of moral issues. The progression depends of the widening cognitive capacity to understand the perspective of others. At the Preconventional Level, moral reasoning is characterized by a concrete, egocentric perspective. Individuals at the Conventional Level are gaining the ability to understand the perspectives of others and an understanding of the norms and laws that are necessary for society to function effectively. At the Post-conventional Level, moral reasoning is based on an understanding of the principles of justice and social cooperation that underlie the norms and laws of society.

There appear to be two key concepts, rooted in a Kohlbergian framework, that will assist in developing an understanding of moral reasoning in the information age. The first is that young people construct their framework for reasoning about moral issues through their interactions with others and these interactions are shaped by their level of cognitive development. This concept raises the need to consider what the impact of electronically-mediated interactions will be on young people as they are in the process of constructing their moral reasoning framework.

Early adolescence appears to be a time when young people who have online access become strongly interested in Internet communications. Their emerging moral framework is being developed in an environment where there is little affective feedback, where there is a reduced risk for authoritarian-delivered punishment but the potential for being ostracized as a consequence of inappropriate behavior, where an individual is judged on the basis of what they write and not who they are, where there is a constant need to authenticate information to determine its truthfulness, where there is a high level of interaction with people from throughout the world and where there is the ability to act out different personas. The impact of interactions in this kind of an environment on the development of moral reasoning is unknown.

The second concept is that cross-cultural studies have found that less industrialized societies tend to have fewer individuals who reason at the higher stage levels. A probable reason for this is that individuals in societies that are not administratively complex do not need to engage in higher level reasoning to ensure the orderly continuance of their society. An optimistic interpretation may be that individuals within a certain society gain the level of moral reasoning maturity that is necessary for their society to function effectively and that as the complexities of society increase, human kind has the capability to expand their moral reasoning capacity to a level necessary to effectively sustain greater complexity. Society's transition into the Information Age may be the ultimate test of this hypothesis.

b. Domain theory

Turiel's domain theory research focuses on the differences between concepts of moral values, social conventions, and personal choice. Moral values are categorical, universalizable, and structured by underlying conceptions of justice, rights, and welfare. Social conventions are arbitrary and agreed-upon uniformities in social behavior that are determined by the social system and which are alterable and context dependent. Personal choice issues are those issues which impact only on the self. Some issues involve domain overlap; they are multifaceted issues that raise moral values as well as social conventions or personal choices. Just as concepts of moral issues undergo development in accord with the cognitive development of the child, so does the understanding of social conventions.

Several key concepts from the domain theory appear to have direct relevance to issues that are emerging in cyberspace. The first concept is that a key factor that appears to be relevant in distinguishing moral values from social conventions or personal choices is the determination of whether a certain action will result in harm to another. The second concept is that social conventions are context dependent and alterable. The third concept is domain overlap or multifaceted issues where an issue may raise moral values, social conventions, and personal choices. Actions taken in cyberspace are distanced from the resulting harm which may impair a person's ability to discern an underlying moral value. Our transition into the information age is resulting in changes in social conventions. Many issues related to the use of information technologies appear to be multifaceted issues. All of these concepts appear to be related to the difficult situation of discerning underlying moral values when social conventions are changing and it is difficult to perceive the resulting harm of actions taken.

2. *Moral motivation*

a. Internal moral orientation

Hoffman has focused primarily on the internal moral orientation and the role of empathy in moral motivation. Hoffman views empathy as the significant vehicle by which external or society based norms become an internalized motivator of action, an internalized moral orientation. Empathic arousal is a trait that humans are born with. Empathy is connected with cognitive development, as humans gain greater abilities to perceive the perspectives of another, this also impacts their empathic response to the perceived distress of others.

The underlying empathic disposition of individuals varies. Life experiences also impacts the level of empathic awareness. Humans have the capacity for representation and represented events can arouse an empathic response. The degree to which individuals actually have the ability for a representative empathic response varies. The internalization of an external moral norm occurs when a person feels an obligation to act in accord with the norm even in absence of concern about being caught and punished if they do otherwise. Internalized empathy is the motivating force behind the internal moral orientation.

Hoffman's research has determined that the disciplinary approach used in response to a young person's transgression impacts the internalization process. Discipline that is focused on how an individual's actions have affected another tends to support the internalization of empathy; whereas, discipline that is rule and punishment-oriented does not. Hoffman's findings are strongly supported by the work of Baumrind who investigated the impact of parenting styles. Baumrind has found that children of parents who attempt to inculcate conventional values through rules and punishment have difficulty in developing an autonomous sense of social responsibility.

Children of parents who support their child's natural empathic response by explicitly confronting them about actions that may be harmful to others tend to have an active sense of social responsibility. In light of these findings, it would appear that young people who have been disciplined in a manner that forces them to focus on the consequences of their actions and who have a well-developed sense of internalized empathy will be more likely to behave ethically in cyberspace, than those who have been raised in an authoritarian environment.

3. Moral control

a. Social cognitive theory of moral thought and action

Bandura has focused his research on an analysis of ways in which social factors and moral orientation combine to effect moral conduct. His research has focused on mechanisms by which internal control is selectively disengaged. Several key mechanisms that allow for disengagement have been identified. Those that appear most relevant to the use of information technologies are:

i) *Moral justification:* The cognitive restructuring of an analysis of a situation that leads to support of immoral acts. Conduct is made personally and socially acceptable by portraying it as being for moral purposes — fighting ruthless oppressors, saving humanity, self-defense, or, in the case of hacking, breaking into computers to find evidence of corruption by government or business. The changing social conventions in cyberspace appears to facilitate cognitive restructuring.

ii) *Disregarding, minimizing, or ignoring the consequences:* If the consequences of one's actions can be disregarded, minimized, or ignored there is little reason for self-censure. Judgments and actions can be influenced by their proximity to resulting harm — a person is more likely to cause or permit harm to occur when they are more remote from the victim of that harm. As we move into the information age, technology will continue to distance people from the harm resulting from their actions, thus facilitating the ability to disregard, minimize, or ignore the consequences.

iii) *Dehumanizing the victim:* The evaluation of injurious conduct partly depends on how the actor views the victim. To perceive another as a human activates an empathic response, but this response can be disengaged by dehumanizing the other. Technology can act to dehumanize others because of the lack of affective or tangible feedback.

iv) *Blaming the victim or environmental circumstances:* People rationalize inappropriate actions by viewing themselves as victims and their inappropriate actions as self-defense due to injurious conduct by another or being forced by the circumstances. Many of the social injustice and corruption rationalizations for inappropriate conduct related to the use of technologies appear to contain attributes of blaming the victim.

Gibbs, who works specifically with antisocial adolescents, reports processes similar to those found by Bandura. Gibbs held discussions with youth involved with juvenile justice systems. These discussions revealed that young people demonstrated a sociomoral developmental delay, that is, the persistence beyond childhood of egocentric bias that appeared to be supported by significant cognitive distortions of situations presented. Gibbs also discovered that what he termed rationalizations. The most common of these, externalization of blame and mislabeling, appeared to protect the individual from considering the factors that might restrict inappropriate behavior, such as empathy for the victim or dissonance with self-concept.

The rationalizations identified by Gibbs are somewhat understandable given that his subject population were youth involved with juvenile justice systems. What is not quite as understandable is why rationalizations in support of "innocent hacking" set forth by college professors are so similar in nature to those of juvenile delinquents.

b. Limited acceptable morality

Nisan has approached his analysis of moral control from a slightly different perspective. His theory of Limited Acceptable Morality is that humans strive for a moral balance — that we each have a personal moral ideal, but we are all willing, under certain circumstances to waiver from that ideal. Individuals appear to set a limit about how far they are willing to waiver from the ideal and this limit protects against unlimited transgressions. The boundaries of this limit vary according to the person. There are three factors that appear to support transgression, these are:

i) The transgression will not cause any perceptible harm

ii) The harm is perceptible, but small in comparison with the personal advantage gained

iii) The harm is to the system, and no specific person sustains any loss.

Thus in Nisan's theory, the issue of the perception of the degree of harm caused is a critical factor that is weighed in decision-making.

5

MORAL EDUCATION AND HUMAN RIGHTS

Human rights education suggests there is a danger in offering programs, such as character education programs, that ignore contextualized historical analysis. Without attention to context there is no basis for offering a critique of unjust systems. In a similar vein, both Dewey and Kohlberg's work arose out of political considerations. Dewey produced an educational philosophy that was explicitly political in its articulation of democracy as the aim of education.

Kohlberg's moral development theory was partly a response to the horrors of Nazism, and arose out of a politically loaded question: under what conditions is it moral to break the law? Teaching virtues through stories will not address the economic ills of society; jobs and education that provides the skills needed in these jobs, are necessary to do that. Furthermore, such approaches have the potential to blame the victim and tacitly support unjust social structures. Human Rights education also offers a corrective to Kohlbergian theory. Human rights workers caution moral educators to stay close to the experience of people, so as not to get lost in immobilizing principles or intellectual abstraction. For example, in the United States, the experience of the poor is one of our most challenging contemporary moral tests.

The human rights work of women who are responding to acts of individual and collective violence offers lessons for moral educators. Furthermore, women are also victim, of public policies that deny them education, health care, and living wages, fail to protect them from physical, economic and sexual violence, and put them at risk for wife battery, incest. rape, and female slavery. In response to such human rights abuses, women´s groups around the world have organized in ways that offer alternative models for correcting human rights violations.

What are rules for? Who makes them? Children, even very young ones, know that some things are just plain wrong. They also know that they have to follow rules. But children also think some things should be up to them, and they begin the process of sorting out the difference early. Thoughtful grownups can help children to understand and appreciate the need for social rules. At the same time, grownups can contribute to children's sense of themselves as socially competent by helping them to sort between when things are to be governed by social rules and when (and in what contexts) a child's behavior is really a matter of personal choice.

Children are acting, do act, and will act according to their understanding of themselves and of the situation. The teacher's job with regard to these issues is two fold:

— to support each child's initiating actions and interactions in a way that fosters their understanding of self, and of others.

— to ensure that the group of people involved runs fairly, safely, and smoothly.

For children, the process of sorting social situations involves negotiations between the adults and other children. Who is involved? What will happen? Grownups have an important responsibility for coordinating the group, and preventing children from being hurt. However they must always be aware that the enforcement power they use may not adequately recognize the needs of children to act on their own understanding.

Children may comply when they are told to do something, but they then incorporate both the telling and the compliance into their own sense of themselves as powerful initiators. In dealing with questions that come up in classrooms, there are often one or more simple solutions to a problem that could be applied by the teacher. But further consideration suggests that the children can figure out solutions for or between themselves if they are given the chance and a little support.

Doing this enables children to begin understanding themselves as powerful in co-operative situations. When we as teachers are faced with a complicated situation that involves conflict or some other problem, it is useful to think about the kinds of issues involved so that, rather than imposing answers, we can better support children's efforts. One way to approach to the question is provided by what is called domain theory. This approach identifies three basic domains of social norms: moral, social conventional, and personal. In addition to these areas of social regulation, teachers need to be concerned with children's personal safety. In domain theory, these are the areas of "prudential" concerns. Actions from different domains call for different kinds of response. In classroom life many issues involve an overlap among one or more domains of social norms. In such cases, knowing how to best respond to a situation is aided by identifying the different domains involved. What follows are specific descriptions of each domain, and ways in which teachers can use domain theory in the classroom. The examples and discussions are all drawn from real incidents involving teachers or home daycare providers, and the children in their care.

MORAL: ISSUES OF HARM AND FAIRNESS TO OTHERS

Most people agree that it is not acceptable to just go off and hit someone. It is not okay to take or destroy something that belongs to someone else. Because they know the consequences of these actions, people consider them wrong whether or not there is a rule. Children come to understand this because they have experience with being hurt. "You shouldn't hit someone—so hard to hurt, because they'll cry". Children's morality is based on their sense of fairness and concerns for others' welfare.

Conventional: Arbitrary uniformities agreed upon to promote order

Should children all come to the table to eat snack at once, or may they come and get it at their leisure, between activities, as they wish? The answer to this question has more to do with the organizational needs of the household or classroom than with moral questions of harm. There probably needs to be a decision about the question one way or another in the above situation, but either way can be appropriate. Neither way can be declared better or worse without regard to the specific context. All social groups have conventional rules of this kind in order to make social interactions predictable and to allow the group to run smoothly. Unlike moral rules, the specific conventions of a classroom or daycare setting must be taught. Children learn the rules of the house or the school by seeing them applied, or hearing them.

Children may or may not be consulted about such practices, but they cannot come to know conventional expectations without some introduction, either by careful observation or though instruction. Adults let children know what the expectation is, and although there may be some reference to different rules in other places, there is little discussion about whether the particular rule can be changed i.e. "It's too noisy. We don't make noise in the breakfast nook. You can make noise out there, but not in here."

Young children have little understanding of the overall social organizational purposes behind conventions. However, all children benefit from, and appreciate rules that provide for predictable and orderly classrooms and family settings.

Personal: individual perogative that is negotiated rather than defined by conventional or moral restrictions

This includes matters of privacy, control over one's bodily state or activities, ideas and their expression, and choice of associates. Children from very young ages begin to have a sense of what should be up to them rather than what will be controlled by others. Control over an area of personal discretion is essential to the child's formation of self.

Personal needs and desires, however, often bump into or conflict with those of others, and with organizational needs for order. Even young children begin to try and negotiate with others over things they think should be up to them. Parents often allow this i.e. "She wants to wear pink every day, so I let her, as long as there is something pink that's clean. She may not wear dirty clothes to school, that wouldn't be accepted."

Prudential matters concern one's own safety. One must decide whether or not to take a possible risk. However, adults must pay attention to this for very young children. Children, in turn, expect that adults will keep them safe. As children grow older, they also expect to be able to make these judgments for themselves more and more often.

Below, we present examples from actual classrooms that illustrate issues within each domain. I will also be presenting ways that teachers have responded to each situation.

Are there any ways you might want to adjust your setup or situation to make things easier for the individual children, or for your group of children as a whole?

Examples: Here are several examples of situations that have occurred in classrooms or in home child care situations After each example, there are 3 kinds of analyses that teachers generated about the situations.

1. Categorizations and Comments lists some immediate reactions about rightness or wrongness, and about rules.

2. Discussion gives a brief summary of conversation that occurred around the issues. Since each example is a very brief description, people sometimes made different interpretations, leading to varying responses. In most cases a primary domain emerged eventually, though other domains were often involved as well. The discussions reflect thinking about the multiplicity of domains involved.
3. Suggestions emerge out of the discussion, and are listed as summaries of possible actions that teachers or children might take to incorporate these multiple domains. In all cases there is provision to allow and support children in negotiating and figuring out their own solutions. As you read these, think about how you view these issues. What do you think you would do, and why?

Most people felt that this was primarily an issue of Rashid's personal expression that should be recognized. The possible work load or health implications made the issue more complicated.

Contemporary wisdom suggests that usually if children are left to choose from a variety of nutritious foods, they'll get around to a reasonably balanced diet. But if she doesn't eat, then she'll be hungry later. Can we allow that? Maybe solutions would be different depending on whether this happens once, or many times. Don't let her have any milk unless she tastes then she'll be more likely to try new things, and perhaps like them. But if she really likes the milk, then is it right not to let her have it until she's done?

In general, what one eats is considered a personal issue. One cannot easily force a child to eat. But there are some other considerations. Perhaps one could discuss with all the children the importance and interest of tasting food, and the possibility of being hungry later.

One could insist that all foods be on the plate, served by teacher or student, (an arbitrary rule). That way they would be available for tasting. Then the child could choose whether to taste or not. Discussion about taste and texture that occurs during mealtime with other children might be inviting.

One could ask Chevy to choose one thing that she might try, or suggest that she serve herself an amount she might want. This also allows her to control the situation. Perhaps, she could propose a limit on the amount of milk that she would drink before eating some other foods. This would also allow her to control her own eating, yet provide clear possibilities for experimenting and trying new things.

How would you approach these examples? While there are no definitive conclusions here, there are possibilities. Most situations in classrooms are complex. In any one situation a teacher may feel the need simply to act. However beginning to consider interactions from the perspective of different domains may allow adults to notice ways in which children can be both engaged in negotiations about their own personal activities, and participate in developing conventional ways of proceeding in group interactions.

DEVELOPMENT OF CHILDREN'S MORALITY: ROLE OF PARENTS

Communities have been concerned with the type of person that children become throughout human history, and scholars have addressed the topic for over two thousand years. Over the past century a wealth of data has been amassed concerning the development of morality in children and adolescents. Throughout this time, the role of adults, especially parents, in the development of children's morality has been a central focus.

The Moral Nature of the Child

Whereas most people would likely agree that they "know a good person when they see one," there is decidedly less agreement as to what characteristics centrally define psychological morality. Psychoanalytic models tend to focus on internalized societal norms for behavior (i.e., conscience or superego) and the corresponding emotions of self-reproach for their violations (e.g., guilt and shame). Behaviorists focus on overt behavior as the core of psychological morality; e.g., sharing, helping, cheating, etc. Socio-cultural theorists emphasize the role of cultural transmission of values, personality traits (moral character), and cognitive patterns. Biologists tend to focus attention on evolutionary functions, genetic selection of moral characteristics, hormones, and neuroanatomy. Cognitive psychologists emphasize moral reasoning and decision-making. This heterogeneity results in a quite confusing picture of the moral person.

Diverse disciplines and theoretical models have generated disconnected, myopic views of the moral person. This is exacerbated by the problem of studying morality with people at different developmental levels. For example, the study of emergent morality in the second year of life (infancy) by necessity emphasizes empathy and self-other differentiation whereas the study of pre-school morality focuses, appropriately, on perspective-taking, self-control, and social behaviors such as sharing. Those who study moral development in adolescence, by contrast, might focus instead on ethical philosophy and moral identity. For these reasons, it is necessary to define the scope of moral development that will be addressed in this analysis.

The goal is to identify how parents can be taught to nurture the development of "building blocks" of morality, a core set of characteristics that either (1) underpin and give rise to moral functioning or (2) reflect fundamental human morality. The focus thus necessarily will be on early and middle childhood, when these characteristics develop. Further, given the interest in the effects of parenting on moral development, only those aspects of morality that are most susceptible to parental influences will be addressed. Consequently, biological and evolutionary perspectives and concepts such as temperament or prenatal teratogens, for example, will not be considered. This nevertheless still leaves a fairly substantial domain of potential scrutiny.

Such moral characteristics, however, do not appear spontaneously nor are they disconnected from the larger core of what constitutes healthy psychology. Rather, the moral nature of a person is fully integrated with other aspects of that person's psychological make-up. For example, Colby and Damon, in their study of moral exemplars, found many non-moral characteristics that were common among their subjects; e.g., a sense of humor, optimism, certainty. The final component of Berkowitz's "moral anatomy", meta-moral characteristics, refer to qualities such as these.

Moral characteristics are matters of morality or ethics, whereas meta-moral characteristics are necessary for moral functioning but are not themselves intrinsically moral in nature. That is, they potentially serve either morality or immorality. For example, to be morally effective one needs self-control. However, self-control can also support criminal behavior, sadistic behavior, etc. Rest incorporates a variety of such characteristics into his model of the components of moral action; e.g., sensitivity and ego strength. In a sense, the first major model of moral character recognized this distinction as well. Aristotle describes practical wisdom or prudence as the intellectual capacity to discern what will and how to serve the moral virtues.

Based upon these criteria, and the emphases in the relevant literature, eight psychological outcomes of parenting will be examined. The first four are meta-moral characteristics: social orientation, self-control, compliance, self-esteem. Understanding these characteristics is important for explaining how parents influence their children's moral development. The next four are components of psychological morality: empathy, conscience, moral reasoning, altruism. All of these components are all well-researched areas with clear relations to parental behavior. Furthermore, all are evident during childhood and collectively span the entire range of childhood, beginning with the first appearance of an attachment bond and a moral sense in infancy and ending with puberty.

PSYCHOLOGICAL FOUNDATIONS FOR MORAL AGENCY

A social orientation

Moral behavior flows from an interest in and concern for other people. Psychologists have long viewed the desire to take part in social interaction, to develop relationships, as critical to psychological health. Indeed, the absence of this desire is viewed as pathological. In the Diagnostic and Statistical Manual of Mental Disorders, a person exhibiting pervasive detachment from and disinterest in social relationships is said to have schizoid personality disorder, and one of the major signals of emerging psychopathology in childhood and adolescence is the onset of an anti-social life-style in which the rights of others are ignored or violated. Given its primacy for psychological health as well as moral development, it is important to understand how a healthy social orientation develops in childhood.

Consensually, researchers and clinicians tend to point to the formation of a secure attachment bond in the first few years of life as the origin of healthy social orientation. Lickona, in his prescription for raising moral children, argues that "given a loving environment, kids make huge strides in their relationships with other people. Babies get attached to those who cuddle and care for them, and that's their first vital link to the human community" Attachment is the special affective relationship that forms between infants and their primary caretakers.

Research with humans and other primates has repeatedly demonstrated that the formation of a healthy attachment bond in the first two or three years of life leads to a broad variety of positive psychological outcomes and that these outcomes are long-lasting. Healthy attachment relationships have been found to predict successful relationships throughout life. For example, Park and Waters notes that preschool children with secure attachments had more harmonious interactions with peers than did children with insecure attachments. Indeed, it has been argued that the attachment relationship is the template for most later relationships. Some argues that the single most consistent cause of childhood antisocial behavior is the lack of a secure attachment bond in infancy, because of the resultant failure to develop a conscience.

It is a bit tautological to argue that parenting influences the development of a social sense, having already established that the core of a social sense derives from the formation of the attachment bond that is formed with one's primary caretakers. Nevertheless, one can examine which features of parenting affect the development of a secure attachment bond. Unlike other species in which the attachment bond is instinctive and very narrow and triggered by specific physical cues, in humans the attachment bond can form in a variety of ways and result in a broad range of outcomes.

Secure attachments are understood generally to derive from the quality of the interaction between infant and caretaker. Although such interactions are best conceptualized as social systems, the contributions of mother can be meaningfully teased out of the system. One of the most widely recognized parental characteristics that predict secure attachment bonds is responsivity. Mothers of securely attached infants tend to respond consistently and rapidly to the infants' signals.

Securely attached infants also tend to have mothers who more accurately interpret the infants' signals and therefore respond more appropriately. Research has demonstrated that this characteristic continues to be present in parents of securely attached toddlers. Not surprisingly, mothers of securely attached infants also are more consistently nurturant, including more loving physical contact, and express less hostility and anger.

Another parental predictor of secure attachment is diligence in physical care of the infant, whereas neglect predicts insecure attachments. As already noted, the influence of the infant is also important in the nature of the relation that produces the attachment bond. Even here, there is useful information in parent training, however. Crockenberg demonstrated that infant temperament interacts with parental resources. Mothers with irritable infants were at risk for not forming secure attachments unless they had ample social support for their parenting. This support allowed the mother to escape the stress of the irritable infant for short periods of time.

Self-control

Self-control is first recognized to develop in the deliberate motor schemes of infants, perhaps most notably in the achievement of toilet training. However, self-control as a personality or character trait has been studied most intensively in the pre-school years. As young children develop the ability to use mental mediators, such as mental imagery and private speech, they develop the capacity to resist temptation, suppress impulses, and delay gratification. The most marked gains in such cognitively-mediated self-control abilities seem to develop between approximately five and seven years of age.

The development of self-control is a gradual and complex process in which maturation and development of the child's capacities plays a great role. Parents also, however, affect the development of self-control capacities, through a process that is consistent with "scaffolding" or guided self-regulation. Both of these concepts refer to a process in which parents provide support for unmastered skills via guidance, feedback, etc.

Along these lines, Schaffer points out that parents can help at each phase of self-control development by (1) creating the external controls necessary before self-regulation is mastered and (2) engineering the situations so that they are more readily controllable, given the nascent nature of infant and toddler self-control strategies. For example, during the first months of life "the problem of regulation involves safeguarding the infant from stimulation that is too strong and which will therefore have too great an arousing effect. Caregivers have a vital role in protecting and soothing".

Maccoby concurs and lists five ways parents can assist in the complex transition from impulsivity to self-regulation: (1)

protect children from the effects of their impulsivity by situational management; (2) provide the ego-controls that children have not yet developed (e.g., soothing children during emotional outbursts); (3) teaching coping skills, like how to shift one's own attention in delay of gratification situations; (4) helping children to anticipate the consequences of their actions; (5) modeling self-control. Block reports that impulsive adolescents come from homes in which there was a high level of conflict, especially about child-rearing values, parents neglected to teach their children, and parents demanded very little of their children both in terms of household chores and school work.

Compliance with external standards

Part of the nature of a moral being is adherence to selected external controls; an effective moral agent must eventually learn to internalize external standards for behavior. For example, children must learn that sharing valued objects in work and play is societally encouraged. The roots of such compliance have been identified as beginning to develop in infancy. Beginning at around 18-19 months of age, toddlers begin to want to comply with mothers' demands. They begin to spontaneously make reparations for their transgressions; e.g., tattling on themselves or soliciting praise when complying.

Parental behavior is highly influential in the development of early compliance. Mother's flexibility, reliance on negotiation rather than direct control, and positive affect when parenting have all been found to relate to higher levels of compliance in toddlers. Furthermore, such behaviors have been linked to the development of conscience six years later.

Self-esteem

Platitudes and "truisms" about self-esteem abound: "You have to like yourself before others can like you," "Be your own best friend," etc. Indeed, research supports the gist of these contentions. Self-esteem in childhood has been related to mental health later in life, while a lack of self-esteem has been related to social dysfunctions and mental pathologies such as depression and anxiety. The relation is not always straightforward as overly high self-esteem has also been found to be dysfunctional in peer relations, but the bulk of the evidence suggests that a positive sense of self is psychologically healthy.

Coopersmith reported that three central dimensions of parenting promote children's self-esteem: acceptance of their children, setting clearly defined limits for the child's behavior, allowing individual expression and respecting the child's unique personality and point of view. These dimensions correspond closely with what Baumrind has identified as the "Authoritative" parenting, a style of parenting that will be discussed later in this chapter.

PARENTAL INFLUENCES ON MORAL DEVELOPMENT

Empathy has been identified by Kagan as one of the "core moral emotions." Damon considers it "one of morality's primary emotional supports" and argues that "because morality is fundamentally concerned with one's obligations to others, it cannot be developed solely through introspection and recognition of one's inner feelings... Children must learn to become attuned not only to their own emotional reactions but also to those of others.

Children must learn to be receptive to the input from others' emotional expressions, modifying their own feelings when appropriate". Empathy has been defined in different ways, but the most widely recognized position on empathy comes from the work of Martin Hoffman. Hoffman considers empathy to be an affective response to another's distress that is "more appropriate to someone else's situation than to one's own". He describes it as a bystander phenomenon, such that empathy is aroused in one who is observing another's plight from the outside.

In a fairly complex model, Hoffman describes five types of empathy ranging from automatic and involuntary reactions of infants to the sound of other infants' cries to mature, reflective reactions to the meaning of others' unfortunate circumstances. Empathic responding has been positively related to altruism and negatively related to antisocial behavior.

Relation to parenting. Where does empathy come from? Clearly, Hoffman thinks it is born in the infant's innate tendency to match the noxious affect of others, what he calls "global empathy." This is fed and nurtured by the cognitive development of the child, most notably the child's developing ability to take others' perspectives. But Hoffman also very strongly emphasizes the role of parental induction, and conversely the avoidance of power assertion and love withdrawal techniques, in the development of empathic responding.

Conscience

Conscience has long been understood as a combination of (1) internalized standards and (2) behavioral and affective results of adherence to or violation of those standards. Much of the literature on conscience derives from a psychoanalytic perspective, but researchers from other perspectives have also found it useful to study aspects of conscience. The most impressive work on the development of conscience, however, comes from the work of Kochanska and her colleagues.

These researchers have described conscience as having two major aspects. The first is affective discomfort which encompasses the emotional results of transgression; e.g., guilt, apology, empathy for the victim, etc. The second is active moral regulation or vigilance, which encompasses the classical internalization of standards along with confession, reparation, and monitoring of others' wrongdoing. Kochanska has demonstrated a link between early temperament, specifically high inhibitory control and low impulsivity, and later conscience development. This substantiates the assertion that self-control is a foundational element in the development of morality.

Altruism

Perhaps one of the most widely recognized and studied aspects of moral psychology is altruism, or the giving to another at cost to oneself. Altruism has been studied in anecdotes of toddlers offering solace to one another, in laboratory manipulations with children, adolescents, and adults, and in real-life acts of common altruism (e.g., charitable donations) and heroism. Altruism may be construed as a behavior (or set of behaviors) or as a personality trait (character). The latter tends to represent an enduring tendency to engage in the former.

An extensive body of research has illuminated the characteristics and determinants of altruism. Eisenberg and Mussen, in a review of the literature, conclude that altruistic children tend to be "active, sociable, competent, assertive, advanced in role taking and moral judgment, and sympathetic". In examining altruism as a behavior rather than a trait, they also point out that there are diverse situational factors that determine whether a child will act altruistically; factors such as the cost to the actor, the nature of the victim, the mood of the actor, etc.

We can also find a link to the foundational elements discussed above. In their classic study of rescuers of Jews in Nazi Europe, entitled The Altruistic Personality, Samuel and Pearl Oliner argued that the rescuers were motivated by strong values of care and inclusiveness which were in large part transmitted to them by their parents through the formation of an early attachment bond, a bond which "shapes personality and becomes the prototype for all subsequent relationships".

Parenting is an important determinant of altruism. Eisenberg and Mussen conclude that parents of altruistic children are nurturant and supportive, model altruism, highlight the effects of actions on others, use induction, establish clear expectations for mature behavior, and create opportunities for their children to manifest responsibility for others. Research also shows that parents of altruistic children tend to moralize, i.e., lecture about right and wrong, using strong affect and use an authoritative parenting style. As noted above, Oliner and Oliner found that WWII rescuers were motivated by "values learned from their parents which prompted and sustained their involvement".

Moral Reasoning

While there are a number of models of the development of moral reasoning, most research on the relation of parenting to moral reasoning development has relied predominantly on Kohlberg's model. This section will therefore describe the Kohlberg model and summarize findings related to parenting and Kohlbergian moral reasoning development, but will include findings about the relation of parenting to some of the other models of moral reasoning development.

Kohlberg has identified an invariant sequence of six stages of reasoning about morality; i.e., a developmental progression of increasingly more effective ways of thinking about and resolving moral problems and issues. Only the first three stages apply to the developmental levels under investigation in this discussion. The first stage represents a very dogmatic, physicalistic, and egocentric perspective on right and wrong. Acts are right if (1) they are sanctioned by authorities or other powerful individuals or (2) they do not result in undesirable concrete consequences to the actor.

At the second stage, right and wrong are still calculated by concrete consequences, but the child has come to see that others may have different perspectives than the self. This opens the door for negotiation. Right is still what maximizes desirable and minimizes undesirable consequences, but authorities no longer have absolute control and consequences are no longer perceived as inevitable. At the third stage, right and wrong are no longer limited to the concrete consequences of actions, nor to consequences to a specific individual. Now morality is based less upon concrete and more upon psychological and covert consequences. Furthermore the consequences are to social units, most notably to dyads. Hence the bottom line for calculating right and wrong is relationships with others; e.g., what significant others think is right, what will happen to the relationship, what will happen to one's reputation, etc. Research suggests that Stage 1 is an early childhood stage, Stage 2 is a middle childhood stage, and Stage 3 is an adolescent stage, although there are quite varied rates of development through these stages.

Relation to parenting. Ironically, the effects of parenting on the development of Kohlbergian moral reasoning were largely ignored for decades. This was due in part to the Piagetian thesis that parents tended to be authoritarian and therefore suppress moral reasoning development, whereas peers were more egalitarian and therefore fostered moral reasoning development. Fortunately, researchers eventually questioned or ignored this position whereas other researchers had studied this with outcome variables other than Kohlberg stage. Hence a substantial body of literature exists. Most research has focused on three principal parent variables: parental stage of moral reasoning, parental discipline style, family communication patterns.

Parent stage of reasoning has been systematically related to child stage of reasoning, but this effect is difficult to interpret. First, moral reasoning has a strong cognitive component and this correlation may be reducible to intelligence. Second, there is a strong relation between parental stage of moral reasoning and parenting style of communication and discipline; hence the variables are confounded. Third, it is clear that parents and other adults adjust the stage of their rhetoric to the level of assumed understanding of their children. Fourth, the results of these studies are quite variable; e.g., Walker and Taylor find the effect only for real dilemmas and not for hypothetical dilemmas and Speicher finds both gender and age variability. When these variables are considered together, however, it appears that the relation between parents' and children's stage is not causal; rather, the other two parenting variables seem to account for most of the development of moral reasoning in children.

Baumrind and others have identified discrete patterns of parental behavior that are referred to as Parenting Styles. Baumrind describes three predominant parenting styles. Authoritarian parents are highly controlling and demanding but affectively cold and hostile and generally uncommunicative. Permissive parents tend to be loving and communicative but wield little control and set few demands for mature behavior.

More recently, Permissive parenting has been differentiated into the more classically warm laissez faire style and the more distant neglectful style; however, the research being reviewed here pre-dates this differentiation. Authoritative parents are loving, controlling, communicative, and set high maturity demands for their children. It is those latter parents whom researchers have found to produce the most positive child characteristics, including higher moral functioning.

Only a few studies have directly examined the relation of parenting style to moral reasoning development; however, numerous studies have examined component variables that comprise distinct parenting styles. For example, Clarity of Communication, a predominant characteristic of Authoritative parenting, includes parental behavior that has been identified most prevalently as Induction; i.e., explaining one's parenting behavior to the child especially with a focus on consequences of one's actions for others. Induction, under a variety of names, has been significantly positively related to moral reasoning development, of both the Piagetian and Kohlbergian varieties.

Three studies have directly examined the relation of parenting style to moral reasoning development. Pratt and Diessner reported that adolescent moral reasoning is predicted positively by Authoritative parenting style and negatively by Permissive parenting style. Boyes and Allen reported similar results while employing different methods of assessing both moral reasoning and parenting style. They found the highest levels of moral reasoning in college students with Authoritative parents and lowest with Authoritarian parents. Berkowitz, et al. however found no relation between parenting style and adolescent moral reasoning; however, their sample was a clinical sample.

Finally, research has demonstrated that parents at higher stages of moral reasoning tend to use more Induction and other Authoritative parenting elements. Hence, it appears that a pattern of Authoritative parenting, especially with its focus on open supportive communication, is nurturing of children's moral reasoning development.

The communicative element of parenting style has already been addressed; however, there is a second way in which family communication has been studied in the development of children's moral reasoning capacities. Numerous investigators have examined the nature of family discussions of moral issues and their relation to children's moral reasoning development. There are two types of such studies: those that use family discussions as interventions intended to stimulate children's moral reasoning development and those that simply analyze family discussions and look for relations to children's levels of moral reasoning.

Two intervention studies have been identified. Grimes found significantly greater moral reasoning development when mothers were included in moral discussion with their children than in a traditional classroom moral discussion intervention. Furthermore, only those parents showed a parallel decrease in authoritarian decision-making in family discussions. Three studies have examined the relation of transactive discussion in family discussions to children's moral reasoning stage.

Transactive discussion is a form of discussion originally identified in adolescent peer moral dilemma discussions. It is defined as speech acts in which the speaker re-presents or actively operates on (e.g., analyzes, extends, logically critiques) the reasoning of a co-discussant. Powers reported that transaction was weakly related to adolescent moral reasoning. The greatest moral development was found in families that are supportive of their children in the discussions and share perspectives. Kruger, in a series of studies, reported that transaction in both peer and mother-daughter moral discussions is positively related to moral reasoning development.

It appears that parents and children naturally tend to regulate they way they communicate when discussing moral topics with each other. Children who are most advanced in moral reasoning tend to have parents who, either naturally or through training, affectively support their children in the discussions, ask challenging questions and elicit children's reasoning, present advanced challenging moral perspectives, and openly reflect on and re-present their children's reasoning.

EDUCATING PARENTS AS NATURAL MORAL EDUCATORS

As demonstrated in the review above, research investigating parental influences on children's moral development consistently identifies a set of processes that relate reliably to moral thought, feeling, and action in children. Within this set can be identified a short list of five parenting processes that relate to two or more of the seven components of moral psychology featured in the preceding discussion.

Parents' use of induction, expression of nurturance and support, use of demandingess and limit setting, modeling of socio-moral behavior, and implemention of a democratic open family discussion and conflict resolution style are each positively related to two or more of the fundamental "building blocks" of morality described above. Thus, by focusing on a relatively small number of parenting dimensions, parents can play a significant role in shaping the moral development of their children. Below we discuss each of these dimensions and provide practical recommendations for helping parents become more effective moral educators.

Induction

Perhaps the single most powerful parental influence on children's moral development is induction. Explaining parental behavior and its implications for the child and others is linked to greater empathy, more highly developed conscience, higher levels of moral reasoning, and altruism. Why should this rather simple process be so potent for shaping moral development? Perhaps because it explicitly links the self and other, simultaneously stimulating children's understanding of the reasons for choosing one behavior over another and the impact of that behavior on another person. Thus, it directly addresses and connects the cognitive (moral reasoning) and affective aspects of moral functioning, and helps children to internalize standards for moral behavior. As Lickona points out, children "need to see us lead good lives, but they also need to know why we do it.

At the same time, induction models a rational, respectful approach to interpersonal relations. When parents take the time to explain their behavior to their children and show awareness of how that behavior affects the child, they implicitly acknowledge that the child's feelings and viewpoint are important and worthy of attention. Indeed, such respect for children is at the heart of both Damon's and Lickona's models of raising good children.

Damon offers the principle of respectful engagement as the underlying model for moral parenting: "respond to the child's own experience without intruding upon this experience, while at the same time presenting the child with consistent expectations, guidelines, and mature insights clearly explained". Lickona argues that respect is the core of morality and parents need to nurture mutual respect in their relationships with their children: "one of the most basic ways to develop kids' respect for themselves and others is to respect them, and require respect in return...Treating kids with respect means treating them like persons...Treating kids like persons means trying to be fair with them". Finally, the discussion of behaviors that parents consider more or less acceptable helps children understand and internalize particular standards for behavior.

There are many opportunities to employ induction. One of the most obvious is in the context of discipline. When children disobey, parents have the opportunity to teach their children about what is right and wrong, and more importantly, why certain behaviors are preferable to others. Taking the time to go through this process will further the child's understanding of moral principles and consequently reduce the need for such interventions in the future.

Of course, at times short-term goals such as stopping a particular behavior take precedence over such long-term goals and make other kinds of discipline necessary. Nonetheless, talking through what happened with the child at a later time will help them better understand the moral implications of their behavior. Induction need not take place only when discipline is required. Discussing the day's events also can involve a focus on the "whys" of behavior and their consequences for other people. Talking explicitly about why the child, parent, or other some other person did something and how it affected other people can flow naturally out of everyday conversations and again make salient the rational and emotional aspects of behavior.

During dialogues generated by parents' use of induction, parents also can help stimulate children's moral development by the use of Socratic questioning within an emotional supportive context. For example, parents can ask children why they think that their behavior led another child to cry, helping children come to the answer themselves.

How parents can do this depends on the child's level of development; parents need to be cognizant of what children can understand and adjust their language accordingly. This is what Lickona refers to as "the moral development approach to raising good children." For example, telling toddlers not to hit another child because it hurts the other child may be sufficient for communicating the message that one's behavior affects others, and is an improvement over simply telling them that such behavior is wrong. Preschoolers with more advanced perspective-taking skills can make the connection between not liking to get hurt themselves and their behavior toward other people. As children get older, engaging them in more sophisticated discussions about why some behaviors are preferable to others becomes feasible.

Another element of parenting related to several core components of morality is Authoritative Parenting. "Maladaptive moral-emotional patterns are prevented in the authoritative type of parenting advocated by Baumrind; for as Baumrind has shown, authoritative child rearing fosters social sensitivity, self-awareness, and respect for rules and authority". This style of parenting has been defined by the intersection of two parental tendencies: responsiveness and demandingness.

We will deal with them separately. Responsiveness is understood as the provision of nurturance and support. Establishing a warm, mutually positive basis for interaction promotes the development of conscience and moral reasoning in children. One effect of warm and responsive parenting is communication of the idea that the child is valuable and worthy of such treatment. "We raise children by giving them love.

The kind of love that helps them develop a positive self-concept. A sense of their worth." A broader message is that people in general are deserving of respectful treatment, and therefore it is wrong to do something that is hurtful to another. Violation of this standard leads to guilt and shame, affects linked closely to conscience. It also provides a basis for moral reasoning: if people are worthy of humane treatment, what course of action is best in a given situation?

Even more than with induction, opportunities to express nurturance abound in parent-child relationships; in fact, the level of warmth and support is a pervasive quality of these relationships. One implication of this is that many interactions not related to the domain of moral functioning will affect children's development in this area. However, the expression of support during interactions around moral issues may be especially important. For example, parents trying to challenge children to think through the moral consequences of some behavior will be more effective if they show support for and interest in the child's point of view and exhibit empathy for the child's feelings.

In addition to providing a supportive platform for children to confront the moral implications of their behavior, parents who take this approach also model concern for others, and so there may be indirect benefits as well. As noted above, parent-child discussions of moral issues seem to be most developmentally nurturing when done in a respectful and emotionally supportive way. What is most interesting about these data is that this pattern is quite different than what one finds in examining the most developmentally productive peer moral discussions, which tend to be highly conflictual and combative in nature.

As noted, the second component of Authoritative parenting is demandingness. Demandingness is more than simply requiring certain behaviors from children. Effective demandingness requires three major ingredients.

First, parents need to set high but realistic goals for their children. This entails understanding what the child can and cannot reasonably be expected to do. Children whose parents have low expectations for them, develop low expectations for themselves. Children whose parents set unreasonable high expectations for them, become frustrated, angry, and develop a sense of self as a failure. Clearly also, parents need to communicate these goals to their children. One of the more common breakdown in all human relations is the tendency to hold others accountable for failing to meet expectations of which we have never informed them.

Second, parents need to provide the support necessary to help children attain these goals. Parental involvement in supporting and monitoring school work is one example. The technique of scaffolding described earlier offers a detailed description of how to provide such support in a way that nurtures development rather than becoming a surrogate for it.

Third, parents need to monitor whether or not children meet their expectations. Children will quickly recognize the impotence of demands that are not monitored and therefore are unrelated to consequences. Such demands will have little impact on the development of morality in children.

If demandingness is appropriately and consistently implemented as part of Authoritative parenting, we have already demonstrated that children will develop greater self-control, altruism, and self-esteem.

"One of the surest ways to help our children turn their moral reasoning into positive moral behavior is to teach by example. Teaching kids respect by respecting them is certainly one way to teach by example... But teaching by example goes beyond how we treat our children. It has to do with how we treat and talk about others outside the family — relatives, friends, strangers. It has to do with how we lead our lives". We have already discussed how parents' behavior during interactions with their children regarding moral issues serves as a model for them; parents who express empathy or discuss moral reasoning also are modeling these qualities.

There also are more direct ways that modeling can influence children's moral development. Children closely observe their parents' interactions with each other, with family members, and with people more generally, and from those observations learn a great deal about how to treat others. As parents can model respect and compassion toward others, so may they model behavior that is harmful or abusive. For example, parents who resolve disagreements by belittling, coercing, or physically dominating their spouse may teach children that aggression is an appropriate response when their interests conflict with another's.

Indeed, families marked by angry, poorly resolved interparental conflict tend to have children who are more aggressive. Grych and Fincham have argued that children actively attempt to make sense of the causes and consequences of parental behavior during conflictual interactions, and that these appraisals can have long term effects on their functioning. Although children may not imitate the specific behaviors they observe, their beliefs and attitudes about how to treat other people may well be shaped by such family experiences. The fact that these "lessons" are unintended makes them no less powerful.

Parents also act as models for moral behavior when they relate events in their lives to their children. Damon offers as the first of his four specific recommendations for parenting moral children that "parents should share openly with children moral reactions to events in their own adult lives. Sharing emotional reactions means demonstrating them when appropriate, describing them clearly, and answering children's questions about them candidly." Similarly, prosocial behaviors, which could involve everything from sharing with their children to discussing contributions to charities, teaches children that they should treat others with respect.

DEMOCRATIC FAMILY DECISION-MAKING AND DISCUSSION

It has often been argued that "you can't legislate morality." This is not necessarily true. It depends on the nature of your legislature. You can't legislate morality by fiat. But you can if your legislature is truly democratic; that is, if all stake-holders are given equal power to enter into the public arena and participate in decision-making. This leads to morality in two ways. First, decisions and rules are more likely to be just. Second, the participation in the process is more likely to stimulate the more development of the participants.

This has been demonstrated empirically in Kohlberg's Just Community school approach. It is equally true, however, in the family. We have seen in our analysis of the components of moral development, that various aspects of such a democratic process produce compliance, moral reasoning development, conscience, higher self-esteem, and altruism in children. Such families respect children's voices as meaningful contributions to family discussions, decisions, and conflict resolution processes. They let children know that their voices are valued and provide affective support for their participation in family discussions.

Thus far we have tried to identify the components of a moral child and the parenting behaviors that foster or impede their development. We also have tried to explicate in more detail how parents can implement five core parenting strategies that have been empirically related to the growth of our eight aspects of child morality. Many parents naturally engage in these strategies, but others may require education or structured training to provide the kind of parenting that supports moral development.

Parent training programs have a well-established place in the treatment of noncompliance, aggression, and other externalizing problems in children. These behaviorally-based psycho-educational programs are designed to teach parents principles of effective behavior management, including but not limited to the proper use of reinforcement and punishment and guidelines for clear communication. Outcome research on the efficacy of parent training programs for reducing externalizing problems in children consistently supports their utility, suggesting that this model also may work well for teaching parents how to foster moral and prosocial behavior in their children.

Parent training programs also have been designed for non-clinical populations as a way of enhancing parents' interactions with their children, and focus more on improving parent-child relationships than on eliminating problem behaviors. These programs provide a preexisting platform for teaching the five parenting strategies described; each above is amenable to presenting in an individual, small group, or workshop format. Although the specific content taught would need to be adjusted to fit the developmental level of the child, the principles are applicable across ages. For example, a 4 year-old may be included in a democratic approach to family decision-making by inviting their opinions and giving them choices. A 14 year-old, in contrast, may be involved in making decisions about an appropriate curfew or reasonable consequences for failing to complete homework. Unfortunately, little attention has been paid to teaching parents how to foster specifically moral characteristics in children. As noted above, two studies have taught parents how to participate in discussions of moral issues with their children. Although both were successful in accelerating moral reasoning development, only Stanley documented a change in parenting style outside of the artificial school-based discussion sessions.

Nevertheless, these studies do suggest that interventions with parents can change parental behavior related to moral development and can positively influence children's moral development. More attention has been paid to teaching parents how to prevent child risk behaviors such as substance use. It is worth noting that one popular model, the "resiliency model", includes empathy and self-esteem as two of seven basic resiliency characteristics in youth. However, even though parent training programs generally are effective, not all children and parents benefit from these interventions. Factors such as marital discord, parental psychopathology, and adverse socioeconomic circumstances can make it difficult for parents to understand and utilize the skills taught in these programs.

Some parent training programs attend to these issues, teaching skills for resolving marital discord and reducing depression, but some parents will need more intensive interventions, such as individual or couples therapy, before they can provide the kind of parenting that promotes moral development. Moreover, parents' behavior, both with their partner and with their child, may go beyond failing to stimulate moral growth and actually undermine their children's moral development. Marital conflict, interspousal and parent-child abuse, and inconsistent discipline are related to aggressive and antisocial behavior in children, and consequently need to be directly addressed before there can be any reasonable expectation that children will exhibit more moral behavior.

Thus, for some families, attention to promoting moral development begins with changing destructive behavior in the family. Finally, cultural norms and values for appropriate parenting may be inconsistent with the goals and methods of standard parent training programs.

The majority of research on links between parenting and moral development has been conducted with White, middle class samples and may not apply to other ethnic or socioeconomic groups. What is viewed as desirable and appropriate behavior in children and parents is not invariant, and for parent education to be effective, educators and therapists need to be aware of and sensitive to the cultural context of parenting. Failure to do so could result in viewing parents from minority cultures as inadequate and teaching them methods that clash with their values.

6

TRANSACTIONAL STRATEGIES FOR MORAL EDUCATION AND ASSESSMENT OF MORAL MATURITY

INTEGRATING STRUCTURE AND CONTENT IN MORAL EDUCATION

One would be hard-pressed not to notice that character education is experiencing a renaissance of sorts, particularly but not exclusively in the United States. At all levels of public experience, the rhetoric of character education can be heard. Local communities and grass roots parent coalitions are imploring schools and civic leaders to support the development of character in our youth. Numerous states have begun to implement character education initiatives, some spurred on by Federal Legislation and funding and others by local interest. And, in his 1997 State of the Union Address, President Clinton emphasized the national need for character education as one of ten central points about education reform, "Character education must be taught in our schools. We must teach children to be good citizens." One is led, obviously enough, to query why such a groundswell of interest and support has emerged.

Clearly there are multiple reasons for it. First, it is partially a reaction against the popularly cited statistics about the deteriorating state of youth in our society. Second, it is a response to the declining confidence in the family to deal effectively with problems of youth misbehavior. Third, it is a product of more politically "ecumenical" approaches to the issue of character education. Groups such as the Character Education Partnership and the Communitarian Network have worked diligently to bring together multi-partisan coalitions that previously had focused largely on their differences, effectively precluding success in wide-scale implementation of character education. This third point raises an historically contentious issue; i.e., the longstanding animosity between different schools of thought on the how to raise and educate future good citizens. Certainly this conflict is neither new nor unique to the United States, as the death of Socrates can amply demonstrate.

Nevertheless, the futility of much of the efforts to make a national impact over the past century underscores the need to examine why so many well-intentioned educators, parents, and civic leaders fell so far short of their mark in trying to positively influence the moral formation of our youth.

SOURCES OF CONTENTION

The competitive relationships between differing schools of thought about the moral formation and education of youth are borne from a variety of sources. Only five sources of contention will be highlighted here, far short of an exhaustive list. First, differing approaches to the issue tend to disagree on the basic nature of the moral person; i.e., on the psychological characteristics of morality. This issue is particularly important because one's assumptions about moral nature define the outcomes that are to guide interventions. Is a good child a compliant, submissive, docile and obedient child? Or is a good child inquisitive, challenging, and assertive? To what degree is conformity to be valued? Are the key indices of success to be seen in the overt behavior of the child? Or are they to be measured by more intangible characteristics such as personality traits, reasoning capacities, and affective response tendencies?

In another discussion, we have attempted to describe the anatomy of the moral person as a complex composite of these and other characteristics, pointing out that the major flaw of most approaches is not incorrectness, but incompleteness.

A second point of contention has to do with the means of nurturing the development of whatever outcomes one endorses. Clearly this issue is largely derivative of the first point. Different methods are warranted for different goals. If, for example, one merely wants to control behavior, then more behavioristic methods (e.g., reward and punishment) would be warranted. Hence some models rely more on authoritarian external controls and standards while others tend to focus on cooperative democratic methods that empower students. Even here the problem again may be more one of myopic incompleteness than of misguidedness. Based on an Aristotelian model, Peters argues that more externally oriented approaches may be more appropriate with younger children and more collaborative egalitarian approaches may be more appropriate as the children mature. A third point of contention concerns the source of moral formation. Does goodness come from within? That is, it is a predisposition or principal potential of the human condition? Or is it something that must be imposed from outside, in essence to subjugate the innate antisocial nature of human beings? There are widely disparate perspectives on this issue and each different perspective greatly influences how one selects both methods and outcomes for a character education project.

Fourth, to make matters worse, there is the ever present problem of language. Already the astute reader can note that we have alternated between the terms moral education and character education. These terms are not fully arbitrarily chosen, but there is indeed a degree of arbitrariness to them. At times they are chosen simply because of current fancy. For instance, in Great Britain currently the term of choice is values education. In the United States it is character education, although for many citizenship education or civic education is the preferred term.

In Japan, a popular term is moralogy. Not too long ago in the US, the term of choice was moral education and before that values education. Sometimes the rubric is selected for its political impact, and sometimes, but rarely, it is even chosen for conceptual reasons. A fifth and final point of contention has to do with specificity. Some would define the domain of character education as encompassing all values that a person holds and all behaviors that impact on others. This might include adherence to arbitrary institutional rules or even to matters of personal taste.

Others rely on a narrower definition, limiting the domain of character education to only those issues for which there is a clear moral focus. Whether one relies on a narrow or broad definition of the scope of character education, it is clear that different domains of social behavior require different pedagogical methods. As noted, these are but some of the reasons for the past failure of character and moral education approaches to be wide-ranging, integrative, and effective. One more issue will be addressed here, and in much greater detail. That is the issue of the role of content in character and moral education

CONTENT IN CHARACTER EDUCATION

Perhaps the most frequently raised challenge to proposed moral education programs is "Whose values?". Polls consistently reveal that the vast majority of Americans support moral education in the public schools, but when a specific proposal is made in a specific community, it invariably raises concerns about the content of the intervention. Some mistake moral education for sex education. Others fear it will be a form of religious education, while still others fear it will not. Some fear moral education will be a form of totalitarian mind control.

All of these concerns, and others, center around what will be taught; i.e., the content of the proposed moral education curriculum. Three basic approaches have been identified in dealing with this issue. First, there is the Indoctrinative approach which presupposes a justified content and proposes to teach that content by a variety of methods. Traditional character education approaches tend to fall in this category.

The second approach is the Romanticist approach. The individual is assumed to have an innate tendency to develop into a moral agent; the role of education is to provide the nurturant context in which this natural "flowering" can occur. Imposing a specific content is anathema to the Romanticist approach. An example would be the values clarification approach.

The third approach is the Cognitive-structural approach. It focuses on the construction of moral reasoning capacities, which are understood to be a product of the interaction of one's genetic, developmental, and biological endowments with one's experience with the physical and social worlds. Content is largely ignored as the focus is on reasoning structures and decision-making processes. Proposed curricula do not endorse specific content; rather they provide the opportunity to apply one's reasoning to a variety of contents. Here content is used as a catalyst for producing development. Kohlberg's Just Community schools are examples of this approach.

Hence we have three quite discrepant approaches to the role of content in moral education. The Indoctrinative approach embraces the teaching of content; in fact, the acquisition of this content is the goal of Indoctrinative moral education, typically highlighting a list of values or virtues that serve as the core of the curriculum. The Romanticist approach avoids providing moral content; it considers content to be idiosyncratic and to be latent in the individual. The Cognitive-structural approach views content as a pedagogical tool; a means to an end. This difference lies at the heart of much of the perceived incompatibility of diverse approaches to moral education. A core issue in disentangling this issue is the concept of moral relativism.

All three approaches have been "accused" of promoting relativism and they tend to reciprocally "accuse" each other of the same failing. Kohlberg has claimed that the Indoctrinative approach is relativistic because of what he labels the problem of the "bag of virtues". He claims that such approaches always face the problem of justifying why they chose a particular set of values or virtues from a very large pool. He felt that such decisions were inevitably ethically unjustifiable.

The Indoctrinative approach has labeled both the cognitive-structural and Romanticist approaches as relativistic. It is argued that by not advocating a specific content set, these two approaches covertly endorse an ethical position that there is no absolute right or wrong. For example, they argue that by using open-ended dilemmas to promote development, such approaches are subtly suggesting that the right answer to such dilemmas is ultimately unknowable.

The problem with this seeming circularity is that content has been assumed to be either intrinsically non-relativistic or intrinsically relativistic. Kohlberg assumed that the incorporation of content had to be ethically arbitrary. Only structure could be universal; specific content could not. Indeed, the advocacy of content was seen to pervert the potential of peer egalitarian discussion for promoting moral reasoning development.

There was an assumed trade-off: more content meant less stage development and vice versa. Character educators and values educators from the Indoctrinative tradition, on the other hand, assumed that a content-less program must suggest to the students that any answer to a moral problem is equally justifiable.

Herein lies not only the problem, but also the opportunity, for a solution. Kohlberg failed to accept that ethical philosophy can justify content as well as structure. And the Indoctrinative educators failed to accept the fact that open-ended discussion can be done in an ethically evaluative context. It should be noted that these positions tend to represent the rhetoric more than the practice of moral education. Kohlberg recognized both the potential and inevitability of teacher advocacy of certain values and behaviors, and incorporated them into his "Just Community" school model. And many Indoctrinative model programs include peer discussion of moral concerns, and do not rely solely on adult advocacy.

INTEGRATING CONTENT AND STRUCTURE INTO MORAL EDUCATION

The critical issue in evaluating the relativism of a moral education approach is not whether or not it relies on a specific content. Rather it hinges on how that content is justified. For those educators who try to identify a content list for their moral education programs, there tend to be two major strategies. The first is to generate a local consensus.

Typically this is done by committee. Such committees tend to vary on the degrees to which they are representative or expert; i.e., the degrees to which they profess to represent a cross-section of the community or to which they represent expertise in the area of moral and character education and development. For example, many school districts will form a representative committee, composed frequently of teachers, administrators, parents, students, clergy, and other stakeholders. They will be charged with generating a list of values and/or character traits around which the moral education program can center. Sometimes this process can be short-circuited by adopting the results of another community's deliberations, with or without editing.

This is by far the most popular approach. Recently the Wisconsin State Superintendent of the Department of Public Instruction, John Benson, appointed a state-wide representative committee, the Wisconsin Citizenship Initiative Task Force, charged in part to "list, define, and recommend a core set of citizenship values essential to our society that need to be part of every child's school, home, and community experiences."

In the final report of the Task Force they list the core set of citizenship values as Courage, Honesty, Respect, and Responsibility.

Two examples of more expert committees are the Josephson Institute's 1992 Youth Summit Conference in the United States and the 1996 National Forum for Values in Education and the Community in the United Kingdom. The former generated the now fairly well known set of 6 values that have become the Six Pillars of Character, which are included in federal education legislation. Those values are Trustworthiness, Respect, Responsibility, Fairness, Caring, and Citizenship. The UK committee generated a separate list of values for each of four domains: Society, Relationships, The Self, The Environment. They specifically concluded that whereas "there could be no consensus on...the source of the values [nor]...how to apply the values...a consensus could be reached on the values themselves."

The second approach is to try to identify a "universal" set of values and/or character traits. Such a set is assumed to be ethically justified, usually based on philosophical analysis. This is rarely done, however. One example where it was done was for the Community of Caring approach, which employed ethical philosophy to justify the five universally-accepted values of Care, Responsibility, Respect, Trust, and Family. Sometimes, however, the assumption of universality is more tenuous. For example, the 1992 Josephson Institute "Six Pillars of Character" were judged to be universally valid, based upon the diversity and expertise of the group formulating them, and upon the process of democratic discussion used to generate the final list. Clearly these six values of the Josephson Aspen Declaration are quite parallel to those of the Community of Caring. This suggests two points. First, expert agreement typically leads to very similar conclusions about consensual values. Second, these similarities do not guarantee justifiable claims of universality. For instance, the most controversial of the Josephson values was Citizenship. This is so because it connotes for many blind loyalty to the community. If such loyalty is not subordinate to ethical values and principles, then one is considered to be universally required to adhere to even obviously despicable community actions and values. We need not look to such blatant examples as Nazi Germany for confirmation of this problem, but instead to our own backyards in Waco (TX), Tigerton Dells (WI), and many other local havens for racist and fanatic communities.

The problems of universality and cultural relativism are perhaps most evident in the report of the Wisconsin Task Force cited above. The Task Force claimed to be identifying "universal values" through "consensus." In the same paragraph they asserted both that "there is a core set of citizenship values essential to our democratic society" and that "each community needs to identify the core set of citizenship values important to them."

If the values are universal, then why should a new set be generated by each community? And if each community is given carte blanche to do so, by what criteria and processes do we preclude the government sanctioning of undesirable values such as child abuse, white supremacy, and terrorism? These are difficult questions and the are rarely answered or even addressed for that matter. Some counterarguments are as follows. First, the local process of creating and endorsing core values is a means of insuring participation and commitment from the local community. This is clearly a valuable goal. Second, local value generation will rarely differ from more centralized control of core values. This is empirically true, but though the risk is low in probability, it is very high in effect. Third, the building of communities is a greater good that needs to be integrated into this process. This Communitarian approach is certainly a viable and popular one, but not without its controversial aspects. It still fails to adequately address the problem of dysfunctional communities.

RELIGION AND CONTENT

One area where the issue of the relativism vs. universalism of content in character education is very prominent is in the role of religion in public education in the United States. This is a complex issue. First, at least in the United States, religion is highly restricted in public schooling. Hence a reliance upon overtly religious content or religious justifications for content could be quite problematic. Second, again most notably in this society, we live in a highly pluralistic world. Religious diversity is quite predominant and increasingly so.

Third, and derivative of the prior point, it is unclear whether religion as a justification for moral content is representative of the local consensus approach to moral content or of the universal philosophical approach. When one is functioning within a homogeneous religious community, then the issue is moot. Religious moral content is both expected and accepted. When one is functioning in a religiously diverse context, however, the problem is often insurmountable.

Some groups, resort to the political blueprints of our society to avoid religious justifications. Others struggle with how to incorporate religion into the public schools. The Williamsville (NY) school district, for example, recently tried to eliminate all religious activities, events, references, etc. from the schools due to the increasing diversity of their community. They eventually had to switch their tactics and try a religious diversity curriculum instead, in which different faith traditions were given their own places in the life of the school. This becomes rather tricky as comparisons are inevitable and often evaluative.

This is exacerbated by the tendency to confuse the moral and non-moral dimensions of religion, even though people intuitively treat them differently. One solution to the problem of religious content is to first differentiate those aspects of religion that are intrinsically moral from those that are matters of religious convention. Additionally, at least in secular and public schools, the moral values and rules of religions require philosophical justification, and cannot be justified merely on the basis of religious authority. This serves as part of the model more generically for dealing with the role of content in moral education.

Ultimately, if one is to be truly moral about moral education, there must be a justification for content that transcends local "tastes". In most cases this is really not a functional need, but a theoretical need. That is so because most communities tend to be well-intentioned and end up with highly similar lists of values, quite parallel to those in the Aspen Declaration or the Community of Caring. However this is not necessarily so. One can readily imagine a community that is relatively homogeneous and holds beliefs that are immoral (e.g., white supremacy, child pornography). The value consensus that such a community would likely generate would not fulfil philosophical criteria for ethical universality; criteria such as the Principle of Generalization, the Golden Rule, or the Principle of Reciprocity. Such rules must be differentiated from the criteria for identifying, for example, objective truth. Whereas, it is certainly not non-controversial, nonetheless it is probably the predominant position in philosophy that one must differentiate between fact and morality. Empirical evidence is relevant to questions of truth, but it is typically held that it is not a basis for moral prescriptions.

Hence, philosophically, the local consensus approach to justifying ethics is not acceptable, whereas practically it may very well suffice in most situations. In fact, as noted above, the local consensus model brings with it many positive side benefits, mostly relating to commitment and community building. It therefore seems imprudent to argue that a select set of "philosopher-kings" should pontificate about what ought to be the single set of universal values that guide all school curricula. On the other hand, it is patently unjustifiable to allow all communities to generate whatever set of value they see fit. The solution would be to allow communities to generate consensual guidelines, but to require justification of their validity beyond mere local agreement. The values must be put to some philosophical tests before they can receive the "stamp of universality."

DOMAIN

Unfortunately, there is yet another distinction that we must address in attempting to generate an integration of content and structure in moral education. Turiel and his colleagues have attempted to differentiate moral concerns from other concerns. They argue that the moral domain concerns matters of welfare, justice, and rights; matters that are intrinsically right and not alterable by consensus. Such matters are fixed and unalterable. The moral domain is contrasted with the domain of social conventions and the personal domain. Social conventions are "behavioral uniformities which coordinate interactions of individuals within social systems... Conventions are relative to the societal context, and may be altered by consensus or general usage within a social system". The examples given above about religious issues, killing and dietary laws, are respectively, examples of moral and social conventional values. The personal domain includes matters that are outside the authority of others. They are matters of personal preference.

Unfortunately, these distinctions are rarely considered by moral educators. As a result, many so-called moral education programs actually include moral and social-conventional content. This is a problem because these social domains are justified differently, should be evaluated differently, and are often intuitively understood differently by both students and teachers.

All to often, the eager character educator is left with merely a list of values or character traits that are to serve as the core of character education. Clearly, an effective program will need to be built on more than a skeleton such as that. The British National Forum for Values mentioned previously asserted that "the statement of values should not be seen simply as an exercise in abstract moral reasoning...the values should be presented in such a way as to exhibit the relationship between values and behaviour."

And in that spirit, for each of their four areas of valuing they offer "Principles for action" that are intended to offer guidance as to how those values should be manifested in action. Other examples of attempts to add substance to the skeletal lists of values at the heart of most character education programs are fairly common. For instance, the Josephson Institute has continued to flesh out their Six Pillars of Character with detailed descriptions of the components of each. Wynne and Ryan offer a long specific checklist of behaviors that should be manifest in a school that embodies their concept of character education.

MORAL PSYCHOLOGY

Moral psychology suggests that to function as a moral agent requires a fairly broad diversity of psychological characteristics. As we have detailed this analysis elsewhere, we will only describe it very briefly here. To be a fully moral person requires more than merely holding a set of values or character traits. We have intentionally avoided the terminological problems of even defining the relations between values and character. Others have attempted to do this, but for the sake of this discussion let it suffice to define values as affectively-charged beliefs and character traits as enduring tendencies to act in certain specific ways. Beyond values and character traits, one also requires moral emotions and moral reasoning. It is the latter to which Cognitive-structural approaches to moral education are directed. Finally, one also needs, at least from adolescence on but likely sooner in a more rudimentary form, a moral identity. This concept refers to a self-reflective and evaluative sense of the self as a morally adequate person. Such a sense will guide the selection of goals and methods.

Given this model of the complete moral person, it should become somewhat clear that the values or character traits that we have been discussing are actually part of a much larger educational agenda. Whereas Kohlberg argued that including character and values in moral education undermined the universality of the enterprise, it should now be clear that (1) values can be justified as universal and (2) both reasoning and values are parts of a larger and more psychologically justifiable agenda for character education. Additionally, it should also be clear that omitting the intentional focus on fostering the development of moral reasoning capacities is likewise a perversion of moral nature.

The most effective models of character education are those that recognize the complexity of human moral nature and attempt to be multi-faceted in their approaches. Excellent examples come from the Child Development Project and Tom Lickona. In other words, by being less narrow, more philosophical and psychological, and less contentious, character education can not only avoid problems of ethical relativism, but be more effective in producing moral citizens.

SYNTHESIS RESEARCH ON MORAL DEVELOPMENT

Educators can help children differentiate between the norms and conventions of their culture and the universal moral concerns for justice and human welfare. Five educational practices enable teachers to engage in moral education that is neither indoctrinative nor relativistic.

— Moral education should focus on issues of justice, fairness and human welfare.

— Effective moral education programs are integrated within the curriculum, rather than treated separately as a special program or unit.

— Moral discussion promotes moral development when the students use "transactive" discussion patterns, are at somewhat different moral levels, and are free to disagree about the best solution to a moral dilemma.

— Cooperative goal structures promote both moral and academic growth.

— Firm, fair, and flexible classroom management practices and rules contribute to students' moral growth. Teachers should respond to the harmful or unjust consequences of moral transgressions, rather than to broken rules or unfulfilled social expectations.

We have known for some time that the overwhelming majority of parents expect teachers and other school authorities to contribute to children's moral development. There is, however, considerable confusion and discord among people about what it is they mean when they talk about morality. In such a context teachers who want to provide moral education have difficulty even deciding what parents want them to teach, let alone how best to teach it.

Recent research suggests that the apparent public confusion is not about what is moral but about what is "proper." Both children and adults generally agree about what is moral; this overall agreement can be seen by differentiating the sphere of action governed by moral precepts from that governed by consensus or social convention. We have attempted to pull together research and theory on children's social development that helps clarify the distinction between the moral and conventional domains.

DISTINCTION BETWEEN MORALITY AND CONVENTION

Children in any society should learn to conform to a number of social rules and expectations if they are to become participants in the culture. In our society, children need to learn that certain classes of adults are addressed by titles. They are also expected to learn that it is unacceptable to be naked in public even if it is 90 degrees and sunny outside, and so forth. Actions of this sort are examples of social conventions. Conventions are shared, uniform behaviors determined by the social system in which they are formed.

Over time, through accepted usage, these standards serve to maintain social organization. While conventions are important, they are arbitrary. This is because there is nothing inherently right or wrong about the actions they define. For example, dresses are worn only by women in American society. The social norm governing this behavior is arbitrary in that another form of dress could be designated to differentiate between the sexes.

In contrast with convention, moral considerations stem from factors intrinsic to actions: consequences such as harm to others, violations of rights, effects on general welfare. Moral issues are, thus, neither arbitrary nor determined by cultural precepts or by consensus. The individual's moral prescriptions are determined by factors inherent in social relationships, as opposed to a particular form of social, cultural, or religious structure.

The following excerpt illustrates the distinction children make between moral and convention issues. The excerpt is from an interview with a three-year-old girl regarding her perceptions of spontaneously occurring transgressions at her preschool.

Moral issues

Did you see what just happened? Yes. They were playing and John hit him too hard. Is that something you are supposed to do or not supposed to do? Not so hard to hurt. Is there a rule about that? Yes. What is the rule? You're not to hit hard. What if there were no rule about hitting hard; would it be all right to do then? No. Why not? Because he could get hurt and start to cry.

Conventional issue

Did you see what just happened? Yes. They were noisy. Is that something you are supposed to do or not supposed to do? Not do. Is there a rule about that? Yes. We have to be quiet. What if there were no rule; would it be all right to do then? Yes. Why? Because there is no rule.

Cutting, charing and consuming a piece of pie are fraught with moral issues: What is fair? Who decides? This kind of distinction between morality and convention is at variance with the accounts of moral development that have had the greatest impact on moral education. Within those earlier views, it is only at the higher stages of moral development that morality (fairness) is differentiated from the displaces convention as the basis for moral judgments.

Over the past decade, however, 27 published accounts have reported research demonstrating that morality and convention are differentiated at very early ages and constitute distinct conceptual and developmental systems. These studies are summarized in several recent reviews. In brief, these studies have found the following.

— Moral transgressions are viewed as wrong, irrespective of the presence of governing rules, while conventional acts are viewed as wrong only if they violate an existing rule or standard.

— Individuals view conventional standards as culturally relative and alterable, while moral prescriptions are viewed as universal and unchangeable.

— The forms of social interaction is the context of moral events differ qualitatively from interactions in the context of conventions. Specifically, children's and adults' responses to events in the moral domain focus on features intrinsic to the acts, while responses in the context of conventions focus on aspects of the social order.

— Individuals tend to treat moral transgressions as more serious than violations of convention and tend to view prosocial moral acts as better and more positive than adherence to conventions.

While the majority of these studies were conducted in the United States, essentially the same results have been obtained in Nigeria, and the Virgin Islands.

Finally, a series of studies involving several hundred Catholic, fundamentalist Christian, and Jewish children showed that children make distinctions between matters of morality and religious doctrine similar to the distinctions secular children draw between morality and convention. Most agreed that moral transgressions such as stealing, hitting, or slander would still be wrong even if there were no religious rules against them, because they are harmful to others. However, work on the Sabbath, women preaching in church or synagogue, and the use of contraceptives, for instance, would be all right in the children's view if there were no religious rules or scriptural injunctions concerning them.

THE MORAL AND CONVENTIONAL DOMAINS

While a young child has an intuitive grasp that actions such as hitting and stealing are prima facie wrong, the child's moral concepts do not reflect a fully developed moral system. For example, although young children view it as wrong to keep all of the classroom toys to oneself and not share any of them with the other children, preschoolers think it is quite all right to keep all of the favored toys to oneself as long as one shares the remainder. Thus, while the young child's morality is structured by concepts of justice, it reflects a rather egocentric moral perspective.

With development, the child's moral perspective gives way to progressively more objective and inclusive notions of equality and reciprocity. With respect to sharing, for example, the four-year-olds' premise - whoever wants the most should get it - is replaced by the idea that distributive decisions should be based on strict equality or reciprocity - everybody should get the same. This strict reciprocity is replaced in turn by a recognition that there can be multiple valid claims to justice by different individuals and that persons with special needs, the poor or the handicapped, deserved special consideration.

The changes observed with respect to distributive justice reflect the more general structural changes in the child's moral understanding. Moral development entails the construction of progressively more adequate conceptualizations of justice and beneficence.

Just as children's conceptions of morality undergo development, so also do their concepts of social convention. Through observation and communication with others, children learn their society's conventions. However, the societal functions of conventions are usually quite complex, and even when children have learned what is "expected," they do not fully understand the reasons why such behaviors are considered reasonable and right. Indeed, to understand the importance of social conventions, children need to understand interpersonal relationships, social systems, and the role of behavioral norms in maintaining both. Such complex constructs take time to develop.

Conceptions of social convention progress through seven development levels reflecting underlying concepts of social organization. Development follows an oscillating pattern between periods affirming the importance of convention and phases negating it. This oscillation indicates the difficulty children have in accounting for the function of arbitrary social norms and illustrates the slow process of reflection and construction that precedes the adolescent's view of convention as important to the maintenance of the social system.

Fostering moral development

If even very young children differentiate between actions in the moral and conventional domains and reason differently about the two, then moral or values education should clearly reflect this distinction. Moral education should move students through progressively more adequate forms of resolving conflicting claims to justice or human rights. Teaching about convention should move students toward an understanding of the role conventions play in establishing social organization, and the importance of convention for organizing and coordinating interactions within social systems.

The first step toward such an approach entails the teacher's analysis and identification of the moral or conventional nature of social issues employed in values lessons. Such an analysis would be necessary to ensure that the issues discussed are concordant with the values domain they are intended to affect. A discussion of dress code, for example, would constitute a poor issue from which to generate moral discussion since mode of dress is primarily a matter of convention. Likewise, consideration of whether it is right to steal to help a person in need would be a poor issue with which to generate a lesson intended to foster students' understanding of the function of social conventions.

Of course, not all issues of social right and wrong fall neatly into one domain or the other. In many cases one can find issues that overlap the two domains. Such issues afford rich opportunities with which to involve students in reasoning, necessitating the coordination of knowledge from more than one social dimension.

Moral development and the general curriculum

Moral education should be integrated within the curriculum and not take the form of a "special" program or unit. A program that is simply inserted into the curriculum carries with it an inherent artificiality and discontinuity that renders such interventions incompatible with the more general aims of teachers and students.

The life of such programs is generally brief. Regarding one of his own early programs of this genre, Lawrence Kohlberg quipped, While the intervention operation was a success, the patient died. When we went back a year later, we found not a single teacher had continued to engage in moral discussion after the commitment to the research had end.

As the Kohlberg quote implies, the central method used to generate moral development has been moral discussion. The use of discussion acknowledges that social growth is not simply a process of learning society's rules and values, but a gradual process in which students actively transform their understanding of morality and social convention through reflection and construction. That is, students' growth is a function of meaning-making rather than mere compliance with externally imposed values.

Despite the widespread and long-standing use of discussion of moral dilemmas as an educational method, it is only in the past five years that careful research of the mechanism underlying the effectiveness of moral discussion has been conducted. On the basis of that research we can discard some long-held notions about moral discussion and focus our efforts on more effective interactional patterns.

The central myth uncovered in the research is that advances in the moral judgment of children are aided by teacher statements one stage above the modal reasoning level of the children. Not only are such statements difficult to generate and therefore rare in classroom discussions, including those conducted by trained experts, but they seem far less relevant to changes in moral reasoning than statements by peers. The research by Berkowitz and his colleagues suggests that teachers serve less as instruments for direct intervention that as agents for the facilitation of peer discussion.

From the research we can identify three characteristics of effective moral discussion. Conflict. According to Berkowitz, stage change occurred most readily in students who disagreed about the moral solution to a dilemma. Consensus on the outcome reduced the likelihood that students would challenge or otherwise respond to one another's reasoning and thus reduced the impact of the discussion on students' existing notions of morality. The educational implication of this finding is that the issues or problems teachers select as the basis for moral discussion should be ones likely to generate disagreement.

A note of caution regarding the use of conflict comes from research with young children. Damon and Killen found that social conflict tended to retard and not to promote stage change in children under eight years of age. Development took place in contexts where children could resolve problems through cooperation and conciliation. Their findings are concordant with other research suggesting that moral development in young children occurs through co-construction rather than argumentation or passive withdrawal.

Stage disparity: The optimal distance in developmental level among students participating in moral discussion is on the order of one-half stage. This stage disparity is about what one finds among students in a typical classroom and implies that normal heterogeneity among students is sufficient for effective moral discussion.

Transactive discussion: In their analyses of student discourse, Berkowitz and his colleagues identified several forms of student statements that are related to moral development. They labeled such statements transacts. Transacts are characterized by listeners' efforts to integrate the speaker's statements into his own framework before generating a response. Transacts are responses that attempt to extend the logic of the speaker's argument, refute the assumptions of the speaker's argument, or provide a point of commonality or resolution between the two conflicting positions. Listener behavior that was not found to be associated with the moral development includes forms of discourse in which the listener restates the speaker's argument or engages in collective monologue in which the listener's statements seem not to have reflected those of the speaker.

Cooperative goal structure

David Johnson has suggested that successful moral discussion is more like to take place in classrooms employing cooperative goal structures in a democratic atmosphere than in the traditional classroom environment. There is a considerable body of evidence to support Johnson's claim that cooperative goal structures contribute to moral development. In a cooperative goal structure, students perceive that they can obtain their goal if and only if the other students with whom they are cooperatively linked obtained their.

In addition to being linked to positive social outcomes (such as increased perspective-taking and moral stage, decrease in racial and ethnic stereotyping), cooperative goal structures have been associated with increases in student motivation and academic achievement. Thus, the use of cooperative education may serve the dual purpose of promoting moral development and linking moral education to the broader curriculum.

Classroom management

Each aspect of moral education discussed thus far is embedded within the more general social climate of the classroom; the rules, structure, and sanctions that make up what Philip Jackson calls the "hidden curriculum." While specific classroom management practices may vary, the overall features of classrooms that contribute to moral development are as follows:

— *Firm:* Classroom rules and expectations are known and upheld by school authorities.

— *Fair:* Rules are limited to those necessary for learning and are evenly applied; consequences are moderate rather than severe.

— *Flexible:* There is room for negotiation between students and teachers regarding the establishment, removal, and enforcement of school and classroom rules.

In addition to the above characteristics of classroom and school climate, practices associated with moral development include the use of reasoning to respond to transgressions. Research indicates that students are sensitive to whether teacher responses are concordant with the domain (moral or conventional) of the breach. Students evaluate not only their judgments of teacher responses but also the teachers as respondents. Students rated highest those teachers who responded to moral transgressions with statements focusing on the effects of acts. Rated lower were teachers who responded with statements of school rules or normative expectations. Rated lowest were teachers who used simple commands.

As one would expect, students rated highest those teachers who responded to breaches of convention with rule statements, or evaluations of acts as deviant, and rated lower those teachers who responded to such transgressions in terms of their effects on others. As with moral transgressions, the use of simple commands was rated the least adequate.

This research suggests that students attend to the informational content of teacher responses to transgressions. It also suggests that the domain of teacher responses to transgression may prove to be an important variable for future studies of the relations between classroom management techniques and social development in children.

The universal nature of morality

The philosopher Alasdair MacIntyre has characterized the current historical period as one of moral dissention. Yet in the midst of this moral Babel, the majority of parents expect schools to contribute to moral development of children. The research indicates that morality is centered on a set of universal concerns for justice, fairness, and human welfare that are available even to young children. Those findings provide a basis for moral education that is both nonindoctrinative and nonrelativistic.

The universal and prescriptive nature of morality means that educators can do more than merely clarify student values. At the same time, the developmental and constructivist basis of moral knowledge is commensurate with interactive rather than directive educational practices.

A SOCIAL DOMAIN ANALYSIS OF MORAL DEVELOPMENT

Although socialization theorists have viewed moral internalization as stemming primarily from parents' influence on children through their parenting practices, structural-developmental theorists generally have proposed that the hierarchical nature of parent-child relationships constrains children's moral development. This has led to a predominant focus on the formative role of peers and social institutions such as schools in moral reasoning development and a relative neglect of the role of the family.

According to social domain theory, children construct different forms of social knowledge, including morality as well as other types of social knowledge, through their social experiences with adults (parents, teachers, other adults), peers, and siblings. In keeping with the focus of this special issue, this article focuses primarily on moral development. But to understand social domain theory, morality must be described in the context of, and as distinct from, other social-cognitive domains. Therefore, in the following sections, the broader framework of social knowledge domains is described briefly.

Then, two propositions about the role of parents are elaborated in subsequent sections. First, it is proposed that the affective nature of parents' interactions may facilitate childrenís moral development, and specific affective mechanisms are described. Second, it is proposed that cognitive aspects of parents' interactions also facilitate children's moral development; the importance of providing domain-specific feedback regarding the nature of childrenís social interactions is discussed.

Domains of social knowledge

According to social domain theory, the social world is not unitary. Children have qualitatively different social interactions that lead to the construction of different types of social knowledge systems, or domains of social knowledge. Thus, children's thinking about and actions in the social world are characterized by heterogeneity and the coexistence of different social orientations, motivations, and goals.

Parents are concerned with ensuring children's welfare, protecting their rights, and helping children learn how they ought to relate to others. According to social domain theory, these concerns are all aspects of the moral domain. Morality pertains to the system of rules that regulates the social interactions and social relationships of individuals within societies and is based on concepts of welfare, trust, justice, and rights.

Morality is defined here as individuals' prescriptive understanding of how individuals ought to behave towards each other. Moral judgements are proposed to be obligatory, universalizable, unalterable, impersonal, and determined by criteria other than agreement, consensus, or institutional convention.

Although morality is constructed from children's reciprocal social interactions, not all social concepts are moral. Parents are also concerned with maintaining appropriate social behaviour and facilitating the smooth and efficient functioning of social interactions. According to social domain theory, these concerns are aspects of individuals' understanding of social systems, social organizations, and social conventions, which are viewed as conceptually and developmentally distinct from an understanding of morality.

Social conventions have been defined as the arbitrary, consensually determined rules, uniformities, and behaviours that coordinate the interactions of individuals within social systems and a set of expectations regarding appropriate behaviour. Conventions are hypothesized to be alterable, contextually relative, and contingent on the rules and dictates of authority. Social interactions also may require an understanding of self and others as psychological systems. The psychological domain pertains to an understanding of self, identity, personality, and attributions regarding the causes of oneís own and othersí behaviour. Two aspects of the psychological domain have been distinguished. Prudential issues pertain to harm to the self, safety, comfort, and health. Like moral rules, prudential rules regulate acts that have physical consequences to persons. Whereas morality pertains to interactions among people, prudence pertains to acts that have immediate and negative consequences to the self.

Personal issues pertain only to the actor and fall beyond the realm of conventional regulation and moral concern. Personal issues entail preference and choice pertaining to such issues as friends or activities, the state of one's body, and privacy. Personal issues are an aspect of the self that forms the boundary between the self and the social world, and these boundaries may be actively negotiated within families. Maintaining an arena of personal discretion is seen as representing an important aspect of the individualís autonomy or distinctiveness from others. Traditional structural-developmental theories have described moral development as a process of increasing differentiation between moral and nonmoral concepts, such as convention, prudence, and pragmatics. Social domain theory departs from this view by proposing that the moral, conventional, and psychological domains are separate, self-regulating developmental systems that are not developmentally ordered. Rather, they are hypothesized to coexist from early ages on, although concepts in each domain are seen to change qualitatively with age. A great deal of research has indicated that from early childhood through late adolescence, children distinguish the domains using the theoretical criteria outlined above. Although most of the available research has focused on white, middle-class children, there is a growing body of research in a range of cultures, as well as research on children from varying social classes, religions, and ethnicities within the United States that provides broad support for these theoretical distinctions.

Most of the theorizing from the social domain perspective has focused on children's development. A corollary assumption, however, is that parents' understanding of social rules, their child-rearing goals, and their views of and responses to children's transgressions likewise are differentiated by conceptual domain. Evidence for this assertion comes from a number of studies of adult and child responses to transgressions, which indicates that parents respond differentially to transgressions in different domains, as well as from research indicating that parents' choice of discipline strategy depends on the nature of the misdeed.

Experiential Origins of Morality

Social domain theory focuses on children's active construction of knowledge from varied social experiences and different interaction partners, including parents as well as peers. Numerous studies have documented that young children have ample social experiences with physical and psychological harm, fair distribution, and the violation of rights through their experiences of rules, rule violations, misdeeds, and peer conflicts. These types of experiences are hypothesized to lead to the construction of moral concepts. More specifically, children's experiences as participants in moral conflicts and as victims of and observers to moral transgressions lead to the construction of abstract notions of fair and unfair, right and wrong.

Children generate an understanding of the wrongness of moral conflicts and rule violations from their experiences of the intrinsic features of those acts, such as their harm or unfairness. The proposition that social interactions form the experiential basis for the development of social knowledge has been tested by examining responses to childrenís naturally occurring social interactions. Researchers have looked for systematic patterns of social interactions that parallel hypothesized distinctions in social concepts. Correspondences between social interactions and social judgements are seen as demonstrating that social interactions provide the experiential basis for the construction of social knowledge.

The results of numerous observational studies are consistent with Piaget in demonstrating that children's conflicts over moral issues such as object possession (taking a toy or not sharing), rights, turn-taking, hurting, aggression, psychological harm (such as teasing and name-calling), and unkindness —all moral issues — do occur primarily in interactions with peers, often in free-play settings. Furthermore, as Dunn and her colleagues have high-lighted, moral conflicts and interactions frequently arise between siblings, whereas the available research has demonstrated that moral conflicts are relatively infrequent between parents and children.

Moral conflicts are often resolved without adult intervention, leading some researchers to propose that peer conflicts play a positive role in children's moral development. Research on naturally occurring social interactions among toddlers and school-age children demonstrates that children (primarily the victims) respond to moral transgressions with statements of injury or loss, emotional reactions, and evaluations of rights, as well as with physical retaliation and commands to cease the offending behaviour. When adults do respond to moral breaches and conflicts, however, the research indicates that mothers (as well as teachers) typically focus on requests to take the victim's perspective and evaluations of rights. As elaborated in the following sections, both the affective context of these interactions and the cognitive features of parents' responses are important in the construction of more mature moral concepts.

Affect may inform moral development in two ways. First, moral conflicts and misdeeds occur in the context of the broader affective climate of parent-child relations. A great deal of research suggests that the quality of the parent-child bond and the degree of warmth in the parent-child relationship affect many different facets of children's development. Indeed, one of the most consistent (and least anticipated) findings from research examining the family interactions that facilitate Kohlbergian moral reasoning stages is that the affective components of those interactions, such as parental warmth, involvement, and support, are related to moral reasoning development. Therefore, a warm, supportive bond between parents and children may enhance the likelihood that children are motivated to listen to and respond to parental messages.

Second, affective reactions are an inseparable aspect of children's experiences of transgressions, and social interactions regarding moral rules, rule violations, and conflicts may be highly affectively charged. Parental affective reactions, in conjunction with reasoning, may facilitate childrenís understanding and encoding of moral and social rules. Research by Arsenio has shown that children may employ affective responses to transgressions to understand, differentiate, and remember moral and social events.

Indeed, previous research indicates that maternal responses to moral transgressions accompanied by intense feelings leads to greater reparation among children than when cognitive messages are not so embellished. Parents are more likely to employ negative affect, including dramatizations of distress and greater anger in response to moral than other transgressions. Such affective responses, used in conjunction with explanations that focus on others' welfare and rights, may increase the effectiveness of reasoning because it helps focus children on the harm or injustice they caused.

However, research also indicates that there are optimal levels of affective arousal. Too much anger may be too negatively arousing and therefore may inhibit children's focus on others' feelings. For instance, a great deal of recent work on vicarious emotional arousal has indicated that too much emotional arousal leads to self-oriented, aversive emotional reactions rather than other-oriented reactions such as sympathy. The assertion that affect may be an important component of moral development is consistent with Hoffman's proposal that witnessing another individual in distress leads to empathic arousal. However, Hoffman has proposed a developmental sequence wherein empathy is transformed with age. In contrast, the view articulated here is that children's affective experiences are part of and influence children's understanding and encoding of moral transgressions, but that conceptual knowledge, not emotional responses, is transformed with age.

Cognitive aspects of parents' interactions

There is also an important cognitive component to parents' interactions with their children that may facilitate children's moral development. Research indicates that children may obtain information about transgressions from varied sources, including observations and direct experiences with moral transgressions. However, direct experiences are not the only sources of moral and social development, nor are they always the most desirable or effective source. In the social domain view, parents' communications with their children are one aspect of children's social experiences that may be used in the construction of moral knowledge. By explaining the reasons for rules and responding appropriately to moral violations, parents can facilitate moral development by stimulating children to think reflectively about their actions.

This assertion implies that the more explicit parents are about the nature of the event and why a behaviour is expected or a misdeed is wrong, the more effective such messages might be, particularly for young children. This suggests, in turn, that reasoning, explanations, and rationales will be more effective than other types of disciplinary strategies in facilitating children's moral development, as well as development in other domains. Although a great deal of developmental research has advocated the use of reasoning as a disciplinary strategy, others have asserted that reasoning is a broad and poorly defined category. The social domain view adds specificity to our understanding of reasoning as an effective parenting practice by suggesting that reasoning will be effective only if it is coordinated with the domain of the act under consideration, because only such explanations would provide the child with domain-relevant information.

More specifically, to effectively facilitate moral development, explanations of moral rules and responses to moral violations need to highlight the consequences of the acts for others' rights and welfare. Support for this assertion has been found in previous research, which indicates that parental reasoning, and in particular, other-oriented reasoning, is associated with greater moral internalization and the development of concern for others, as well as greater resistance to temptation. Observational studies of responses to transgressions indicate that mothers (and other adults) naturally coordinate their explanations with the nature of the misdeed.

They rarely focus on the intrinsic consequences of acts for others (a moral concern) in response to conventional events, nor do they reason about social order (a conventional concern) in response to moral transgressions. Considered alone, these findings do not definitively support the assertion that responses that are coordinated with the domain of the transgression are perceived as more appropriate by children. However, several experimental studies have tested this proposition more explicitly.

The results of several studies suggest that children actively evaluate social messages in terms of their domain appropriateness and reject messages that are domain inappropriate and inconsistent with the nature of the event. In one study, children evaluated teacher responses to moral and conventional transgressions that were concordant, discordant, or undifferentiated with respect to the domain of the transgression. For instance, children evaluated statements focusing on the intrinsic features of acts in response to moral or conventional transgressions.

Conversely, they evaluated statements indicating that the act was creating disorder in response to moral transgressions or conventional transgressions (domain-appropriate). Children rated domain-appropriate teacher responses (and the teachers themselves) more favorably than domain inappropriate or domain-undifferentiated teacher responses (and teachers). Similar findings were obtained in a more recent study of preschool childrenís evaluations of teacher responses to peer conflicts and replicated in a study of Japanese preschoolers in Tokyo. Therefore, these studies indicate that across ages, children make prescriptive judgements about adults as social agents and evaluate adult messages in terms of their domain appropriateness.

Social domain theory also suggests that effective parental reasoning needs to consider the child's developmental status. At the most basic level, parental reasoning may not be effective until young children develop the verbal capacities to comprehend such messages. Studies suggest that during the second year of life, parents shift from employing physical strategies for intervening in children's transgressions to employing verbal strategies. These findings suggest that parents naturally respond to developmental changes in childrenís comprehension, but they also may reflect parents' increasing expectations for morally and conventionally appropriate behaviour.

Structural-developmentalists have provided evidence that reasoning slightly above the childís own level stimulates development, although research has varied as to the degree of discrepancy that is optimal. The findings suggest that parents' messages need to be somewhat more sophisticated than children's level of understanding, but not so much above that children will assimilate parental messages to their own level. Research also indicates that parents typically do accommodate their level of reasoning to their childís level when reasoning about actual moral dilemmas in their children's lives.

These findings and the research reviewed previously on reasoning provide an additional explanation for the consistent associations found between authoritative parenting and moral internalization. Recent research indicates that authoritative, authoritarian, and permissive parents differ in the domain appropriateness of their social judgements. In contrast to other parents, authoritarian parents of adolescents were found to moralize social-conventional acts in their judgements and justifications; for instance, they treated conventional transgressions such as cursing and putting elbows on the table as prescriptive acts that were obligatory and universally wrong.

Authoritarian parents also were more likely than other parents to treat personal issues (such as choice of clothes and hairstyle and how to spend allowance money) and friendship issues (such as choice of friends) as conventional and legitimately subject to their authority (rather than as personal and up to the child). Taken together findings are consistent with Baumrindís description of authoritarian parents as moralizing, overintrusive (especially in terms of the child's personal domain), and valuing obedience as a virtue. Permissive parents, in contrast, were more likely than other parents to construct broad boundaries of personal discretion for their children and treat a range of issues, including personal, prudential, and friendship issues as personal for the child.

Only authoritative parents drew clear boundaries between moral, conventional, and personal issues in ways that were consistent with domain-theoretical expectations. These parents clearly distinguished moral and conventional regulations, but they also were responsive to the child's need for an arena of personal control and choice, treating personal issues as adolescents' personal prerogatives. At the same time, they treated friendship and multifaceted issues, defined as issues containing both conventional and personal components (such as the child's room, which can be seen as either the child's personal territory or part of the household) as conventionally regulated. These findings are consistent with Baumrind's assertion that authoritative parents negotiate more with their children, but they also suggest that parents negotiate primarily over personal issues.

Social domain theory also accounts for the consistent finding that power assertion is associated with poorer moral internalization. Some forms of power assertion, such as commands, statements of rules, references to parental authority, and some types of sanctions may be ineffective in inhibiting antisocial behaviour or facilitating moral development simply because they fail to communicate the reasons for the rule or prohibition. This may explain why power assertion successfully terminates unwanted behaviour and induces short-term compliance but does not facilitate moral maturity. More extreme forms of power assertion, for instance, responses that are extremely negative, angry, or coercive, may scare the child and threaten the childís sense of security, thereby hindering the child's moral development.

Parent-child relations also may influence children's social understanding in more subtle ways. As others have noted, families consist of complex social arrangements that entail hierarchical social roles and power relationships. In most families, there are gender inequalities in the distribution of power, the way resources are allocated, and how opportunities are encouraged or discouraged. Children do not necessarily accept these structural arrangements as given. An emerging body of research suggests that children and adults also construct notions of the fairness of different social arrangements and that these evaluations depend on oneís position in the social hierarchy.

Those in more subordinate roles, who may experience greater restrictions in their choices and freedoms as a function of their social position, tend to evaluate social practices as more unfair than do those in more dominant positions, who may be accorded greater entitlements and choices. Thus, children receive many tacit social messages that may be used to construct moral knowledge. Furthermore, the results indicate that individuals do not unquestioningly accept the social messages they receive.

To summarize, in prohibiting actions, giving instructions, and responding to transgressions, parents are an important and, because of their emotional bonds to their children, valued source of children's social experiences that lead to the construction of moral concepts throughout childhood and adolescence. In the view outlined here, parents are not the sole sources of influence on childrenís moral development, nor is morality seen as directly transmitted by parents; moral transgressions and conflicts are seen as originating primarily in interactions with peers and siblings. Rather, parents underscore and amplify the lessons that are constructed from these interactions.

Parents are centrally important by virtue of their concern with their child's development and welfare, their affective relationship and extensive interaction history with their child, and their ability to provide the types of interactions that facilitate moral development. The research reviewed here suggests that parents' responses to children's transgressions and moral disputes and their explanations of the reasons for rules and expectations may facilitate children's moral development.

The proposition that parents' domain appropriate and developmentally sensitive reasoning and explanations helps to promote childrenís moral understanding is consistent with previous research from socialization perspectives but expands on this prior research by providing greater specificity regarding the types of reasons that may effectively stimulate development. Reasoning and explanations must be domain-appropriate to help children focus on the consequences of their actions for others and delivered at a cognitive level that is comprehensible to the child.

This prescription does not mean that effective facilitation of moral development necessarily entails rational discourse devoid of affect. As the research reviewed here demonstrates, affect is an important component of these social interactions. Parents' affective reactions to children's behavior — including negative affect, within reasonable limits — in conjunction with reasoning, may facilitate children's moral development by signaling to children that parents' messages require attention. Although the focus here has been on parenting, it should be clear that the same prescriptions are relevant to school-based moral education curricula. As noted earlier, much of the research discussed here has been conducted on white, middle-class American children, and more research on children from different cultures, as well as children from diverse groups within the United States is needed. The social judgments of individuals within and across cultures are heterogeneous and contain diverse social orientations that may involve conflicting concerns with justice, interpersonal obligations, conventions, autonomy, personal choice, and personal entitlements. Research needs to examine how these different social concepts are applied in different social and societal arrangements.

LIMITATIONS OF THE MORAL SELF CONSTRUCT

Accounting for moral agency has proven to be a complex and difficult problem for moral psychology. How is it that we move from knowing right from wrong to acting in relation to that moral understanding? Are differences in the tendencies to engage in moral action a function of differences in kinds of people, or differences in kinds of knowledge that people have? Can we even successfully pose such a dichotomy? What we hope to accomplish within this next hour is to examine recent attempts to resolve these questions through work that is being done on what is referred to as the "moral self."

The effort to define the moral self, and related work on moral identity has been offered as a counterpoint to more traditional conceptions of moral agency framed in terms of personal character and moral virtue.

This structuralist alternative to these traditional approaches has its roots in Kohlberg's devastating critique of traditional character education, and his subsequent account of moral development. Therefore, to get us started, let's look at the notions of moral virtue and character, and the response to virtue theory offered by Kohlberg's structuralist moral theory.

Aristotle and Virtue

Socrates, we are told, held the view that, "nobody does wrong willingly: we choose the lesser good only as a result of ignorance". Aristotle, in contrast, rejected this view as simply inconsistent with the phenomena. On Aristotle's account, good and right action are not simply a question of epistemology, but result from being a particular kind of person for whom virtuous conduct is part and parcel of the person's very being. Essentially all contemporary western virtue theories are grounded in Aristotle's viewpoint.

Aristotle's approach to ethics begins not with the question of what it means to act morally, but with the more general question, "What does it mean to lead a good life?" Aristotle held that all things in nature are always moving toward a flourishing of their own nature. That is to say, that all living things have a telos. Trees grow up to be grown up trees. The business of leading a good life is to move toward the human telos and to achieve eudaimonia or a flourishing With respect to ethics, the process of flourishing entails the gradual development of virtues, or personal characteristics that will support ethical conduct. In youth, this process involves the building up of habits that in time translate into ways of being that constitute virtuous conduct.

Because Aristotle wrote so long ago, and because most of his surviving works are in the form of lecture notes, rather than the equivalents of articles or books, his ideas have become a sort of Rorschach of the given time period. Aristotle's notion of habit, and his emphasis on the phenomenological, have led to an assimilation of his positions to logical positivism and behaviorist theories of learning and development. His notion of human flourishing has been adopted by utilitarians as in support of the pursuit of happiness, and an ethics based on outcomes.

Modern translators of his work, such as Nussbaum, have taken issue with these various assimilations. On Nussbaum's reading, the child according to Aristotle, is not simply a creature who is causally affected and manipulated, but an active, cognitive being that responds selectively, and whose actions are explained by his own view of things. Thus, Aristotle's approach to habit formation has more in common with such notions as the construction of cognitive schemata than it does with behaviorist notions of association.

This non-behaviorist view of habituation allows for Aristotle to propose a developmental progression in which such habits become subsumed within reasoned judgment. In terms of ethics, the core or master virtue is justice, around which the other virtues serve supporting roles. The development of the virtuous person, then, involves the cultivation of the right set of habits , ethical values, and a conception of the good human life as the harmonious pursuit of these. Such a person will be "concerned about friendship, justice, courage, moderation and generosity; his desires will be formed in accordance with these concerns; and he will derive from this internalized conception of value many ongoing guidelines for action, pointers as to what to look for in a particular situation". Because Aristotle perceived these values and commitments to be trans-situational, he took them to be what the person is in and of himself.

Kohlberg's critique of virtue theory was not aimed directly at Aristotle, but at American traditional character education. The traditional view combined elements of Aristotle's conception of virtue with behaviorist and social learning theory conceptions of socialization. Kohlberg's critique responded to both elements of traditional character education on four main points. First, Kohlberg established that the definition of what counts as a virtue varies as a function of cultural and historical setting.

A humorous updating of this critique has been offered by Daniel Lapsley who compared the checklist of virtues from his own elementary school report card, against the list of 23 virtues to be used as core values in character education classes, that had been compiled in 1988 by The Panel on Moral Education of the American Association for Curriculum Development

(ASCD). The only virtue that overlapped between the two lists was "courtesy." In addition, the list compiled by the ASCD panel left out 9 of the 11 values in "The Children's Morality Code," an earlier effort to guide teachers similar to the ASCD list published in 1924 by W. J. Hutchins.

The second issue raised by Kohlberg was the empirical evidence provided by Hartshorne and May's research in the late 1920s and early 1930s challenging the assumption that there were such things as character traits. This carefully done series of studies demonstrated convincingly that whether or not a person engaged in a particular form of conduct presumed to be consistent or inconsistent with a particular character trait or virtue depended upon the context.

Faced with the evidence from their series of studies, Hartshorne and May were left to conclude that there was no such thing as character. For example, they concluded there were no people with the character trait of honesty. People were honest in some situation, and dishonest in others. These findings of Hartshorne and May were subsequently buttressed by the research conducted in the second half of the century on the related notion of personality traits. The results of these studies led researchers to concluded that people cannot be accurately described in terms of stable and general personality traits, since people tend to exhibit different and seemingly contradictory aspects of themselves in different contexts. In place of trait theories, contemporary personality psychologists tend to view personality as something one does in particular settings, rather than as something one has independent of context.

Kohlberg's third point builds from these conclusions about personality and virtue. The application of virtues always occurs in context, thus requiring an application of judgment not only as to which virtue is applicable, but often to determine which of two or more competing virtues should hold sway. Actually, this contextual aspect of the application of virtue was anticipated by Aristotle who saw the application of virtue as entailing the use of practical wisdom. Kohlberg's insight into this issue was to recognize that moral virtue essentially reduces itself to the structures of reasoning that people employ to resolve moral situations.

Kohlberg's final point is that moral reason does not emerge spontaneously as a result of environmentally evoked hard wired modules or Platonic forms, nor is the capacity for moral reasoning the result of the gradual building up of habits, but rather the construction and reconstruction of forms of understanding that emerge through processes of cognitive equilibration as outlined within Piaget's genetic epistemology.

Kohlberg's alternative to the morality of personal virtue is his six stage theory of moral development. The brilliance of Kohlberg's theory is that it offers simultaneous resolution to nearly every conundrum faced by moral psychology. Kohlberg's structuralist theory accounts for the contextual variation in people's morality through the application of moral reasoning. Moral maturity is understood as the progressive development of more morally adequate forms of moral judgment.

The invariance of personal virtue is replaced by the contextual invariance of cognitive structure, and the telos of eudaimonia or human flourishing is replaced by the telos of equilibration. This is not say that Kohlberg was opposed to the notion of the development of personal goals and projects as a part of self actualization. It was that Kohlberg did not see how one could define that aspect of personal development in any but the most individual of ways, and that such aspects of personal growth were not in and of themselves aspects of morality.

In essence Kohlberg agreed with the philosopher William Frankena's distinct between leading the "good life" in the Aristotelian sense of flourishing, and leading a life that is good in an objectively moral sense. In what is one of the most important of his works, Kohlberg argues in his "Is to ought" paper that the process of equilibration of structures of moral thought moves inevitably toward a philosophically defensible moral ought. In this, Kohlberg is in agreement with the notion that there is but one moral virtue, and that is the virtue of justice. Thus, he ends up in alignment with Socrates view that to know the good is to do the good.

Inconsistencies, contradictions and heterogeneity

Unfortunately, Kohlberg's theory does not fit the phenomena. Kohlberg acknowledged early on that there were certain minor contradictions with his theory regarding the binding nature of stage six. He mentions in some of his early work the well known contradiction between the principled moral positions of Thomas Jefferson, and his relationship with his slave, Sally Hemmings.

Kohlberg explains this contradiction as evidence that persons knowing what is morally right may not have the will to act on that knowledge if they are under great social pressure. Kohlberg saw this as particularly the case when a person takes a moral stand at variance with generally held social convention. Kohlberg dealt with this type of contradiction by invoking the construct of "ego strength" - a psychological notion quite divergent from his structuralism.

The problem of social pressure came up again in the results of Milgram studies on authority and social conformity when it was found that a portion of subjects judged to be stage six moral reasoners were nonetheless willing to go along with social authority and continued to shock the supposed "learner" in the study to the point where the shocks caused great pain and discomfort and posed physical danger to the person supposedly receiving the shocks. However, the fact that any post-conventional reasoners went along with the authority would seem to be a problem for the theory. Moreover, the fact that a considerable number of people at lower developmental stages resisted the authority, suggested that personal features other than moral stage may have been involved in guiding people's behavior.

Gus Blasi, provided the first comprehensive review of the relationship between moral stage and behavior that looked not simply at post-conventional reasoning but at the entire developmental progression. Blasi's review concluded that there was in fact a general trend for moral behavior to be associated with developmental stage; that in fact, people at higher stages of development were less likely to engage in various forms of moral misconduct than were people at lower stages. This was particularly the case if one looked at forms of behavior that had moral consequences for the welfare of others.

Nonetheless, the power of the association was far less than perfect, and suggested that other factors beyond moral judgment, as assessed by Kohlberg's stages, were involved in generating moral actions. These results led some followers of Kohlberg to generate multi-factor models of moral reasoning. With some variation in the exact number of steps, a distinction is drawn in these models between the deontic evaluation of the morally right thing to do, and evaluation of whether or the moral judgment, once made, poses a responsibility for action upon the person. In these formulations, then, Kohlberg stage accounts for the judgment of moral right and wrong, while some other factor accounts for the actual judgment that one is personally responsible to act in a manner consistent with that deontic moral judgment.

Moral self/identity

It was Blasi who presented the first comprehensive review of the judgment-action research on Kohlberg's stage theory. It was also Blasi who offered the first effort to fill in the perceived missing step between moral judgment and action by bringing in the connection to the moral self, and more particularly to moral identity. Blasi's approach builds from Erikson's work on identity formation, but is most heavily influenced by Loevenger's theory of ego development. Loevenger's theory can be read as providing for a compatible bridge to Kohlberg in being constructivist and transformational, rather than logical positivist and behavioral.

Employing Loevinger as a starting point, Blasi began to look at the possibility that the link between moral judgment and action lie in the degree to which morality and moral concerns were integrated into the person's sense of self. The basic idea here is that from moral identity derives a psychological need to make one's actions consistent with one's ideals. Thus, in Blasi's words, "self-consistency is the motivational spring of moral action". In a similar vein, Clark Power redefines character as the specifically moral dimensions of self. Like Blasi, Power states that the motive for moral action is not simply the direct result of knowing "the good", but from the desire to act in ways that are consistent with one's own sense of self as a moral being. As Power puts it, "Individuals may undertake a particular course of action, even at some cost, because they want to become or remain a certain kind of person".

In contrast with the traditional character construct, the approach taken by Blasi, and joined now by Anne Colby & Bill Damon, Dan Hart, Monika Keller & Wolgang Edelstein, Gil Noam, and Clark Power "does not attempt to replace moral ideas with a set of non cognitive personality characteristics: it sees personal identity as operating jointly with reason and truth in providing motives for action". Thus, one's moral "character" is not something divorced from moral cognition, and the complexity that it entails. General issues in the construction of self. While the notion of the moral self has its roots in Blasi's work, cognitive theories of moral identity are not constrained by Loevenger's theory of ego development. If we look more broadly at cognitive accounts of self, we see that the construction of personal identity is itself multifaceted, incorporating values and social roles from a number of contexts. Research on the development of children's conceptions of self provides evidence that with age, children construct increasingly differentiated notions of themselves as actors within different contexts or domains.

These differentiated constructs emerge as a result of children's efforts to interpret their differential competence, and involvement in various areas of activity (academic, making friends) and a corresponding tendency with age to assign meaning to those levels of competence and commitment. Harter has suggested that development of self-concepts may very well entail a reiterative process whereby a child's initial attempts to construct an integrated notion of self (e.g., in terms of characteristic behaviors) is followed by a period of differentiation (e.g., good at some things, bad at others).

These differentiated general descriptions are then incorporated within a higher level of integration (e.g., general traits), which are then subsequently differentiated. This process eventuates at the most advanced levels of development in a conceptualization of self in multidimensional and contextual terms. The inherent complexity of self-definition has its counterpart in efforts at self-evaluation. Current evidence, supports the proposition that we construct both a general sense of self-worth, and domain-specific evaluations of our own competence. This in turn suggests that it is possible for us to have a positive view of ourselves, while still having a sense that we are not very good in a particular area of performance. In other words, it may be that we can feel good about ourselves if those areas of performance in which we are not so great, are not terribly important to who we are.

As a way of beginning to think about how this might apply to the area of morality, let's look for a moment, by way of analogy, at the highly researched area of how children apply their sense of self to academic performance. It turns out that there is little evidence to suggest that a students' view of themselves in terms of academic capabilities (academic self-esteem) is necessarily tied to students' general sense of self-worth. For students for whom school matters, performance in school has a relation to the students' self esteem. For those for whom school matters little, their academic performance has little relationship to their more general sense of self esteem.

Those of you in the audience with teenagers already knew this without hearing the results of research. The question is whether something like this can be operating with respect to morality. If we move from the area of academics back to the issue of the moral self, one can see both parallels and differences. One significant difference is that people aren't as free to discount their moral selves as they are to discount other aspects of their personal endeavors such as their performance in mathematics, or the dance floor.

This is because morality is inherent in human interaction, and engages us in binding "objective" ways. Perhaps, however, the objective or binding nature of morality may be overstated as a basis for presuming its centrality in the construction of personal identity. Whether one attends to the moral implications of events may be more compelling than whether one develops skill as a dancer, but it may not attain the same degree of salience or centrality for everyone. There is no reason to assume that the basic process of constructing the moral aspect of self is fundamentally different from the construction of other aspects of personal identity. Thus we should expect interpersonal variations in the connection between self and morality.

This assumption of interpersonal variation in moral identity has not been extensively researched. However, recent work by Agusto Blasi and his colleagues has provided evidence that some individuals let moral notions penetrate to the essence and core of what and who they are, while others construct their central defining features of self in other ways. This is not to say that morality is somehow absent from many people, but rather that the moral aspects of self may be subjectively experienced in different ways Blasi puts it this way, "...several individuals may see morality as essential to their sense of self, of who they are. For some of them, however, moral ideals and demands happen to be there, a given nature over which they feel little control. In this case moral ideals exist next to other characteristics, all equally important because they are there. Others instead relate to their moral ideals as being personally chosen over other ideals or demands, sense their fragility, and feel responsible to protect them and thus to protect their sense of self."

Morality and the self

This variability in the centrality of morality within one's personal identity is of interest for the present discussion only if there is also evidence that it matters for moral action, and that it serves as a bridge between moral judgment and behavior. Here the evidence is less than compelling. What is usually presented as evidence is some association between personal definition, and prosocial conduct. Hart and Fegley, for example, studied the moral identities of a group of inner city adolescents who exhibited a high degree of community service voluntarism, and care for others. These adolescents were identified by community leaders, teachers, and churches as youth who had done such things as organize youth groups, and work in homeless shelters. They and a comparison group of adolescents from the same community were asked to generate a list of all of the important characteristics that they could think of that described themselves as they are in the present, the person they were in the past, the person they dreaded becoming, and they kind of person they would ideally like to become.

What Hart and Fegley assumed was that persons whose actual selves incorporate a subset of their ideal selves will be more driven to realize the goals of the ideal self, than persons whose ideal self and actual self are unrelated. What they discovered in their study was in line with that hypothesis. Two thirds of the adolescents high on voluntarism and care, and less than a third of the comparison adolescents exhibited overlap between the characteristics of their actual and ideal selves. Moreover, there was very little correlation between these adolescents' moral stage, as measured within the Kohlberg framework, and their involvement in community service.

A second, widely cited illustration of the connection between moral self and conduct is Colby and Damon's study of moral exemplars as recounted in their book "Some do care." What they report are a series of biographical sketches which purport to demonstrate that the decision to become active in community service, or civil rights activities are linked to the ways in which these individuals constructed their own personal identities. As with the Hart and Fegley study, Colby and Damon report that their morally exemplary people ranged widely in their Kohlbergian stage of moral development from lower conventional stages to post-conventional. These two studies, and other similar ones lead one to the conclusion that moral development seems to matter little when it comes to moral action, and that what does matter are the qualities of the person. But there are several problems with such a conclusion. First, it is not clear that the actions described constitute moral conduct. Second, one can come to moral conclusions at any Kohlbergian stage of moral development. Colby and Damon recognize this, but do not provide convincing evidence whether there is or is not a linkage between the moral decisions of the person's they studied, their self definitions, and their actions.

Actually, the only work that we know of that has tried to systematically explore the relationship between moral identity and motivation for moral action has been done by Blasi and his colleagues, and their findings and interpretations are much more nuanced that reported in most other research. Blasi and Glodis examined whether people who define morality as a central part of their personal identity experience a sense of "personal betrayal" when they act in opposition to those moral values.

They hypothesized that such a sense of personal betrayal would be more evident in person's whose sense of identity stemmed from their own active efforts at becoming the person they were, than among persons whose identity emerged from a relatively passive, unreflective acceptance of themselves. In their study, they asked 30 women to indicate an ideal that they considered to be very important to their sense of self, one that she cared deeply about, and to which she was deeply committed. Among the ideals listed were: friendship, caring for others, morality and justice, self-reliance, and improving one's mind and knowledge. Six to ten weeks later, each of the women was presented with a story in which a fictional character chooses a course of action advantageous financially and career-wise, but which compromised her ideals. The compromised ideal in each case was the one listed by the subject as a central value in her earlier interview.

What Blasi and Glodis found was that some of their subjects tended not to see the situation as relevant to their ideals. Instead they focused on the pragmatic consequences of the decision presented in the scenario, and expressed feelings of satisfaction with the protagonist's pragmatic choice. Others, on the other hand, saw the situation as entailing a serious contradiction of their ideals, and expressed such feelings as shame, guilt and depression over the protagonist's choice to violate those ideals. The feelings expressed by subjects in the study were a function of whether their own sense of identity was one for which they were actively involved.

Subjects whose ideals were not experienced as passively received from outside influences, but rather as central concerns to be pursued were those who reported the most distress in response to the scenario entailing a contradiction or betrayal of those ideals. Now it is important to note that in discussing their findings, Blasi and Glodis avoid claiming that it is essential for a person to have constructed a moral identity of this sort in order for someone to act in morally consonant ways.

They recognize that morality may be viewed as important for other reasons, such as social approval, or simply out of concerns for the objective consequences of actions. The latter, of course, is a way of saying that individuals might act morally simply for moral reasons. They also suggest that such intense personal involvement may not be implicated in many day-to-day moral interactions that don't entail dilemmas pitting one's pragmatic self interests against the needs of someone else. The authors suggest that one's personal identity may only become at stake in cases requiring substantial subordination of other motives.

Of course, whether one views such situations as placing the self at risk, are a function of whether morality exists as an ideal central to one's self definition. Blasi asserts that moral and other ideals are chosen as core values because they are understood to be important. As Blasi puts it, "to some extent personality is shaped by what one knows to be worthy of education and commitment". Blasi's work is provocative in that it may be seen as linking Aristotelian notions of eudaimonia to the work that has been done on moral cognition. It also implies that constructivist assumptions of how one generates moral knowledge are also important to the active construction of the moral self, and consequent moral responsibility, and character. The moral self and moral identity leaves open a set of important and as yet unanswered questions:

1. It does not resolve the question of moral judgment. It simply pushes things back one step. One's structures of moral judgment do not result in action, but rather one's perceptions of whether or not an action comports with one's sense of self.

2. It reduces questions of morality from questions about one's obligations to others through judgments of fairness and human welfare to judgments of whether or not the actor will "feel right" about him or herself. There are, of course, behavioral psychologists who believe that such positive and negative consequences are at the core of all human motivation. From such a psychological premise, all morality is reduced to instrumentalism, and ethical egoism.

3. It is reductionistic and mechanist by reducing all complex contextualized moral judgments to the simple evaluation

of whether the action is or is not consistent with one's sense of self.

4. It comes very close to adding a "homunculus" on the scene. "Self" is nearly reified. It is the "ghost in the machine" to borrow from Gilbert Ryle, - a sort of moral Mini-me - that actually makes the decisions after whatever other cognitive mechanisms get finished.
5. Some versions commit the nominal fallacy of naming a phenomenon and thereby claiming to explain it.

Contextualist theory of moral cognition

What we want to propose is that the shortcomings of present efforts to integrate some account of personal agency, and perhaps self and identity with moral judgment can be overcome if we let go of Kohlberg's account of moral development, and move toward a more contextualized structuralism, and a more contextualized view of moral identity. Kohlberg's resolution of the shortcomings of classical views of character formation, bound up all forms of judgments of social right and wrong within a single developmental system which moved progressively to a point where morality triumphs over convention, personal interest, and pragmatics. What we have come to realize is that what Kohlberg treated as a single structural system was in fact several systems, or domains of social judgment, of which morality was one. We now have extensive evidence that concepts of morality center around issues of fairness and human welfare, and that they emerge as distinct from conceptions of societal convention at very early ages. Moreover, both morality and convention are distinct from a third conceptual framework concerning issue of personal prerogative and privacy that we spoke of at the JPS symposium several years ago. Each of these domains: morality, societal convention, and the personal undergoes structural developmental changes with age. Each, however, is a distinct conceptual framework with an independent developmental course and sequence.

We now know that Kohlberg's formulation of moral development captured typical age-related coordinations of moral and non-moral concerns for children and early adolescents, and for adults within modern cultures. What he failed to recognize is that people's moral judgments could be employed in simple situations in the absence of recourse to other social concepts, and that contextualized social judgments by people at all ages, including childhood could be dominated by moral considerations or by non-moral ones. In other words, understanding moral decision making requires a much richer appreciation of how moral and non-moral social factors are evaluated in context.

That social roles blind us to the "objectively" moral elements of the context is not new. Nicholas II, last of the Russian tsars as described by John Lawrence in his history of Russia, conceived it to be his duty and his fate to carry on his shoulders the whole burden of the Russian aristocracy. His duty to his family, to his country, to God were indistinguishable to him. He felt bound unconditionally to his office and by his coronation oath to preserve Russia holy and Orthodox under his absolute rule while he lived, and to hand undiminished powers to his son when he died. To limit his own powers by the acceptance of basic laws that even the tsar must not break, to accept the merest shadow of a constitution or even to appoint a prime minister would be an offense against God and against his own son even more than a political imprudence.

Talk about moral identity! we leave it to you to decide whether or not poor Tsar Nicholas was a person of character. And we can take this a bit further. All of us lead lives that are multifaceted. We are parents, spouses, children, teachers, researchers, scholars of different sorts. Some of us are community volunteers, some are not. each of these role relationships places different demands upon us that have different mixtures of moral and non-moral elements.

The self-same person, to use Michael Chandler's phrase, can appear to employ morality in inconsistent ways across these contexts. This was the very essence of Hartshorne and May's discoveries. And, what are we to make of this? Has our moral identity shifted? Or, is it the case that as the self-same person the salience of morality shifts with the context?

Now at this point, we can begin to hear the chorus of concern that a contextualist structuralist account of moral development and moral reasoning is relativistic. Well, yes, it is in the sense that an honest moral psychology does not presume that morality is always prior to non-moral concerns. However, it is not relativist in its view of the moral, nor in its assumptions about the directionality of individual or social practices when moral concerns are taken into account. Let us take the case of the hierarchical status of women as a case in point.

The moral arguments of the women are not made on the basis of consensual agreement. They are based on non-relativist moral arguments of inequities, harm, and injustices. Those men open to hear the arguments of women are not simply persuaded by the fact that many of the women seem to agree on a particular point, but by the non-arbitrary and non-relativist force of morality itself.

Moral priority and identity

The question for moral psychology is how to account for when we prioritize morality, and when we don't. Whether or not we act on the basis of our moral judgment is a function of whether or not we are attending primarily to the moral aspects of a situation, and we render a moral judgment. There is no second layer to it. Given that morality operates independently of our other social cognitive systems, we can expect morality to guide our actions at any point in development. This is why correlations between moral stage and behavior are often so meaningless. Domain theory unfortunately undoes Kohlberg's unified moral stage telos.

However, domain theory opens up a second possibility that moral reflection is a capacity available in different forms at all points in development, and that people at all points in their social growth can evaluate social situations from a moral point of view. This is not to say that the moral reflections of a typical four year old are the same as those of a typical adult. But, that the capacity to attend to prioritize the moral is available at all ages.

This opens an interesting possibility for the role of self and identity in the construction of one's morality. It has to do with the very nature of moral openness. Whether we are born male or female, tsar or serf will affect our reading of the moral meaning of situations. Within those broad social categories and social roles we also operate as individuals. We are capable of independently assessing the moral meaning of practices and social events. Just as these larger external forces shape our view of things, so also do our own individual biases, opinions, and interests alter our orientation toward the morality of social situations.

Who we are as individuals, and not simply "where we sit" in relation to the social system affects the way in which we read the salience of the moral elements of situations. It is this reading of the moral weighting of the situation that impacts moral action. In this way, we can argue that identity affects our moral actions. Of course, we can and do make decisions in context that we come to regret. We may even engage in actions that shake our belief in ourselves as moral actors. But this can only come after the fact, and does not constitute "moral" motivation.

If self and identity are a matter of connecting up who we were, with who we are, and who we are becoming, then the possibility exists that we can construct notions of ourselves that allow us to be more or less open to changes in our moral orientation - both in a developmental sense - and in terms of the ways in which we frame or attend to the moral and non-moral elements of given situations. It is possible that we can so define ourselves that we freeze our morality in dysfunctional ways.

We have already spoken of tsar Nicholas as an example of someone whose sense of himself so tied him to a conventional moral system that he was unable to respond to the moral contradictions inherent in his own position. But, it can work the other way as well. One can become so focused on a sense of moral outrage and so identified with a moral cause as to become a one-dimensional moral zealot such as the anti-abortion extremists, or the animal rights zealots who in their sense of moral purpose engage in acts of violence in the name of morality.

If instead of adopting a static moral identity, we remain open to the ways in which we attend to moral components of social life, then the possibility exists that we will be open to moral disequilibration. In essence, we can be more or less open to moral self-improvement - not only in the sense of development, but in the ways in which we frame the moral meaning of social events or relationships. When we change those ways in which we orient toward the social world, we change a part of who we are.

The direction of change will generally be toward the moral. That is because the dialectic between moral concerns for fairness and harm to person's, and non-moral considerations such as social hierarchy is not an arbitrary one - so long as we are open to hearing the moral voice in the dialogue. When this occurs we are simultaneously altering how we think morally, and the person in and of himself. They are complementary aspects of one and the same thing. And, perhaps, this is how best to think of moral teleology, and the notion of moral flourishing.

7

Making Education Morally Constructivist

The moral domain is characterised by issues of universal prescriptivity deriving from intrinsic harmfulness. Furthermore moral issues are unalterable in their rightness or wrongness. For example, killing is a moral issue because the ban on killing is applicable to all humans regardless of nationality, race, gender, religion, or ethnicity. It is wrong because it intrinsically robs victims of their mortal existence.

And it is unalterable; i.e., no authority has the power to make killing morally right. The domain of social-conventions is a bit different. It concerns issues that are considered wrong not because of their intrinsic nature, but rather because of social agreement that they are wrong. They are therefore alterable by the appropriate social authorities and only apply to those within the purview of the social agreement. In some cultures, for example, it may be scandalous for an adult male to hold hands with an unmarried, unrelated adult female. In others it would be perfectly acceptable. The same may be said for two adult males holding hands in public as they walk casually down the street. Holding hands does no intrinsic harm, but it can be harmful if there is social agreement banning it.

Without such agreement, it is perfectly acceptable. The critical point is that such social agreement does not make it morally wrong. Therefore, when schools teach social conventions, they must be prepared for moral evaluation of the validity of those conventions, no matter how widely accepted they may be. The personal domain is concerned with those issues which should not be socially regulated; i.e., matters of personal preference and taste.

Schools certainly should not teach children which flavours or colours they ought to prefer. Now it should be clearer that values, for example, may fall into any of these domains. Does values education therefore refer to all values? One should hope not, for as we have just demonstrated, some values should not be socially regulated or indoctrinated.

Does values education refer then to moral and social-conventional values, or only to one or the other? You will find little agreement about this, indeed little discussion of this, in the literature. Yet it is a very important issue. For not only is there a lack of truth in advertising when we offer values education but include different contents in the package, but we need to be concerned about the fact that moral values and social-conventional values need to be educated in different ways, at least in part because they require different justifications. Furthermore, research has demonstrated that very young children, teachers, and very religious individuals, among others, recognise that fact spontaneously in both their actions and their judgements.

Unfortunately, most educators are apparently not aware of this. For example, Lickona titled his book Educating for Character, the first section of the book is "Educating for values and character", and, throughout, the terms "values", "character", "moral values", "moral education", "values education", "moral reasoning", etc. are used seemingly as synonyms and with little definition. Ryan and Lickona, in the opening paragraph of Ryan and McClean's Character development in schools and beyond, use the following pot pourri of terminology:

> Concern for the values and morals of the young is an enduring adult preoccupation. Down through recorded history, this worry about the character of the younger generation is evident. Concern, however, has never been enough to ensure that the young possess the type of character that can sustain the individual and society. Some societies have failed to transmit their values to the young.

Other authors equate non-equivalent terms. Carr suggests that "virtues are values". Others adopt terms merely because of their lay connotations or political effect. William Bennett, former US Secretary of Education, has argued that. The term "values" may suggest that judgments of right and wrong, noble and base, just and unjust, are mere personal preferences, that things are worthwhile only if and insofar as individuals happen to "value" them...

We need to reach for a new term. Because these issues are not matters of mere personal taste, let me propose that we reconsider the enterprise now known as "the teaching of values". Let me suggest that we relabel that enterprise as the effort to help form the character of the young.

Indeed, parallel with Bennett's wishes, the terminology in the United States has shifted from the former preference for "moral education" to the current favouring of "character education", whereas in Scotland the terminology has moved from "moral education" to "values education". Nevertheless in neither country is the issue settled. This is partly due to the continuing existence of factions and to the failure to define terminology.

Even when a term is generally widely accepted, as the term "values" is in Scotland, there is still dissent, as exemplified by the debate between whether we should be doing "values education" or "values in education". Humpty-Dumpty has not only broken into pieces, but we find ourselves unable to agree on the names of the pieces or even what the task is. No wonder the field is so fractionated. There is yet another side to this problem that will be addressed before we move on to attempting the beginnings of a solution.

THE BLIND MEN AND THE ELEPHANT

The parable of the blind men and the elephant attributes the blind men's failure to accurately describe the entirety of the elephant to their physical handicap of a lack of sight. Would that the reasons for social scientists' and educators' failures to describe the entirety of the moral person were so obvious and guiltless. Rather it appears that the theoretical parochialism and arrogance of many of them are the root causes of the problem.

The typical scenario is for various factions to propose diverse competing theories of moral development and moral education which are intended often as solutions to the problems of youth and society. Unfortunately, too much emphasis is placed on the "competing" and not enough on the "solutions". What results is a professional dialogue laden with antagonism, "cheap shots", and rather close-minded competition for the status as the "right answer".

William Perry demonstrated that such a search for the ultimate single right answer reflects a rather immature sense of knowledge. Such a "dualistic" epistemology should be more representative of early adolescent thinking than of high level academic discourse. Yet the field is rife with such perspectives. Asking which theory is right is simply asking the wrong question. Rarely is there simply a choice between a single right theory and a set of wrong theories. Rather, the question should be how best to explain and influence moral growth given all the available knowledge and theoretical perspectives. Such a more dialectical approach makes optimal use of knowledge from all the diverse "camps".

Certainly there are incompatible aspects of some approaches, but that simply makes the task more difficult, not impossible. The challenge is to sift through what each approach has to offer, find the commonalties and adjudicate between the discrepancies. This is a decidedly more productive course of action than the wholesale rejection of seemingly opposing theories, an approach that has unfortunately been so typical of the field.

It is important to note that there are attempts to be more integrative. For example, the single most impressive and successful program in moral education, the Child Development Project in San Ramon, California, is a quite eclectic and wide-ranging approach to child moral development. James Rest was one of the first theorists to attempt a bridging of domains and Lickona is the single most successful writer in the field while integrating Kohlbergian structuralism with character education and a variety of other perspectives, although his rather strident stances on specific cultural issues often precludes some readers from noticing how successfully he has integrated such perspectives.

One way out of this morass is to look for a grand theory that can encompass the major aspects of moral growth and moral education under one conceptual umbrella. Unfortunately such a grand theory is no where to be seen. Teachers tend to ignore theory and focus on the technical aspects of practice. Theorists, as already noted, tend to fall into one or another of various warring camps. To make matters even more difficult, this field actually spans a number of disciplines, most notably psychology, education, philosophy, and theology, and has its roots in quite contrasting philosophical models.

Grand theory is important in part because so many of the failures in the field are due to the failure to build upon sound justifications derived from sound theory. Models instead ignore the fundamental nature of child development or rely upon an unexamined or misguided ethical theory (such as relativism), or fail to distinguish between morality and other social domains, etc.

Until we systematically reflect on the theoretical groundings of our educational work and on the ways in which we can benefit from the work of others, we suffer the problems of the blind men and the elephant. Not only do we describe only a piece of the phenomenon we intend to understand in full, but we desperately refuse to listen to others who are privy to a different perspective on the broader issue, thereby impoverishing ourselves but more importantly our children and our society.

THE MORAL ANATOMY

Just as the description of the problems with moral education began by focusing on the nature of the moral person, so must the offered solution begin. For any reasonable approach to education must be based on a clear and accurate understanding the nature of persons. Hence, an effective and justifiable approach to moral education must begin with a clear and accurate understanding of the nature of the moral person. We have already suggested that such an understanding is sorely lacking, but have pointed to some recent attempts to more adequately categorise the diverse aspects of moral personhood. Here, we shall offer a somewhat overlapping alternative scheme for categorising the components of the moral person; i.e. an "anatomy" of moral personhood.

This model is not intended to represent some "truth" about the parts that comprise the morality of a person; indeed, that would be quite contradictory to the dialectical and integrative approach we are advocating. Rather this is more of a taxonomy than any sort of true anatomy.

Some organisational scheme is required to make order and sense of the diversity of moral characteristics. This seven part model seems as good a place to start as any. At the very least it should suffice to cover most of what comprises the moral person and as a basis for generating further discussion about the nature of moral personhood. The seven parts of the moral person are as follows: moral behaviour, moral values, moral character, moral reason, moral emotion, moral identity, meta-moral characteristics. Each will be discussed in turn.

It is difficult to dispute the fact that the ultimate goal of moral education is behavioural. This is not to say that we should focus exclusively or even predominantly on behaviour control or behaviour management. It is merely to acknowledge that moral education that doesn't affect behaviour is toothless and largely irrelevant. Two points may make this particularly evident. First, many of the opening rationales for moral education programmes focus predominantly, if not exclusively, on a litany of the behavioural ills of today's youth.

Second, many of the criticisms levelled at competing models focus on their inability to influence behaviour. Now this is a particularly tricky issue which warrants some elaboration. It is tricky in part because of the lack of meaningful behavioural outcome research (or any meaningful outcome research for that matter) upon which to base valid conclusions. It is further complicated by some fairly inaccurate accusations. For example, Kohlberg was criticised for educating for moral reasoning which was unrelated to behaviour. The rationale was that,. even if Kohlberg and his fellow structuralists were successful in promoting the development of moral reasoning capacities, it was a wasted enterprise because such capacities had nothing to do with what people actually do.

Unfortunately, this assessment was quite inaccurate, because there is a very substantial body of literature demonstrating a significant relation between one's capacity for moral reason and one's moral behaviour. This misinterpretation was due both to the "Blind men" syndrome described above and to the fact that critics mistakenly assumed an isomorphism between reason and behaviour, when, as has been suggested here, the relation between reason and behaviour is complex and indirect due to the complexity of the moral person.

We shall include here all behaviour, overt or covert, physical or verbal or mental, that affects the rights or well-being of either oneself or others. Unfortunately this definition is not fully adequate and there is strong disagreement on the criteria for moral behaviour. It is worth noting the bases for such disagreement even if we cannot resolve them here.

Three such issues will therefore be identified. First, can one identify a moral behaviour by its intrinsic nature, or must one know the actor's intentions. Aristotle argued that behaviour can be classified as moral or not without reference to the actor. Kohlberg argued that intentions were critical to any definition of an act as moral or immoral. For example, if were to try to maliciously steer you to an investment that was sure to lead to your poverty, but discover after the fact that this investment miraculously became sound and led instead to your fortune. Even if many acts are fundamentally morally ambiguous without reference to the actor's intentions, many other acts are at least probabilistically classifiable on moral grounds. It would be an absurdly bizarre and improbable set of circumstances that would lead to a moral intention to torture a young child or rape a woman, for example.

Second, must the locus of acts be other humans for the act to be eligible for classification as moral or immoral? Some have argued that acts are only moral if they affect other humans whereas others suggest that self-harm is also in the moral domain. Some argue that only acts that affect human beings are in the moral domain whereas others include acts that affect animals or even the environment.

Third, do all behaviours that a particular tradition, culture or religion deems moral or immoral warrant that status? Some argue that morality is culturally justified whereas others suggest that morality transcends social definition. It is impossible to resolve these issues here, but it is nonetheless important to be aware that such conceptual problems exist.

Moral Values is probably the most ubiquitous term in this field and certainly is so currently in Scotland. It is the term of choice for the SCCC and for the Gordon Cook Foundation. Nonetheless, it is very difficult to find any semblance of a consensus on what a value is or to agree on what types of values should be educated. Let us begin our examination of moral values by trying to define the term. There are generally assumed to be two fundamental aspects to a value: cognition or belief, and emotion. Others include behaviour as well. Certainly a value entails cognition, for a value is centrally a belief in the desirability or lack of desirability of the focus of the value. It does not seem controversial to argue that values also entail emotion. As a verb, valuing refers to caring about something, feeling that it is important. As a noun, a value entails a feeling that something is worthwhile or not. It is less clear that values fundamentally entail behaviours other than the covert feelings and cognitions that have just been described. For instance, efforts to prevent undesirable behaviours such as unsafe sexual practices and substance use often change one's attitudes toward such behaviours without actually affecting the behaviours themselves.

Rokeach is recognised as the foremost theorist and researcher of values. He defines a value as "an enduring belief that a specific mode of conduct or end-state of existence is personally or socially preferable to an opposite or converse mode of conduct or end-state of existence". He further argues that such values are organised into a value system on a "continuum of relative importance". Notice that Rokeach does not suggest that values are behaviours, rather that they are affectively-loaded cognitions about behaviours. Researchers in parallel fields, such as the study of attitudes, make the same point; i.e., attitudes or values do relate to and predict behaviour, but are mediated by a variety of other variables so that the relation is not direct and certainly not isomorphic. This is much the same argument as offered above in defence of the relation between moral reasoning and behaviour.

Despite this definition, there is much disagreement as to what counts as a value. Rokeach felt that there are few values, that they are enduring, that they are universal, and that they are central. Others list many values. Some define values differently; e.g., the SCCC defines values as "principles or sets of principles which are consistent and which inform and direct our actions and activities". Carr argues that virtues are values, a sentiment that seems to be consistent with Lickona's failure to differentiate between values and character. Despite all of these apparent disagreements, it is possible to look for common denominators among these definitions. Clearly, as already suggested, values entail beliefs and emotions. Whether character traits or behaviours are part of values is less a matter of agreement. Hence we will rely on Rokeach's definition offered above. Values are enduring tendencies to believe in the desirability or lack of desirability of a behaviour or state of being.

If we take the SCCC's use of the term "principle" to refer to such a belief, then the definitions are largely in agreement, because the SCCC suggests that values guide behaviour, not that they entail behaviour. In fact, an examination of the SCCC's five central values supports this conclusion. Those values are: appreciation of learning, respect and caring for self, respect and caring for others, a sense of belonging, and social responsibility. These are closer to beliefs than principles, in that principles usually refer to rules for decision-making. Another interesting slant on values comes from the structuralist camp. Kohlberg's Just Community schooling approach is based in large part on the development of norms. Norms are affectively-laden beliefs about how people or institutions ought to be or ought to act. Kohlberg has long argued that moral values are at the heart of moral education.

> The school, like the government, is an institution with a basic function of maintaining and transmitting...the consensual values of society. The most fundamental are termed moral values.

The norms or values that Kohlberg and his colleagues focused on in moral education via the Just Community approach are caring, trust, collective responsibility, and participation. What is particularly noteworthy about the Just Community approach to norms is that they are analysed at both the individual and school level. In fact, one aspect of school norms that Kohlberg and his colleagues focused on was their development from individually-held to communally-held status.

Furthermore, they study the justifications for values, recognising that the endorsement of a particular value may be for quite variable reasons. Finally, they examine the relation between moral reason and values. This once again underscores the complexity of the moral person and brings our attention to the inter-relatedness of the various components of the moral anatomy.

This still leaves us with the ongoing problem of the type of values to be included in a program of moral. education. If one is to be true to the term "values education" or "values in education" then one is not limited to moral values, but is limited to values and not reasoning or character, etc. If, on the other hand, one is to use the rubric "moral values education" then it is clear that the purview is even more limited; i.e., to values and to only those values in the moral domain. "Moral education" can include values among other components of the moral person, but those values must be in the moral domain.

Thus far our moral person is comprised of behaviours and beliefs about the desirability of those behaviours or states of being. What is missing? Actually quite a bit. Let us then turn to moral character. Character is clearly related to both values and behaviour. As Wynne notes, "The roots of the word character are taken from the Greek 'to mark'. It suggest a focus on observable conduct". There are typically two major, and closely related, ways in which the term character is used.

First, there is the notion of ways of acting. Character is the way one tends to act. If one acts dishonestly, cruelly, or selfishly then one manifests bad character. If on the other hand one behaves altruistically, honestly, and lovingly, one manifests good character. Note the strong focus on behaviour. The second major use of character refers to personality. One is a person of character. Lickona defines character as "stable dispositions to respond to situations in moral ways—manifested in observable patterns (character traits) of kindness, honesty, responsibility, and a generalized respect for others".

If one takes a behavioural perspective, it seems plausible to divorce character, at least potentially, from cognition. Hence one could have the character trait of honesty without valuing honesty. One might consistently tell the truth without believing in the moral goodness of truthfulness; for example, in the case of one who is afraid to be punished for lying but believes there is nothing intrinsically wrong with lying.

This notion of character is far from what most character educators mean by character. In fact, this is closer to what Aristotle might call a habit, an unreflective or unjustified tendency to act in a certain way, than to a virtue. Aristotle clearly argued that reflection, as we shall see later, is central to virtue. There must be awareness of the value of the behaviour. In this sense, a value is actually embedded in a virtue. Perhaps that is what Carr means when he says that a virtue is a value. But it must be emphasised that virtues are not reducible to values, for values do not necessarily entail behaviour while character traits do. In psychological terminology, character refers to personality and value refers to cognition.

It is important to once again refer back to our ongoing distinction between the moral and other domains. Moral character obviously refers to the moral domain. We can clearly have non-moral character traits, such as endurance, passivity, or sloppiness. Just as for values, whereas schools may choose to educate for non-moral character, the justifications for such an endeavour must be different. Endurance is not a desirable end in itself; one can endure simply to be vengeful or can endure a particular tedious TV program simply out of laziness or a lack of creativity. But endurance can serve moral purposes. We will return to his issue in the section on meta-moral characteristics.

In a sense, by introducing moral values and moral character, we have already introduced emotion. We have seen that valuing entails feeling and that character entails valuing. Lickona considered part of the triumvirate of the moral components to be "desiring the good". Walker et al. include emotion in their five part taxonomy. It is difficult to imagine a moral person who is unfeeling.

Recent books about extremely violent children describe their lack of morality or conscience rooted in a lack of feeling about the welfare of others. They simply don't care. It is not merely coincidental that the title of Colby and Damon's book about moral exemplars is Some do care. Now the notion of emotion that has already been introduced in our discussions of values and character is really a second-order sense of specifically moral emotion. Caring about moral values is no different than caring about amoral or immoral values; i.e., returning to our definition of values, "an enduring tendency to believe in the desirability" of a moral behaviour is not different than the parallel tendency to believe in the desirability of an immoral behaviour.

In other words, it is the object of the belief not the emotional charge of the belief that gives it moral focus. Indeed, we can see this lack of specifically moral specificity in the description offered by Samay in considering the role of emotion in moral development. "Besides enumerating the reasons for which people act or should act, ethics must also call attention to the energies through which people are enabled to act for those reasons". Moral emotion is considered to be "the general power supply of all behaviour,...the integrating force of all knowledge and valuation".

There is another sense in which we may discuss moral emotion, a sense in which there is a specifically moral nature to the emotion. This refers to the subset of emotions that are generally considered to be areas of morality or immorality; emotions such as guilt, shame, empathy, sympathy, and compassion. There are two types of such moral emotions. There are the aversive moral emotions that signal some form of self-censorship or negative self-evaluation in reaction to an undesirable thought or action.

Here we refer to emotions such as guilt and shame. There are also emotions that are fundamentally prosocial. They tend to reflect an emotional reaction to the plight of others. Examples of this second type of moral emotion are empathy and sympathy. It is worth noting that all theories recognise some form of emotion as central to moral personhood. Even predominantly cognitive theories, like those to be discussed in the next section on reason, recognise emotion at least in the sense that Samay does; i.e., as an energy source for moral functioning.

Others coming from the same tradition go further in recognising the more central role of emotion in the development of moral reason. Others suggest that these models are more accurately understood as the cognitive results of prior affective sensitivity. However, one prioritises reasoning and affect, it is unlikely that any sound theory will not include both. Let us therefore turn to a discussion of moral reason.

After all, we now have a moral person who engages in moral behaviour, believes in the desirability of moral behaviours and states of being, manifests an enduring tendency to act in moral ways, and feels moral emotions. Surely this is sufficient to send our moral person out in the world to be an effective moral agent. Unfortunately it is not enough. This perhaps becomes clearest when we consider the situation in which one either has to adjudicate between conflicting moral values or moral character traits or has to generate values or behaviours for situations that were never anticipated; i.e., for novel moral dilemmas.

How does one decide whether to act honestly or caringly in a situation where either choice precludes the other And how do you decide who gets custody of the frozen embryos left from a prior failed in vitro fertilisation attempt when a couple decides to divorce? It is necessary not only in these extreme circumstances, but in many moral situations, to be able to reason about right and wrong, to figure out what is right or wrong in a particular situation. This is the role of moral reason.

Moral reasoning is the most studied aspect of the moral person and relies upon the strongest theoretical framework. Kohlberg, the most influential thinker in the field of moral reason, describes moral reason as the logic of justice; the logic that one utilises to figure out what is fair or just, to balance the claims in a given moral conflict. He describes six stages of natural development of such forms of justice logic, moving from a calculation of self-interest, to a calculation of social interest, to a reliance upon abstract universal logical principles of justice. Kohlberg is often accused (by both foes and friends) of being monomaniacal and seeing the moral person purely as intellect.

This is actually quite far from the truth. Kohlberg has clearly related moral reason to behaviour, emotion, character, and to values. Indeed in Kohlberg's last major work on moral education, it is argued that he is not advocating a literal teaching of the (US) Constitution. Rather, he sees the Constitution as representing the moral principle of justice and claims that it is by teaching "justice" that the schools can legitimately transmit "the consensual values of society". For justice, seen from the perspective of moral development theory, is not a given value, which can be concretely transmitted to or imposed upon children, but it is a basic valuing process that underlies each person's capacity for moral judgment.

It should be clear then that values are highly related to moral reason and that reason is applied to the interpretation and evaluation of values. The same can be said for behaviour. Aristotle introduced the concept of practical reason, which he differentiated from scientific reason. The role of practical reason was specifically moral. It provides the individual with the rational capacity to figure out how to apply the virtues in any given situation; i.e., to figure out what is the right thing to do in a given situation. Perhaps this similarity is what led Power et al.

to attempt to integrate Aristotelian virtue theory with Kohlbergian cognitive-structuralism. Others argue that these two approaches are fundamentally incompatible due to their differing philosophical assumptions. We cannot resolve this issue here, and it really is the domain of philosophers like Carr, but in the service of our integrationist orientation we will accept at least the plausibility of finding useful common ground between the character/virtue educator's notion of reason and the cognitive-structuralist's notion of reason.

Moral Identity

Up to this point, we have endowed our moral person with five anatomical components: moral behaviour, moral values, moral character, moral emotion, and moral reason. Once again we can recognise that we have done a fine job in constructing the core of a moral person. Someone who does the right thing, believes in and cares about goodness, consistently shows the personality traits of goodness, feels regret for transgressions and concern for others, and who can effectively figure out what is good or bad is certainly someone whom we would welcome to my world. Yet our anatomy is still incomplete. The sixth component, moral identity, is a bit different, however, from the five preceding components in three ways.

First, it has only recently been taken seriously by psychologists, despite earlier statements about its importance by Erikson. Erikson has long argued that the core of the adolescent's central developmental task of self-discovery is development of an ideology; and this ideology is what holds the self (the "identity") together. Second, and related, this component may be the only one that does not develop until relatively late in the formative years; i.e., it may be dependent upon, as just noted, a developmental task of adolescence. It requires, at least for its fullest manifestation, powers of self-reflection which do not develop fully and are certainly not manifested fully until adolescence at the earliest.

Third, most recent mentions of moral identity come from the literature described earlier on moral exemplars. That is, moral identity seems to be a salient characteristic of the most highly developed moral individuals. That is not to say it is not existent in others, merely that it seems necessary for moral excellence.

Colby and Damon suggest that the notion of moral identity they have observed in moral exemplars is a sense of self as centrally a moral being. Moral exemplars, when they think of themselves, think of a self that strives to be moral and for whom being moral is critical to their sense of self. For some people beauty, or intelligence, or athletic acumen, or wealth may be critical to the way they see themselves, but to the moral exemplar being good is at the core of their sense of self.

Now we can see from the data collected by Walker et al. that this characteristic of the moral person is not salient to most people. Of the 568 nominated characteristics of moral exemplars, only 6 may be representative of the concept of moral identity, and these are only tangentially related at best. We can clearly see that one's self-concept is related to one's behaviour; indeed Aronson based his model of cognitive dissonance on the assumption that we all try to be consistent with our self-concepts and that we generally have self-concepts that suggest we are "good" people. Nisan argues that we want to think of ourselves as good people and are more willing to forgive ourselves our transgressions if we have been particularly good lately. Morality is more a characteristic of the agent than of either action or thinking; the ultimate source of goodness lies in good will, and good will is at the core of what a person is.

What is most troubling for these authors is how to relate moral identity to moral reason, a problem that we cannot hope to resolve here, but a problem that once again underscores the complexity of the relations among the components of the moral person.

META-MORAL CHARACTERISTICS

The notion of moral emotion presented by Samay may actually be an example of this, for the emotions are not in themselves moral, but rather are a form of impetus for moral functioning. And Aristotle's notion of practical reason may be construed as non-moral reason in the service of moral character. All of the discovered attributes of moral exemplars reported by Colby and Damon may also be candidates for this last component. In fact their identification of faith in moral exemplars is very close to the notion of spirituality in McGettrick's article in this series, an article with a very similar theme to the current argument.

It is very important here to differentiate between non-moral characteristics that one may choose to include in a program of moral education and those meta-moral characteristics that are intrinsically non-moral but serve to aid in moral functioning. Rest presented a broad model of moral functioning that includes processes of perception, moral judgement, moral will, and moral behaviour, but which includes many processes that are not moral in nature but that clearly influence whether one's moral judgement will lead to right action.

Etzioni, Berkowitz, and Wilcox, suggest that self-discipline and empathy are character traits that lie outside of the moral domain yet are critical to the flowering of moral personhood. One could be self-disciplined and empathic in the service of cold-heartedly "conning" an elderly person into giving one all of their hard-earned life savings by employing self-discipline to slowly develop a relation of trust and employing empathy to better understand one's victim in order to more effectively trick her. Clearly then, self-discipline and empathy are not intrinsically moral; however, it would be difficult to imagine an exemplary moral person without self-control and who has no ability to figure out other's private emotional states.

In a similar way, Grim, Kohlberg, and White demonstrated the rather complex role that attention plays in controlling cheating behaviour. Interestingly they called this attribute "moral will" when in actuality it was not moral at all. For intelligent but low moral reasoning individuals, attention actually aided in effective cheating whereas for high moral reasoning stage individuals it aided in resistance to cheating. Wynne and Ryan suggest that moral education is "such long-honoured educational concerns as teaching character, academics, and discipline", a rather broad and atypical definition, but one that may at least suggest the inter-relatedness of moral and meta-moral characteristics. It is clear that we can identify fundamentally moral components of the moral person but that we must not ignore those characteristics of the moral person that are not themselves moral in nature but are essential to effective moral functioning. It takes more than morality to be an effective moral agent.

In the narrowest sense moral education refers to the explicit curriculum of the formal school. In a somewhat broader sense, it includes the implicit curriculum of the school; what is often referred to as the school ethos, the moral atmosphere, or the hidden curriculum. But in the broadest sense, one is remiss in not acknowledging that the school plays only a part in the moral education of our youth. Family is clearly the strongest and earliest influence, but peers, church, society, and the media also are strong influences.

In fact much of the rhetoric about school's role in moral education centres around whether they are in fact being asked to do someone else's "job". Schools blame parents for both the need for schools to do moral education and the fact that children are often so immoral that the schools cannot ignore moral education.

Teachers also often lament the fact that they are fighting "an uphill battle" because of all the countervailing forces in society providing messages contradictory to the moral messages imparted in the schools. One of the most frequently asked questions in the series of seminars for Scottish head teachers organised by the Gordon Cook Foundation in 1995 is whether moral education is futile or unfair because the pupils must go out into immoral communities and eventually an immoral adult world. Response is that it is far better to present such students with a vision of a better world than simply to train them to fit into an immoral one.

Furthermore, the more immoral their context, the more they need moral education. Those pupils who live in morally idyllic families and communities are likely in little need of intensive moral education programmes. Nevertheless, despite all of these caveats, we will now turn to an attempt to sketch out a programme of moral education that will address the complexity of the moral person. School-based sources of moral education One way to divide up the school as a moral influence is by differentiating between the informal and formal curricula.

The formal curriculum entails that which is taught in a way that is clearly intended to be a systematic educational activity. The informal curriculum entails the influences generated from the life of the school, such as rule-making, school norms, and modelled adult behaviour. Now some, quite rightly differentiate between the hidden curriculum and the informal curriculum. We shall not do so here because it will be argued that a central aspect of any effective moral education institution is to make the hidden curriculum an explicit aspect of the informal curriculum; that is, effective moral education entails, in part, uncovering and reflecting on the hidden curriculum, so it no longer remains hidden.

The formal curriculum can support moral education in a variety of ways. First, it can systematically incorporate lessons about morality; e.g., through the historical study of notable moral events and decisions, through the literary study of moral heroes or villains or great moral dilemmas, through the theatrical depiction of great moral narratives or conflicts, etc. Second, lessons may be created which examine moral concepts and the classical thinking about them.

Third, peer interaction around challenging moral issues can be woven into many classes. Fourth, courses specifically concerned with morality can be added to the curriculum. Fifth, service learning and other forms of institutionalised moral action can be made an explicit curricular requirement.

The informal curriculum is probably even more influential however. This is quite widely recognised as can be noted from the following pair of quotes, the first from James Coleman's preface to Wynne and Ryan's quite conservative character education statement and the second from Kohlberg's quite liberal moral education statement. The act of educating another is a moral act...Teaching is itself a part of the moral message transmitted by a teacher to a child... That moral message may be strong and clear if the teacher is dedicated to the task of teaching, or distorted if the teacher has largely given up on the task... But the message contained in the act of teaching is only part of the values teachers and schools transmit. Teachers and schools, like parents and families, cannot avoid teaching values... Yet this teaching often goes unnoticed, unintentional and unreflective. Even if the values of justice were discussed in classes, if the students perceive that getting along in school runs by a quite different set of norms, they will tend to perceive the latter as the real rules of the game and the former as nice talk one engages in with teachers. So how does one influence the informal curriculum? There are four inter-related aspects that must be considered: (1) the explicit school ideology or mission, (2) the behaviour of adults, (3) the governance structure, (4) peer norms. We shall treat each of these in turn.

School ideology should be clearly developed, articulated, and disseminated. That is, the school should have a clear statement of its purpose and values; what it is trying to achieve, why those are its goals, and how it intends to go about reaching its stated goals. Such a statement should be developed by the entire school community and the broader community of which it is a part. The second element, adult behaviour, is one of the most contentious yet most important.

Some argued that the modelled behaviour of adults in schools is the single most significant influence on the development of moral character. In the field of professional ethics education, faculty modelling is seen a critical to the effective education of ethical professionals. Similarly, Nicgorski has emphasised the importance of university faculty as role models in the moral development of university students. As noted in the quote from Power et al. above, if students perceive the real actions of the school to be different than the espoused actions, then they will readily discount the latter and heed the former. Even young children learn more from what you do than from what you say. It is thus critical that adults in schools practice what they preach.

School governance refers to the ways rules are made and enforced in the school. In traditional schools these processes tend to be quite authoritarian and hierarchical. Piaget noted long ago that such a relation to children impedes their moral growth and their growth as autonomous personalities. Rather, children should be welcomed as participants in the governance of the school or classroom, at levels appropriate to their developmental capacities.

The serious work of deliberate moral education entails...opening up that process and dealing with the ways everyday rules of behavior are made and enforced. for it is those rules that define the moral atmosphere—the context for moral learning—in the school. The most comprehensive study of, and most elegant statement about, the governance structure of schools as a moral agent is offered by Power et al. in their reporting of work in establishing three Just Community schools in the USA.

They describe a process of democratising schools with an explicit emphasis on promoting justice and a sense of community. Such schools promote moral growth through participation, open discussion of moral issues, exposure to differing perspectives and ideas, and living in a moral community. One only promotes the development of respect in children by first treating them with respect. Empowerment is a form of respect.

Finally, peer norms are also at the heart of the informal curriculum. It has long been acknowledged that what peers value and hold to be right has a great impact on how they develop and influence each other. Kohlberg has explicitly focused on the norms of the students in his Just Community schools, norms such as caring and participation. Peer norms both affect the moral atmosphere of the school and are affected by it. It is clear from the research on Just Community schools that such a governance structure nurtures the growth of desirable peer norms. Even more significant, from a sociological perspective, the norms shift from being individually held norms to being collective norms shared by members of the school.

Having thus identified the major influences on moral development in schools, let us turn at last to how such influences may impact on the components of the moral person. Before we do so, however, let us reiterate our caution that the field of moral education is woefully deficient in valid outcomes research. We often do not know what works because either it hasn't been studied or the studies that exist are unscientific or biased. Educating for moral behaviour There are two ways of considering this issue: direct and indirect influences. The former generally is construed as behaviour control, and focuses on discipline, reward and punishment, and authoritarian rule-setting. It can effectively produce greater adherence to the desired norms of behaviour. The second type of influence, informal influence, is derivative. It assumes that education that fosters the development of moral character, values, reason, etc., will consequently lead to more responsible behaviour.

Certainly some schools and classrooms may be in more need of direct behavioural influences, but all schools require indirect behavioural influences. Therefore, schools should model moral behaviour and teach about moral behaviour as well as generally promoting the full growth of the moral person. Because indirect behavioural influence is assumed to be derivative of the influences affecting other parts of the moral person, we shall shift our attention to those other components.

Educating for moral values Values are beliefs and can be affected both by introspection and by social influences. Introspection was largely the domain of the Values Clarification movement. It recommended classroom activities that lead to introspection of one's values. The problem with this approach, insofar as it is applied to specifically moral values is that is offers no guidance as to what ought to stand as an acceptable moral value. Remember from our discussion of domains of social knowledge above, that moral values are universal and unalterable whereas social-conventional and personal values are alterable. Pure introspection then is inappropriate for the development of moral values, but may be an effective technique when coupled with other techniques that provide a means of judging the adequacy of moral values.

One source of moral values education is the explicit advocacy of such values by the school and school authorities. Schools should stand for something and that something should be explicit. The difficulty here is in choosing what that something should be; i.e., the eternal question of "Whose values?". There are generally two accepted solutions to this problem. One is to look for community consensus; i.e., teach those values that the community agrees are important.

The second is to identify an ethically grounded set of core values. Neither are perfect solutions, because neither has ever produced a non-controversial set of values; however, philosophically, local consensus is much more susceptible to moral error than is some abstract ethical scrutiny. Many communities throughout history and today endorse some fairly reprehensible values.

A second, and decidedly more controversial, approach is to make valuing a part of the school's governance agenda. That is, to let the school's democratic process examine and generate the school's moral values. There is clearly a trade-off here, with an increase in the nurturance of moral character and moral reason and moral identity at the possible expense of a justifiable moral values agenda. That is to say, participating in such a process will powerfully influence these other parts of the moral person, but the values that are endorsed may need continual examination and development. Nevertheless, values that one participates in generating or endorsing are more likely to influence one's behaviour than values that are foisted upon you by an authority in a hierarchical power structure.

Regardless of how the moral values are generated, for them to become internalised, they must be made explicit, must be endorsed by the authorities (adults in a traditional school, entire community in a Just Community school), must be modelled by the adults in the school, and must be enforced. Both the formal and informal curricula are part of this process.

The primary focus of moral character education is the development of moral habits that will hopefully become character traits or virtues. The school programs' emphases are on establishing early good habits in a controlled setting so that when their young students mature, those habits will be ingrained and generalize. As already noted some believes that such ingrained habits or virtues are predominantly influenced by teacher modelling. Such social learning processes are indeed very powerful.

Furthermore, advocacy consistent with teacher modelling is very important; i.e., as Lickona argues, teachers must not only practice what they preach, but must preach what they practice. In a school with an explicit open focus on the moral atmosphere, such as a Just Community school, there is a check on whether teachers are being sincere or hypocritical and whether the behavioural tendencies they espouse and/or manifest are indeed justifiable. In such schools, hypocrisy or injustice is quickly rooted out and discussed.

Clearly, the promotion of unreflective habits is more developmentally appropriate in primary schools whereas the active reflection on the moral validity of habits is more appropriate in the secondary school. Lickona, for example, describes an effective primary level classroom practice in which a Primary 7 teacher regularly schedules "appreciation time", a time for students to publicly acknowledge how others have helped them. Lickona suggests that this generates the habit of affirming others, which is assumed to potentially develop into the moral character trait of respect for others. It is worth noting that this activity is simultaneously promoting self-esteem in those students being appreciated. Furthermore, it is publicly advocating the value of helping and serves to reward helping behaviour. This, once again, underscores how the components of the moral person and the processes of moral education are complex and inter-related.

At the secondary level, on the other hand, greater emphasis should be placed on reflecting on the moral adequacy of patterns of behaviour, so that habits may evolve into ethically justifiable character traits. Such reflection may come from learning about behaviour and character through the formal curriculum, or through participation in evaluation of actual behaviours and of norms in the school itself.

Student participation in school judiciaries and legislatures may serve this purpose as well. Educating for moral reason This may be where we are on our strongest empirically-grounded footing. There is a vast educational and psychological literature examining how to promote moral reason.

The more practical and therefore more widely implemented technique is peer moral dilemma discussion. Appropriate moral dilemmas are selected from anthologies, current events, history, literature, or the curriculum or are created by the teacher. Classes are then guided through a critical but respectful discussion of the dilemma with the explicit aim of trying to figure out what the best moral solution is.

The Just Community is a much more ambitious project but has been successfully carried out in a variety of contexts including schools, residential treatment centres, prisons, and workplaces. The core of the Just Community approach is democratic self-governance tied to promotion of justice and a sense of community. Decisions are made by a direct democracy and parliamentarian procedure, but with an explicit focus on maximising justice in decisions and attempting to create and affirm a sense of the communal identity of the group. Educating for moral affect.

In some senses, moral affect is the most difficult part of the moral anatomy to account for in education. There are several reasons for this. First and foremost, most psychological accounts of moral emotions suggest they develop prior to the entrance to formal schooling. Second, there is little research on educating for moral emotion in the schools. Third, much of the literature on moral affect concerns remediation and the lack of a typical emotional life.

Nevertheless, we can offer some guidelines concerning educating for moral emotions. Let us begin with the pre-school experience. It is clear that emotions, including moral emotions, emerge in the first and second years of life. One of the most frequently cited affective components of moral development is empathy. Typically empathy is understood to be natural and to have a biological base as well as to be a source of moral reason and more mature moral affect. It is also assumed by many to have origins in the early attachment bonding of infant to caretaker. Hence children should enter school with empathic capacities.

Clearly, other moral emotions should also be present when the child enters schooling; emotions such as guilt, shame, hurt feelings, pride, etc.. What then can the school provide beyond remediation? Perhaps this is best answered by turning to the notion of moral sensibility offered by Caputo but having its roots in classical Greek ethical philosophy as well as in other prominent ethical theories such as utilitarianism. The notion is that one must "love the good" as well as simply knowing it. Affect is infused in moral knowing. Hoffman argues that moral principles are "hot cognitions" because they are bound to moral affect. The question then becomes one of guiding the moral sensibilities through education. That is, the role of the school is to direct the child to care for the good and abhor the bad; e.g., empathise with victims and despise injustice.

Unfortunately, it is quite unclear how this is done. The literature on moral education pays little attention to this issue. Some argue that humans have a natural tendency to desire the good; exposure is sufficient. Others argue that such moral "tastes" must be cultivated. For example, Bennett argues for promoting "moral literacy" in our children as a means of teaching them what the good is.

From this perspective schools should teach children about moral virtues, about moral heroes, about great moral acts, and should expose children to great moral literature. There is also a need to help children identify their moral emotions. Often they do not have verbal labels for what they feel or do not know which labels apply in a given instance. Talking about moral feelings and labelling them not only reduces a child's confusion about her feelings, but also can serve to legitimise them.

The child who is torn between empathy for an outcast child and a fear of ostracising by the peer group that is engaging in the bullying may feel that his empathic feelings are signs of weakness or wrong in some other way. Discussing and labelling them may serve to reduce the child's doubts about the value of his own feelings.

There is also a need in schools to allow children the opportunity to express their feelings. Schools tend to strive to avoid affective displays by children. They are messy and disruptive. A more appropriate approach is to redirect emotions in more acceptable ways. Ginott often reminded us that we should express our emotions but be sure they are verbalised in appropriate ways. Teachers of pre-school children, for instance, often tell them to "use your words, not your hands" when angry or frustrated.

Similar to educating for moral emotion, when discussing educating for moral identity, we are again in a domain about which little is known. Erikson has suggested that adolescents will naturally attempt to form an identity and will do so most effectively if (1) their prior personality development has been healthy and (2) they are given the opportunity to experiment and explore options. Clearly as well, providing the options and models for adolescents to consider and evaluate will also serve their formation of a moral identity.

INDEX

Altruism 166
Authoritative Parenting 174

Character education movement 8
Character education programs 3
Character Formation 66, 84
Child Development Project (CDP) 20, 119
Clarification programs 2
Classroom management research 22
Clinton 98
Community schooling approach 245
Community service 2
Conceptual differences 68
Constructivism 114
Constructivist approach 113
Constructivist teaching principles 19
Contemporary wisdom 156
Controversial moral issues 17
Conventional
    domain 79
    expectations 76
    understandings 78
    wisdom 10
Cultural transmission 158

Democratic society 83
Developmental discipline 26

Educational policies 67
Educational psychology 66
Educators 2
Ethical theory 240
Extrinsic incentives 99

Good liberal education 7
Grand theory 240

Heterogeneous social contexts 76
Homosexuality 15
Humpty-Dumpty 238

Incompatible aspects 239
Indirect control 27
Individual personality 86
Individual responsibility 90
Interpersonal behaviors 68
Isomorphic 244

Kohlberg system 79
Kohlbergian theory 151

Martin Hoffman 164
Meta-moral characteristics 159
Meta-moral characteristics 253
Moral
    anatomy 241
    development theory 151, 250
    discussion 94
    domain 236

- education 1
- emotion 248
- enterprise 1
- Identity 251
- judgment 67
- normative components 71
- Reasoning 167

Multiple-choice tests 109

Normative conceptions 70
Normative regulation 78

Organisational scheme 241

Pedagogical philosophy 110
Personal autonomy 26
Personal needs 155
Prudential matters 155
Psychological distinctions 70
Psychological terminology 247

Relativism 114
Rote memorization 107

Self-control development 162
Sequential acquisition 107
Sexual behavior 12
Sexual morality 14
Sexually Transmitted Diseases (STDs) 11
Social agreement 236
Social convention 71
Social norm 69
Socialization practices 23

Teaching social behaviors 28
Theoretical perspectives 239

Unquestionable importance 13

Values clarification movement 4
Values Clarification 2, 114